THE BIRTH OF GOD

THE BIRTH

JEAN BOTTÉRO

OF GOD

THE BIBLE AND THE HISTORIAN

TRANSLATED BY KEES W. BOLLE

THE PENNSYLVANIA STATE UNIVERSITY PRESS
UNIVERSITY PARK, PENNSYLVANIA

Cet ouvrage publié dans le cadre du programme d'aide à la publication bénéficie du soutien du Ministère des Affaires Etrangères et du Service Culturel de l'Ambassade de France représenté aux Etats-Unis.

This book, published as part of the program of aid for publication, received support from the French Ministry of Foreign Affairs and the Cultural Service of the French Ministry in the United States.

LIBRARY OF CONGRESS CATALOGING-IN-PUBLICATION DATA

First published in France as *Naissance de Dieu: La Bible et l'historien* © 1986 Editions Gallimard, Paris

Bottéro, Jean.
[Naissance de Dieu. English]
The birth of God : the Bible and the historian / Jean Bottéro ; translated by Kees W. Bolle.
p.   cm. — (Hermeneutics, studies in the history of religions)
Includes bibliographical references and index.
ISBN 0-271-02060-1 (cloth : alk. paper) — ISBN 0-271-02061-X (pbk. : alk. paper)
1. Bible. O.T.—Criticism, interpretation, etc.—I. Title.—II. Hermeneutics, studies in the history of religions (University Park, Pa.)
BS1173 .B6813 2000
221.6—dc21
00-021352

It is the policy of The Pennsylvania State University Press to use acid-free paper for the first printing of all clothbound books. Publications on uncoated stock satisfy the minimum requirements of American National Standard for Information Sciences— Permanence of Paper for Printed Library Materials, ANSI Z39.48–1992.

אם-אשכחך   ירושלים

HERMENEUTICS: STUDIES IN THE HISTORY OF RELIGIONS

CONTENTS

I owe at the outset a word of explanation with respect to the title and the purpose of my book.

The reader will find five essays collected here, of various lengths, all dealing with the Bible—by which we mean what Christians call the Old Testament.

"The Account of 'Original Sin' in Genesis 2:25–3," written in 1949, has never been published before. "Ecclesiastes and the Problem of Evil" appeared in 1955–57 in volumes VII–IX (pp. 133–49) of *La nouvelle Clio*, a Belgian journal for the history of religions that no longer exists; it was published once more in *Recherches et documents du Centre Thomas More*, no. 11 (1976). "The Origins of the Universe According to the Bible" appeared under the title "La naissance du monde selon Israël" in *Sources orientales I: La naissance du monde* (Éditions du Seuil, 1959). "The Oldest Biblical Poem" I wrote in 1960 at the request of my lifelong friend Francis Ponge, for *Tel quel*; it came out the following year in the sixth issue (pp. 81–91). And in 1969, when I was charged with organizing—around an extensive series of photographs by E. Lessing and new and remarkable syntheses, such as those by P. M.-J. Stève ("La Bible du champ de fouilles") and J. Koenig ("Le texte de la Bible")—a collection to be called *Vérité et poésie de la Bible* and published by Éditions Hatier, I inserted there, in addition to a number of translations (pp. 93–273), "The Universal Message of the Bible" (pp. 17–75).

My foremost obligation, and a most agreeable one, is warmly to thank the managers of Éditions Hatier and Éditions du Seuil for granting me the freedom to reproduce my texts—which, moreover, I have sometimes slightly changed to integrate them better into the present work.

With respect to the studies in this book, my plan, from beginning to end, was simple: to take up the Bible from that standpoint by which it constitutes, not the domain reserved for its believers, whatever confession they claim, or the private slash-and-burn preserve of its detractors, from whatever horizon they may appear, but the common property of all people—in the spirit in which we go beyond our own belles lettres and classics to take up the universal treasures of world literature.

When this spirit arises, two ways open up. More obvious, and more commonly taken, is the way of the gentleman not plagued by prejudices, who reads Aeschylus and Tacitus, Plato and Dante, Rabelais and Shakespeare, the *Jin Ping Mei* or the pre-Islamic poets, seeking and holding on to heart-warming or refined emotions and lessons, direct or indirect, that, no matter how far we may be from them in time, place, and culture, the text of their authors places within our reach today. On the whole, such a reader of the Bible is satisfied with a good translation, dependable and well enough rendered into his language—indeed, even with light comments at its more obscure passages—to be at once intelligible and gratifying.

But another way of reading is possible, and preferable, which too few undertake with these same writings. This way is followed when, aware of the vast distance in time and culture that separates us from the authors, we nonetheless attempt to read them with a perspective and mental attitude as close as possible to the perspective and mental attitude with which they composed their works. In other words, through *the texts* we seek to discover *the people* who mused on them and couched them in writing, and *those* whom they thought of while they wrote. Reading in this way, we may hope, on good grounds, to draw from what they wrote, not what we, in our century, can effortlessly recognize or fancy as our own experience, knowledge, reason, taste, but what *they* meant within that enormous heritage that the long line of our ancestors since the dawn of time has never ceased to enrich and that is passed to us together with the life and the culture we receive at our arrival in the world.

This second way of reading ancient books is in fact the way of history. History takes those books, like everything else that comes to us from times past, as relics, remains, vestiges rolled for so long along the roads of time that they have amassed an ore, from which they must first be extracted if we are to make contact with their authors, who have disappeared, and their bygone universe. Cleansed and collected, these *membra disiecta* remain to be pieced together, now like the scattered bits of a venerable mosaic lying in ruins that one would try to restore, in order to recover from the past not only isolated moments, instantaneous, in themselves without great interest, but sequences: calm, enduring periods, and moments of progress, and also times of decay or falling back. Such sequences raise a living and moving world, a series of long adventures that our fathers went through on the path of "progress" of which we, in our place, are the beneficiaries.

But few venture into such deciphering. And this is because history, like all scientific disciplines, demands the practice of a true "profession": a complex, arduous, and subtle technique, with an array of routine procedures that eye and hand have made their own, and, in addition, to ensure their proper function, a preliminary accumulation of masses of data of all kinds—linguistic, epigraphic, philological, chronological, archeological, sensational, cultural— all the more difficult to master, the greater the distance in space, time, or "mentality" that separates us from the authors of those ancient pieces of work.

If the average person can hardly be expected to take on such a task all by himself, even though he may recognize its fruitfulness, are we not right in expecting professionals to introduce that average person to it, sharing with him what they have collected on their long journey? That is *precisely* what I wished to do here with my subject of the Bible and its significance for our history and our future.

At this point, I must dwell for a moment on the fragility of my endeavor. Not only does history concern human affairs, entangled, troublesome, and usually impossible to unravel entirely, the more so when, in order to discern them at all, we must make conjectures in the face of innumerable silences, empty spots, and unanswered questions that envelop on all sides the documentation that is accessible to us when it comes from such a distant past; but in addition, in a field so completely devoid of the constancy of geometry and the unvarying claims of mathematics, each historian is necessarily conditioned by his own time and place, which determine his angle of vision upon the object of his study, and in all he perceives or decides about his object, there is always some intervention of his experience, view, and hierarchy of things, his temperament, his own way of envisioning problems. To the extent that he is competent and has executed his task properly, he, as an individual, resonates the chorus of expert historians, the common voice of history, and one is well advised to listen to him. But I state this without losing sight of the fact that as surely as he has added his own voice to the choir and would abide by the insights he is convinced of, so must he be ready to abandon them should his colleagues demonstrate to him an oversight or error he has made. Inscribing this minor key at the head of my sheet of music is meant to mark only caution and honesty. Circumspection has led me to underline this fragility of the historian's work. It is why I did not add to the title of this volume "the Bible and History," but *"The Bible and the Historian."*

One important point remains to be made.

The nation that for a thousand years lived and wrote these many works that were subsequently collected in the Bible brought us nothing, left us nothing, if not the idea, which they discovered and proclaimed and, in the final analysis, imposed upon us, of God's absolute *Uniqueness and Transcendence*:[1] without any doubt the spiritual conception that pulls us in a direction most opposed to our natural inclination, that most exceeds us, that most elevates us beyond ourselves, and that, for this very reason—whether we see the existence of God or of the supernatural world as confirmed, in doubt, or a fabrication does not matter—merits beyond all other ideas our amazement, admiration, and praise, that is, unless we are partial to seeing ourselves as two-legged computers. This legacy and this essential "message" of the Bible are what I wished to bring to the fore throughout these pages and what I have meant to reflect in my title, suggesting that, thanks to those ancient writings studied on the level of history, we can be present at the actual *birth of God* in the human spirit—whether, I repeat, the God in question may be an unknown Being who has gradually disclosed Himself to us in the course of this history, or simply an ingenious, brilliant, and fascinating idea, a sublime accomplishment of the mind, without any other reality or value than the emotions it is capable of engendering in us.

Whatever way this last point is decided, it is incontestable that in the eyes of the Bible's authors, and their people, God was a Person, a Personality in true existence and wholly real. In Him centered, in their view, the total potential of the Sacred and the Numinous that constituted the

---

1. Another novelty of major importance that we owe to Israel is the moralization of religion— good conduct, right conduct, introduced into religious practice: the "cult" rendered to the supernatural world no longer consisted only of offerings, sacrifices, munificence, and so forth, but required that life and behavior conform to a series of precepts that were primarily moral (see pages 24ff.). But despite the enormous step forward taken by religiosity because of a discovery like this one, I do not dwell on it in my book. There are two reasons. First, regardless of the emergence of monotheism, Israel and the religions that issued from her message never succeeded in establishing a cult that was purely spiritual and, above all, "moral." And then, because such a "moral" view of things— more insidiously than an entirely material and ostentatious cult—so very often led to a perversion of what can and should be most noble, most elevated in religiosity, by shifting toward an appeal to the "stake" one has, one's "merit," and the expectation of a "reward." See also pages 26f., 60ff., 90ff., 95ff.

object of religious experience, which is as ineradicable from Man—whether one likes it or not—as the sentiments of love and beauty. Turning to the Bible, to read it or to seek the evidence it presents, in accordance with the "first" or the "second" way of reading, we would go astray at once if we did not treat it first and foremost as the expression of a *religious* sensitivity and ideology. But in that immense sector of our life where the heart plays its role and leads the way, nothing of what we do or say or think can be understood if the vault is not unlocked with the only key that opens it: sympathy. A historian of religions who neglected this rule would resemble a gastronomic critic who suffered from stomach problems and had never been able to delight in the pleasures of the table! I would have failed in my principal duty had I not chosen to "sympathize" in the highest possible degree with the ancient authors of the Bible, as if placing myself in their skin in order to feel and see things as much as possible as they did. And yet I would also have failed had I ever set aside my professional obligations of caution and rationality! I have always believed that the very best history resides in this equilibrium.

How could one venture to hold forth on the Bible without presenting some of its most typical and most beautiful passages? The rules that guided my translation of these passages I have tried to explain here and there within this book (see pages 110ff.).[2] Whoever has occupied himself seriously with a foreign language, especially one very different from his own, knows from experience—above all when he finds himself before a work of literature that he truly "feels"—that apart from stammering out a word-for-word rendition as lifeless and even repulsive as a body laid out for autopsy, just to give philological comfort to the experts, he can *never* succeed in rendering all that he understands: thus he must, at one and the same time—again the search for an equilibrium, hard to achieve, yet obligatory!—"stick" as much as he can to the original, all the while *transposing* it into his own language. In short, he must absorb the text, in all the nuances and subtleties that linguistic, philological, and critical efforts have opened up for him, to the point where

---

2. In the framework of the present book, it would not have made sense to include systematic justification, with notes and technical explanations, for my choice of specific passages in the text tradition or for my recourse to this or that correction I judged indispensable in an established but corrupt text. The same holds true even more for my way of interpreting and translating a particular word or passage. Of course, specialists will understand, and the trusting reader will be grateful that I spare him the depressing "tour of the kitchen."

I have expressed my principles of translation in S. N. Kramer, *Le mariage sacré* (Paris: Berg International, 1983), and J. Bottéro and S. N. Kramer, *Lorsque les dieux faisaient l'homme* (Paris: Éditions Gallimard, 1993), 16ff.

he can, as it were, re-create it in his own speech. Whoever does not feel himself, in a way, as the author of the text he translates is no better in the final analysis than a translating computer: such machines give you everything and all there is, except the main thing—the soul.

In transliterating Hebrew names, I have simply followed current usage, as chosen in the best-known Bible translations, such as the Jerusalem Bible [and the Revised Standard Version—Trans.]. [As to pronunciation, *u* sounds like *u* in the English *dune*; consonants are always hard; the *g* is always pronounced as in English *go*; the *h* sounds almost always like the *j* in Spanish *Juan*; *q* has no equivalent in our phonetic system, but sounds like a sharp *k*, as in *Qoheleth*.—Trans.]

Finally, I ask for clemency with respect to some things that are said more than once, or repeated in various parts of the book. It did not seem necessary to rewrite or change them, and I told myself that, after all, repetition is the backbone of education.

I do not want to close this long preamble without expressing my heartfelt gratitude to P. Nora and M. Gaucher, who found matters of interest in these pages, since they were the first to urge me to bundle them together in a book.

The principal periods of the history of Israel's life and thought and of the development of the Bible follow below. Here and throughout the book, numbers as a rule indicate years, centuries, millennia B.C.E.

Before the 13th century, for a duration we cannot determine with accuracy: about two or three centuries.	The ancestors of Israel live a nomadic life, moving from east to west along the Fertile Crescent, before entering Palestine.
Beginning of the 13th century.	Moses.
End of the 13th–end of the 11th century.	"Conquest" and settlement in Palestine.
End of the 11th–middle of the 10th century.	Kingdom of Israel. First three rulers.
Second half of the 10th century.	Schism and two separate kingdoms: Israel (north) and Judah (south).
The 9th century.	The first great Prophets.
End of the 8th century.	Fall and disappearance of the Northern Kingdom.
Beginning of the 6th century.	Fall of the Southern Kingdom and the Babylonian Exile.

End of the 6th–second half of the 5th century.	Beginning of the return of the exiles. Organization of Judaism.
First half of the 4th century.	Completion of the selection process of the main Biblical writings.

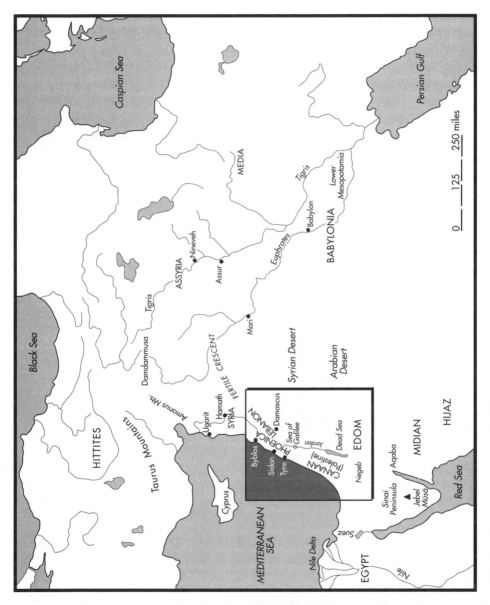

Biblical Palestine in its geographical setting.

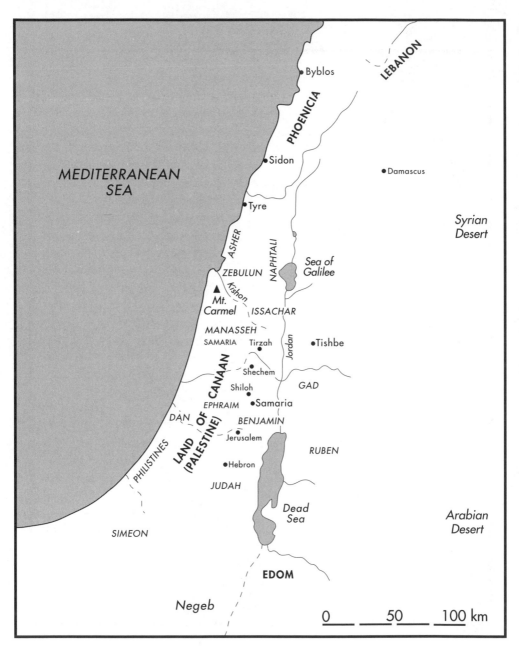

Principal place names for the subject of this book.

ONE

THE BIBLE AND HISTORY

On December 3, 1872, the Bible forever lost its immemorial prerogative of being "the oldest book known," "a book unlike others," "the book dictated, written, by God Himself." The first Assyriologists had been at work for fifty years stubbornly and brilliantly deciphering cuneiform script. Now they had begun to catalogue a wealth of tablets from the soil of ancient Mesopotamia. And on this particular day, before the Society of Biblical Archeology in London, one of their number, G. Smith, announced his extraordinary discovery: a history that was strikingly close to the biblical narrative of the Flood, even in details, but that preceded it and had obviously inspired the story in the Bible.[1]

At a stroke, the Bible entered the stream of world literature and took its place in the endless chain of works issued in that entanglement of original creativity and dependency on previous sources, of fallibility and clairvoyance, which marks all advance in human thought.

As a result, it became no less clear that the Bible, like all that has been produced by men, contained a value that belonged to all, and a universal message.

The Bible's origins here on earth, now verified, could hardly be invoked without temerity or foolhardiness in the face of the venerable belief of millions that the same Bible is the Book of God. It is in the nature of faith to add to the world and to things as they are a supernatural dimension that is visible only to believers: to link the universe to a suprauniverse that faith alone can see and know. The human lineage and behavior of Jesus have never prevented the faithful from seeing in him a divine nature and power as well. On the contrary! How, then, could the human quality of the Bible ever discourage them from perceiving the Word of God? However, that Word they alone, the believers, are able to hear.

But from the moment when we were informed that the Bible is part of that ancient and vast heritage our ancestors passed on to us, like so many other monuments of their thought, their literature, and their art, we had once again the same sort of duty not only to find out what *they* wanted to tell us, but to inquire with all the means at our disposal into that heritage itself, just as we do for our understanding of the sense and meaning of the *Aeneid*, the *Odyssey*, and the Epic of Gilgamesh.

Perhaps even the believers, who are also in the first place human beings, will discover that they are interested in the endeavor to understand what the

---

1. We know today that this narrative makes up the eleventh and final tablet of the celebrated Epic of Gilgamesh in its "classical" version of the end of the second millennium, and that the authors of this epic drew on an equally famous composition, of which the earliest manuscripts go back to about the seventeenth century B.C.E., *The Poem of the Supersage* (*Atrahasis*). The latest serious translation into French is by R. Labat, in the collective volume *Les religions du Proche-Orient asiatique* (Paris: Fayard-Denoël, 1970), 145–226 and 26–36. On the most ancient narrative of the Flood, see *L'histoire*, no. 31 (February 1981): 113–20.

[Translator's note: For English translations of the Mesopotamian flood stories, see Stephanie Dalley, trans., *Myths from Mesopotamia: Creation, the Flood, Gilgamesh, and Others* (Oxford: Oxford University Press, 1989); W. G. Lambert and A. R. Millard, *Atra-Hasis: The Babylonian Story of the Flood* (Oxford: Oxford University Press, 1969); James B. Pritchard, ed., *The Ancient Near East: An Anthology of Texts* (Princeton: Princeton University Press, 1965).]

Bible in itself means, in its true, one might say, carnal, reality, which was to serve as the way appropriated by God to encounter and instruct them.

In the interminable unwinding of literary creativity—from its beginnings in the invention of writing by 3000 B.C.E.—the Bible represents, certainly not *the* literature of Israel, but a sort of anthology of pieces chosen from all that the Israelites wrote during the first millennium of their autonomous existence. This selection, the result of human orientations that inevitably had to occur in the ceaselessly changing ordinary world, came about on the basis of considerations that were above all religious; biblical literature, from the most ancient to the most recent pieces to be found there, was tied above all to the religious thought of those who did the collecting and editing and of those who passed it on.

The very essence of the documents that have preserved for us what I call "the universal message" of the Bible could not be understood apart from the religious level. Certainly, man is not pure spirit, and his relations with his gods cannot be separated from his economic, social, political, intellectual, and emotional life; they are profoundly affected by every crisis that occurs, and consequently, the entire history of Israel is reflected in the Bible. Just the same, what that history brings to our attention first of all is the progress of a people, among ancient peoples, in its religious sensations, its religious ideology, its religious attitude. Here, then, is the aspect by which the Bible assumes its place in the history of human beings, who have always been religious animals, whether we like it or not.

The Bible presents us with only a minuscule fragment of human history. How much is the one thousand years it recounts, next to the aeons anthropologists must posit as the span of humanity on earth? However, we should not speak of quantity outside the spiritual dimension, where it becomes a false and ludicrous criterion. May one weigh on the scale five hundred thousand years, and more, of a quasi-animal existence, nomadic, cave-dwelling, over immense stretches of the planet, alongside the one century and the barely visible little canton of the globe that saw the rise of Socrates, Plato, and Aristotle?

We all know that of this million years since our "origin," 95 percent or more stretched and stretched itself out into interminable stagnations, punctuated by slow and modest advances toward our recent promotion to dominion over the universe. It is less than ten thousand years ago that we began to be what we are today. The first time man arrived at the level of a high and thoroughly civilized state, in which he left behind the uncertainty of day-to-day survival, the isolation of small groups, powerlessness before the elements, that state of a prolonged animality, and gained access to social and political organization, to the sense of duty and law, control over nature, the well-thought-out production of tools, an intelligent arrangement of things, was between 4000 and 3000 B.C.E., in southern Mesopotamia. This first civilization was soon followed, afar, possibly in imitation, by Egypt, then the Indus valley, then China. It was then, and only there, as we now have learned, that the great adventure of our existence began, leading us to where we are today. The adventure is still brief, but how much fuller than the millennia that went before it!

If, in our endeavor to account for our present riches, the wealth of Western civilization, which seems about to complete its conquest of the universe—no doubt before fading in its turn—we search beyond techniques, beyond material riches and scientific accomplishments, if we seek to find its real sources of power, those sources are no mystery. The real foundation of our thought—whether one accepts it for what it is or would wish to recast it— was constituted at the beginning of our era. It resulted from the formidable revolution unleashed by Christianity. And Christianity came at the confluence of the science of the Greeks and the wisdom of the Jews. Greek science, characteristically, places man in and confronts him with the universe, which he is able to know and must know and master. It disposes our spirit and our knowledge to lucidity and rigor; it is the search for a perfect equilibrium of our being and our life. The wisdom of the Jews is that profound attitude of our heart which places itself no longer before the visible world but before the Other who transcends and guides the world, who reunites us all and makes us equals under His irresistible sovereignty, that thickness of mystery which is laid around all we see and know, that counterweight of humility protecting us from the excesses of our pride and dominion. The science of the Greeks is the fruit of a thousand years of progress, battles, various points of view, and discoveries in intellectual reflection. The wisdom of the Jews is the fruit of a thousand years of progress, battles, various points of view, and discoveries in religious experience.

Direct inheritors of the one and the other as we are, the millennial Jew, no less than the millennial Greek, gives us one of the most loaded, most poignant moments of our past. We still live off this double capital, willingly or not, accumulated by the double lineage of our ancestors.

If our origin and our formation hold any interest for us, if we want to know what we are made of, to see once more the time of our adolescence, all of us, whoever we may be, whatever the opinions, the religious or philosophical convictions we harbor, simply by virtue of being human beings, must claim this chapter of world history as our own. The adventure of the Israelite and Jewish people, decisive moment of our past, constitutes our patrimony, and it is virtually a duty for us to return to it in order to know it and relive it, in the way one returns and searches for the most cherished memories in the home of one's birth.

The past is dead. Endless drama on each of whose acts the curtain falls every day, it knows no encores, no revivals. We cannot be present to watch the actors. We can only perceive them through what they have left of themselves, which, less ephemeral, has persisted until our own days.

Of the biblical drama, there remain some of the décors and props: landscapes, sometimes barely changed for millennia, and a number of vestiges collected from the depth of the earth by archeologists in the course of centuries of discovery. Their feverish excavations continue still. Above all, what is left to us, apart from the scattered footnotes of the epigraphic finds that have surfaced parsimoniously in Palestine, and some sort of supplement that has come to us from the "apocryphal" literature (see note 21 on page 90), is the libretto of the piece: the Bible.

It is not easy to discern from these remains how scenes and acts followed one another and what profound meaning resides in them.

To begin with, this "libretto," written in a language and in accordance with a vision of the world that are separated from us by more than twenty centuries of accelerated evolution, is not complete: a thousand years or more of history cannot be compressed into a thousand pages without substantial loss.

In addition, the Bible's arrangement of materials is not in perfect order. It is true that it presents to us, grosso modo, in its "historical books," a scheme of events (among vast lacunae) in a plausible sequence, according to a certain chronology. But how to relate to this sequence the "nonhistorical books," each one in its time and its milieu, as one should if one cares for clarity? As for the "Prophets," matters are sometimes made easier because their names are mentioned in the historical accounts, or because of the concise biographical notes that occur in the opening of each book under their names. But where in the trajectory should one insert, for example, the Book of Job?

Moreover, the "historical" part is so full of repetitions as to drive us to distraction. Not only is the long sequence from the beginning of the world to the first fall of Jerusalem, narrated from Genesis to the Second Book of Kings, repeated, very abridged on the whole but with additions of many unedited or contradictory details, in the two books of Chronicles (or "Paralipomenon");[2] but as well, one finds a single episode repeated, almost word for word, two or three times in the same writing: could we make anyone believe that one and the same scandalous adventure of Abraham happened to him twice? Wanting to avoid trouble with the sovereign, who loved attractive women, Abraham, traveling through his territory, decided to pass off his wife as his sister. It happens first in Egypt, with the pharaoh (Genesis 12:10–20), then in Gerar, before the local king Abimelek (20:1–18), and a third time, it happens to Abraham's son, Isaac, in the same place, before the same petty monarch (26:1–11).

Most often, such reiterations are less flagrant and accede to camouflage in a story that appears to be homogeneous but in which an attentive eye, especially if it reads the text in its original language, can quickly tell the details that do not fit the context or that betray inner contradictions. If one looks closely at the account of the famous "Dream of Jacob" (Genesis 18:10–22), one becomes aware that part of the story (vv. 11, 12, 16a, 17, 20, and the end of 22) makes clear reference to a dream at night, in the course of which Jacob sees himself at the foot of the ladder that leads to the House of God— which in Hebrew bears the name Elohim ("God")—but another part mixed into the story (10, 13, 14, 15, 16b,19, the first words of 22), in which God receives His "proper name" Yahweh (see page 20), makes no reference to sleep: Yahweh appears suddenly to Jacob, and from His presence in that place, Jacob infers that He resides there.

The Prophetic books and Wisdom books are not devoid of similar "doublets" and likewise show an abundance of problematic or quite incredible elements. How could Isaiah, between 760 and 700 B.C.E., have known King Cyrus by name—for he mentions it in two places and in a context that leaves no doubt (44:28–45:1)—when Cyrus, founder of the Persian Empire, lived two centuries later (558–528)? And insofar as one insists on the first verse of Ecclesiastes, where the author says that he will transmit "the words" of Solomon (there is no other *"son of David"* who *"ruled in Jerusalem"*), one gets entangled in linguistic puzzles—to say nothing of other, more serious problems on an ideological plane; and the book becomes a burlesque of sorts, by 950 B.C.E. full of words and phrases borrowed from Aramaic, as unthinkable in

---

2. [Translator's note: The term "paralipomenon," things left out, was used to describe the books of Chronicles, so as to suggest that these books purposely tried to add material that was omitted from the earlier Bible books.]

Hebrew as a sermon by Bossuet studded with American slang (see pages 183ff.).

These problems of time and context are not the only ones, or the most serious problems, that await the reader of the biblical "libretto." Others come with the issue of meaning itself, the question of the realness of what one reads. Without invoking the first chapters of Genesis, as is done again and again— the light *preceding* the heavenly bodies (1:3ff. and 14 ff.); the "tree in the middle of the garden," with its forbidden fruit (2:9ff.); the ever-hilarious "rib of Adam" (2:21); the Serpent-tempter (3:1ff.); and the celebrated universal Flood, together with the ark and its menagerie (chaps. 6ff.); all of which have caused floods of ink to flow for centuries—there are a thousand other questions, no less crucial and no less obscure. For example:

Did Moses really exist? Undoubtedly—but what was his role? Must we really imagine him parting the Red Sea with a gesture, to let his people pass through in regiments, and then walking for forty years, *"six hundred and three thousand five hundred and fifty persons, without counting the tribe of Levi"* (Numbers 1:46), in a desert that could not possibly feed one thousand?

Is David the author of all the psalms that bear his name? Quite a few of them suggest a political, economic, and social situation in total decay and delivered to misfortune (9, 10, 14, 25, 28, and more), diametrically opposed to what 1 and 2 Samuel depict of the rule, prosperous and glorious, of this great king.

Was it really Solomon who constructed the first Israelite Temple (1 Kings 5:15ff.), or should we believe the end of Exodus (chaps. 25ff.), according to which, more than three centuries earlier, the throng of humanity taken along by Moses, without roof or fire, on their trek through the desert land of Sinai, already carried a sanctuary about as vast, as complete, as sumptuous, as Solomon's temple, but collapsible?

From the moment one reads the Bible for the purpose of knowing the actual life of those who wrote it, the entire book bristles with doubts and uncertainties. For the artless reader the Bible remains an enigma. Some have claimed in a frenzy to see nothing there but an enormous mystification, thus resolving the problems in one stroke by annihilating the data. But so many features the Bible reports, sometimes the most unexpected and minor ones, have been startlingly confirmed, directly or indirectly, by archeological excavation or by the decipherment of extrabiblical documents that we may not doubt (while keeping our *reason*) that in fact it contains the elements of an authentic history.

However, they are there in disorder and unrefined.

It is not as if the authors of the various biblical books, the compilers and reeditors through whose hands they passed before finding themselves incorporated in the "canon," had not provided a certain arrangement in the parts and in the whole. But their goal was pragmatic; it was fixed on the religious level, which was their sole interest. They did not seek to find and establish the past of their people in its prosaic reality. It was their religious universe that they wished to call forth, demonstrate to their readers: the supremacy of their God, the choice He made of their people, the sanctity and antiquity of the precepts He had given them, the necessity to obey Him. From the start, in the first chapter of Genesis (see also page 150), the filigree of this apologetic concern shows through in the narrative: the work of the Creator comprises really *eight* stages, yet perforce it is compressed into *six* days, followed by the seventh, when "God rested." The seven-day rhythm of time was a fundamental principle of the religion of Israel. Six days for work, then one for rest and cultic observance (Exodus 20:8ff.; see page 25): the author of the narrative manifestly wished to base this duty upon the conduct of God Himself, in order to confer a value on it that was built into the cosmos.

In a time that had become fully historical, the entire Book of Judges is cast in a scheme that is repeated ten times, setting the names and great deeds of the various judges in a certain frame: the Israelites turn from Yahweh and let themselves be carried away toward other gods; Yahweh chastises them, and abandons them to their enemies, who oppress them; in their misfortune, they return to Him; then He is moved and delivers them by means of a "judge" whom He raises up for them. The names of the enemies and of those who set the Israelites free differ in each case, but the scheme is identical throughout the book (Judges 2:11ff.; 3:7ff.; 3:12ff.; 4:1ff.; 6:1ff.; etc.).

Composed as it is, the Bible throughout bears the imprint of its authors' faith—nay, even their credulity, which is like the ever-present shadow of their faith. And we find ourselves still a long way from our goal, we who wish to uncover, by means of this book, what really transpired in the past of its authors. How can we accept what they say, *ut iacet*, as unique and infallible? In truth, the history of Israel *is not given in* the Bible. It *is arrived at by making use of* the Bible. The latter is no more than its repository.

Thus, with the stubbornness and cunning of an examining magistrate, we must discern each author's purpose and make use of what he presents us in this enormous affair.

To discuss, evaluate, and understand a collection so large and intricate is an enterprise that is not within the reach of just anyone. A *métier* is called for: a tested technique, applied by professionals trained in its practice and able to devote to it their entire energy.

This technique exists, in full possession of all the means it needs. It is history, whose "scientific" role is to take all that the past has left us—material traces and written documents—and to classify, analyze, and penetrate these "witnesses," in order to rediscover through them the time from which they came and which in their way they convey to us and make present.

Especially for the last century and a half, since the "genetic sciences" developed a sharper focus, a large number of scholars, including some authentic geniuses, have labored mightily to bring the methods of history to bear on the Bible. Through these methods and these methods alone, a collection of documentary fragments, a dossier of witnesses, was restored to coherency. And though the task was gigantic, it has been pushed much further since. Of course, for all that, we would err in presuming that henceforth biblical history is perfectly integrated and clarified. In the first place, that would be a miracle! Infinite is the past, and it leaves no more than traces, like a destroyed mosaic whose few surviving bits would not enable us to restore more than fragments, separated by enormous spaces uncrossable except by reckonings more or less well founded—and, in the final analysis, subjective. Furthermore, one must recognize that history is governed by the spirit of finesse, and one does not find in the historian's work forthright geometric pieces of evidence that impose themselves at once on every intellect. The grounds for history's appraisals are so manifold and tenuous as to lead historians into frequent conflict with each other, over details, conjectures, and interpretations. Especially at the end of a long and scrupulous inquiry, when historians must align their scattered findings into a coherent view for the sake of the point that matters, to give the idea, to give the sense, of a segment of human life, large or small, inevitably their personality, their outlook, their preoccupations, their own priorities in raising questions—all the more so in the complex, subtle, and finally subjective areas concerning our intellectual and spiritual life—create within their work something personal to each of them, indeed something involuntarily biased, which here and there flavors the thesis they aver.

When one steps back a bit before their work, in the final analysis there does emerge from it, at least in outline, the thousand-year history of which the Bible in its entirety is the ore and the archive. If the image scholars depict is not always what was expected by familiars and devotees of the Bible, and if they are disappointed, this is not surprising. It is proper for science to look beyond the appearances that hold back the man in the street, and to search for things as they are.

We have noted before that to various degrees the books of the Bible, in their narrations, all bear the marks of the practical purposes of their authors or compilers. The radical preliminary discovery made by historians of the Bible lay precisely in tracking down these redundant interventions, which could only obfuscate the search for what really happened, and gleaning the elements of primary documents, which are the basis for a sound reconstruction of history. This is not the place to relate how this reconstruction succeeded, or even to sketch a picture of this "Bible set in historical order." It is devoutly to be wished that some day an intelligent and intrepid publisher might provide us with such a Bible instead of the everlasting stream of reeditions of the "canonical text." Let it suffice, here and now, by means of two or three examples, to suggest the entirely renewed idea of the Bible that historians have provided us.

With regard to the historical books, it was not difficult to remove the dogmatic, supererogatory schemes into which pious editors had inserted preexisting documents. (We have just noted such a scheme in the Book of Judges.) Once the recurrent theological frame was taken away, together with the artificial, misleading idea it implied of the time, real progress could be made on two fronts. Not only were the "witnesses" freed from the deceptive veneer and returned to their "native" state, appropriate for shedding an authentic light on the period (see, for instance, pages 10 and 26f.), but the artificial scheme itself, singled out from the text, now showed us the idea its authors formed of the history of events that unfolded centuries earlier, namely, a rigorous demonstration of God's retributive justice (see page 60).

What has been more troublesome is the study of "double narratives" of the same event, mingled together, like those that make up the canvas of the "Dream of Jacob" (pages 8f.), which one comes upon at every turn of the page, especially in the ensemble of the Hexateuch, the first six books of the Bible, from Genesis through Joshua. Once the texts and vocabulary have been properly ascertained and examined in each case, including their language, stylistic characteristics, and individual ideology, then, even as geologists can identify a terrain, though it contains great gaps, by its mineral composition and its characteristic fossils, it has been possible to verify that the "doublets" are coherent within themselves, in autonomous bodies of literature, so that instead of *one* history of ancient Israel, as it appears in the Hexateuch, we can single out several histories, written in different times and moods, each with its own language and its own typical way of viewing events. Only, rather than let them exist side by side, as in the case of Chronicles (see page 8 above), the authors of our Bible preferred to extract episodes from the various histories, which they then devoutly interlaced like strands of a rope, so as to present a narrative that is smooth and coherent in appearance but does not lose anything from what each independent story has to say. They went about their task in a manner similar to that of Tatian, who, in the second century C.E., dealt with the four gospels so as to weave a "gospel harmony" out of them: the result is the *Diatessaron*, a unique account that is as smooth as it is composite.

As with the *Diatessaron*, the biblical root documents number four. (There the analogy ends.) The most ancient of these, known to us as the *Yahwist* (see pages 34ff.), goes back to the ninth century B.C.E. and must have been composed in or around Jerusalem. The author is he who in the "Dream of Jacob" (pages 8f. above) calls God by his name of Yahweh and does not shrink from making Him appear in person to Jacob. The rest of the same story, where God bears the name Elohim and where every personal contact between Him and Jacob is carefully avoided, comes from the *Elohist* (see pages 45f.), written approximately a century later, in the Northern Kingdom, which commences its history only with Abraham, while the account of the *Yahwist* begins with the creation of the world. The third literary source, the *Deuteronomist*, which is much more devoted to religious legislation than to history properly so called, consists especially of almost the entire mass of materials that we have in Deuteronomy (see page 59); the author of this material, like the *Yahwist author*, is from Jerusalem, and his documents date for the most part from the seventh century. Finally, we have the *Priestly Document* (see page 84), so named for its clerical interest, concerned with theology and legality, precise, dry, with a great weakness for numbers and schemes. This last document, in which history also begins with Creation, must have been written during the great Exile or a little later, approximately two centuries after Deuteronomy.

One ought not to assume, by way of these demarcations, that the union of the four works is simple and that to isolate them we need only separate some four perfectly consistent, perfectly autonomous strands. Not only do they generally depend, to some extent, on their predecessors, but often we find, inserted in their common web, other documents, partial or complete, older, or, at least initially, independent. This is the case especially with parts of the legislative corpus, such as the Renewal of the Covenant (Exodus

34:10–26) in the *Yahwist*; the Decalogue (Exodus 20:1–21; see page 25) and the Book of the Covenant (or Code of the Covenant; Exodus 20:22–23:19; see page 32) in the *Elohist*; and the Code of Holiness (Leviticus 17–26; see page 84) in the *Priestly Document*. Moreover, the conjuncture of the sources was achieved in more than one step. The *Yahwist* and the *Elohist* had become amalgamated before the Deuteronomist was joined to them, and the *Priestly Document* in its entirety was added later on. Thus we see how twisted the track becomes, and how it leads us to posit that each of the works involved, and above all the juncture of each to the others, is not the work of one author but of a group of contemporaries working in the same spirit—in others words, "a school" (see, for instance, page 60). We should mention that these "schools" have played their part likewise in the elaboration or revision of other historical books following the Hexateuch.

Given all this, there is no hope of seeing these four documents precisely separate and presented with their original texts intact. Only geometers can view their subject matter in perfect parts. For historians, accustomed to shadings and objects that blur into a surrounding darkness, the recovery of the four basic elements of the Hexateuch and of the stages in their development toward the shape in which we have them in our Bibles is not only evidence enough (irrespective of disputes over details, and variations from one critique to another) but a great step forward in the orderly arrangement of the biblical record with respect to its impact on the plane of history. This historical vision presents one by one events that preceded their earliest narration by several centuries, and helps critical scholarship to evaluate the veracity or improbability of the earliest narration. Moreover, since the steps in the process are spread out from the beginning to the middle of the first millennium, we now have at our disposal valuable beacons to follow in the historical development, especially the development of religious thought.

To the extent that success has been achieved and a first progression established in the cultural and religious development of Israel, analogous research in sorting out and redistributing elements in the nonhistorical books of the Bible has been facilitated and stimulated. By way of example: we can no longer ascribe to the prophet Isaiah the authorship of the "oracles against Babylon" (Isaiah 13:1–14:23; see page 69 below), because they imply a political situation that prevailed two centuries later—as is the case with the passage where Cyrus is mentioned (see page 8 above).

And better yet, with respect to these verses in Isaiah, if one carefully studies the context, one observes that they are part of a coherent and sequential whole (Isaiah 40–55), whose language, style, imagery, religiosity, and ideological milieu—to say nothing of the historical and political situation (the end of the great Exile; see pages 73ff.)—are quite different from those of the old Prophet, two centuries earlier. So what we have here is a complete, independent, and much more recent prophetic work (see again pages 73ff.), *attributed* to the great man, indubitably for the same reasons of admiration, piety . . . and endorsement that motivated those who attributed to Moses a large number of laws that were worked out well after his time (see pages 33 and 59), and made David responsible for quite a number of psalms inconceivable during his lifetime (see pages 9 and 91).

In other words, the compilers of our Bible had their hands just as much in other texts as in the historical books proper, especially in the Prophets, and even in the Wisdom writings, although in those, with their generally rather recent composition, the interference seems less frequent and more discreet. We find in the Prophets or the Wisdom writings no trace of the process of interconnecting preexisting works. But the insertion of entire passages or of tendentious glosses and comments (see, for instance, pages 99 and 184), and the attribution of such superadded passages, even entire sections, to weighty characters who could not have been responsible for them (see, for instance, pages 8 and 184), are phenomena throughout the *prophetic* and *wisdom* parts of our Bible, just as they are in the historical part.

Here too, the critics have had their role, by patient inquiry rearranging the chronology of pieces mixed together by compilers. The compilers betrayed their own preoccupations, especially their religious preoccupations, which we can discover in making our way through these entanglements. Here, as elsewhere, there is still uncertainty, conjecture, and blur; but also, as elsewhere, there is no real barrier to an adequate regaining of temporal order in the biblical record.

In sum, thanks to the enormous, quiet activity by historians, it is possible from now on, in their footsteps, "to engage in biblical history with the help of the Bible."

One should not expect to find in the present book any more than a synopsis of this history, centered solely on the religious development that is the basis of the "universal message" of the Bible. The account will not escape the weaknesses that by nature attend any historical synthesis. Without insisting on a meticulous chronology, we will find it more worthwhile to depict the principal parts of the immense trajectory, basing our depiction as much as possible on biblical passages selected for their suggestive power and translated from their original language into our own with a special concern for the force and beauty of what is said in them.

BEFORE MOSES

As we look upon her across more than three thousand years, Israel before Moses had at best a *potential* existence; to our eyes, dazzled by the great empires and heights of millenarian civilizations, of Mesopotamia in the East, Egypt in the Southwest, Anatolia in the Northwest, Israel seems one more tribe astray among the countless, inconspicuous seminomadic groups that roamed the Fertile Crescent, the northern flank of the great Syro-Arabic desert.

Almost all are Semites: herders of small cattle, caravaneers, or pillagers, living on the margin, often off the surplus of a firmly rooted, urbane, and highly civilized agricultural society that does not look kindly upon them. *"Those nomads from the West, who infest the steppe, know nothing of grain, houses, or cities, eaters of raw meat, uneducable, ungovernable, and who, when they die, are not even interred in accordance with the rituals."*[3]

If some of them, individually or in groups, are tempted and allow themselves to be absorbed by city life, many constitute a danger for those who are settled there, and officials charged with maintaining order do not hesitate to inform the proper party of their movements, in order to ward off any occurrence: *"Let my Lord the King know that the hordes of the Hana nomads, who are on the banks of the Euphrates, have crossed the river and have ascended the wadis. These people are going to feed their sheep and goats around Fort Iasmahaddu. . . . They are bandits! Let us take care that they do not turn to plunder or commit other crimes! And since my Lord the King finds himself at that place, and in view of the present report, which he has requested of me, may he take counsel on the subject of the small livestock [and counter the threat they present]."*[4]

We can hardly be mistaken when we imagine the ancestors of Israel as one of these turbulent tribes, always in search of new pastures and new spoils. Destitute of literature, certainly even ignorant of the art of writing, so rough and vagrant their existence, they have left us no direct testimony of their sayings and doings. However, because of the oral tradition, which is always alive and abundant with nomadic and nonliterate peoples, there are some

3. This is how the citizens of Mesopotamia at the beginning of the second millennium saw them, judging by what their learned individuals tell us: see the Sumerian texts assembled by J. Cooper in *The Curse of Agade* (Baltimore: Johns Hopkins University Press, 1983), 31ff.

4. Letter, in Babylonian, from a steward of King Iasmahaddu of Mari, around 1800 B.C.E. Published in G. Dossin, *Archives royales de Mari*, pt. V (Paris: Imprimerie nationale, 1952), 110–13, no. 81.

scattered outlines, more or less embroidered, that, among the writings of their descendants, recorded in the Bible, emerge here and there, assembled around a series of great sheiks, the "patriarchs," dating from the beginnings of their tribe as an autonomous entity: Abraham, Isaac, and Jacob. In the fashion of Bedouins even today, they kept a lofty genealogy and some elements of a "history," on which in the course of time a whole folklore came to be grafted, as one can see especially in Genesis, beginning with chapter 12.

What we retain are just the memories, probably faithful ones, of a nomadic and trans-Euphratean origin: *"In former times, your ancestors lived beyond the Euphrates, and they served other gods. I took your father Abraham across the Euphrates, and I made him come into the midst of the land of Canaan, where I multiplied his offspring"* (Joshua 24:2f.; *Yahwist* + Elohist).

> *Leave your native country, Yahweh said to Abraham, your kindred and your father's house, to go to the land that I shall show you. I shall make a great people of you; I shall bless you; I shall make your name great, and it will become a carrier of blessings:*
>
> *I shall bless those who bless you;*
>
> *those who scorn you, I shall curse!*
>
> *Through you all the peoples of the world will be blessed!*
>
> *And Abraham set out, as Yahweh had ordered him, accompanied by Sara, his wife, and Lot, his nephew, with all the possessions they had set aside and all the servants they had acquired. They traveled toward the land of Canaan, where at last they arrived.* (Genesis 12:1–5; *Yahwist*)

Once in Canaan—that is to say, Palestine, especially the southern part of that land—by, as we think, approximately the middle of the second millennium, they grew and diversified into clans (which will come to be known as "the tribes"; see page xviii). The majority remained herdsmen and followed their flocks from one pasture to another, from one watering place to the next, often at war with other nomads and especially with the sedentary occupants of the land.

At the time, the country was occupied notably by "Canaanite" peoples (see pages 26f. and 31), also Semites in origin, but who had been settled there for a long time. They had redivided and lived in fortified cities, which were like small kingdoms, sometimes independent, sometimes vassals of one another or of some great sovereign abroad, especially the king of Egypt. The nomads in the country, including perhaps certain Israelite clans, must have taken part in the wars in which the Canaanites were involved, whether they fought in the service of the settled populations or were in search of a bit of land for themselves. Must we not think of them when we read the following letter, which was written in the fourteenth century B.C.E. by the governor of Byblos to his patron, the pharaoh? *"Let my Lord the King know that, though everything goes well in the city of Byblos, which is a faithful servant of the King, the pressure of the brigands and vagabonds on me is increasing more and more. May my Lord the King not turn his eyes from the city of Sumur; otherwise the city might find itself, before long, entirely in the hands of these Brigands."*[5]

Taking the entire region into account, however, it hardly seems as if the descendants of Abraham had obtained a notable foothold in Canaan. Scattered through the land and about the two major centers, Sichem in the North and Hebron in the South, they seem to have led a precarious and inglorious existence.

Some of the groups in the utmost southern area, where the land bordered on the Negeb desert, were more exposed to the droughts that brought famine and decimated livestock. For them, it was natural to push westward, toward the humid regions and the grassland of the Nile Delta, in Egypt.

> *When Jacob learned there was grain for sale in Egypt, he said to his sons: "Why stay and look around you? I hear there is grain in Egypt. Go down there and buy some of it, so that we may stay alive instead of starving to death." Hence ten brothers of Joseph went down to Egypt to purchase wheat. But Jacob did not let Benjamin, the youngest brother of Joseph, go with them. "Out of fear," he said, "that something bad may happen to him!" In the company of others who went the same way, the sons of Israel set out to purchase grain, because there was famine in the land of Canaan.* (Genesis 42:1–5: *Yahwist*)

"Others who went the same way." This clearly means that what happened was not exceptional—barely different from a change in encampment or pasture. The functionaries of the pharaoh, in the Northeast of the country, must have registered the movement of such Eastern nomads into the delta many times. Thus, by the end of the thirteenth century, one overseer of the

---

5. Letter, in Babylonian, from the El-Amarna collection, no. 68, in J. A. Knudtzon, *Die El-Amarna Tafeln* (Leipzig: Hinrichsche Buchhandlung, 1907), I:360ff.

area whose report has been preserved says: *"One more piece of news for His Majesty; we have allowed the Bedouins coming from Edom to pass . . . as far as Pools of Per-Anti . . ., in the region of Teku, so that they and their animals can stay alive."*[6]

This was no doubt occurring at the same time, in the course of the thirteenth century, perhaps under pressure of troubles in international policy, things were taking a turn for the worse in Egypt. The government became more rigid. Attempts were made to keep back by force the flocks and herds from Palestine in search of fresh pastures, and foreign residents were constrained, perhaps even more than the pharaoh's Egyptian subjects, into forced labor and servitude, a state of affairs that was particularly painful for the nomads, who until then had lived without being tied down: *"The Egyptians forced the Israelites to work and made life harsh for them with cruel labor, in clay and brick-making, and in all sorts of fieldwork"* (Exodus 1:13f.; *Priestly Document*).

MOSES AND THE COVENANT WITH YAHWEH

Later, a fantastic halo would light up around basic memories of those heroic times that had always been preserved in Israel.

In fact, everything began here. Among the oppressed in a hostile land, a leader had to arise, a chief of genius, a great man, who assigned to himself the task of delivering his compatriots out of their servitude and joining them to their own who were living in the ancestral territory, so that all together they could conquer and appropriate the land of Canaan. Their fathers had lived in the margin of that land. The originality of this political design, in our eyes, is that it had to be realized under a religious inspiration, in the name of a "new god."

Moses, for such is the name of this ancient genius, the true creator of Israel, had in the course of his journeys most certainly learned of the existence of this god, who was unknown to his kinsmen and whose cult center must have been, as so often among the ancient Semites, a "high place," a mountain, apparently in a wild desert region, the Sinai, or, perhaps more likely, of the northern Hijaz,

6. Papyrus Anastasi vi:51ff.; after J. B. Pritchard, *Ancient Near Eastern Texts Relating to the Old Testament*, 2d ed. (Princeton: Princeton University Press, 1955), 259a.

on the other side of the arm of the sea of Akaba (see page 23). There perhaps the future chief had found the inspiration that would take him so far. He heard this God declare to him:

> *"I have seen the misery of my people in Egypt. I have heard their cries before their jailers. Yes, I know their sufferings! And I have come down to pull them out of the hands of the Egyptians and to let them ascend from that land to a superb and wide land, to the land flowing with milk and honey!" Moses answered God: "Who am I, to go and stand before Pharaoh in order to bring the Israelites out of Egypt?" He said to him: "But I shall be with you! And when you have brought this people out of Egypt, you will all come here to this mountain to worship God." (Exodus 3:7–12; Yahwist + Elohist)*

Considering that no people in the world will willingly change its gods, Moses must certainly have reflected that in order to bear such a message to his people, he must underscore the identity of its author with the principal traditional deity of their ancestors, their brethren, and themselves, appearing now under a new aspect. And this aspect as yet unknown of God shone forth through His very name, for, among the ancient Semites, the name of a thing was not, as for us, a casual epiphenomenon but a true emanation of its essence. The name, then, "Yahweh,"[7] could make one think of a verb that, in the ancient idiom of the Israelites, meant "to exist," "to be."

> *Then Moses said to God: "Here I am, ready to go and find the Israelites and tell them: 'The god of your fathers has sent me to you!' But if they ask me: 'What is His name?' what should they be told in response?" And God said to Moses: "I am who I am!" And he added: "This is what you will have to say to the Israelites: '"I am" has sent me to you. . . . "He is"* [in ancient Hebrew: Yahweh], *the God of your fathers, the God of Abraham, the God of Isaac, the God of Jacob, has sent me to you.' Thus is My name forever!" (Exodus 3:13–15; Elohist)*

To think that this is "primitive," this intuition, an extraordinary presentation of this God's character, at the same time unique and mysterious, of whom

---

7. "Yahweh" is the authentic reading of the Hebrew word, considered the "proper name" of God. For this reason, the ancient Jewish copyists of the Bible, wanting to avoid the possibility that people might pronounce such a "sacred" designation, wrote it down in such a way that for a long time God's name was spelled "Jehova."

all one could and should know was that He existed, that He was there, would be to misjudge a remarkably profound conception: the religious history of Israel, and consequently our own, is presented here in its seed, and centuries would be required for us to arrive at our idea of its meaning, to make its riches explicit. This conception in its essence suffices to account Moses as one of the paramount geniuses of our race—that is, as long as a sound and serene vision of things causes us to hold the religious sentiment among our very highest powers, even in the excesses that it, just like the sentiment of love, throws us into now and again.

How did the first act actually unfold, in this play that Moses put into motion? Most notably in this case, all is covered by the heroic and the miraculous haze of folklore. That cloud does seem to harbor a real memory of a prime and extraordinary chance that made this small band of wretches the conquerors, in a sense, of the enormous people of Egypt and of pharaoh in all his splendor. Could the story follow upon some untoward accident that mired in the marshes near Suez the patrol that was sent out to bring the fugitives to their senses? The feeling of victory, the first gesture of the new Protector of His people, the first sign of His power, breaks forth in this eulogy, which, nevertheless, in its present form, postdates by several centuries the events it narrates; it is the song that the fifteenth chapter of Exodus places in the mouth of Moses and his liberated companions:

> *I celebrate illustrious Yahweh, Him who is full of glory,*
> *Who has hurled horses and riders into the sea!*
> *He is my strength, my song of praise,*
> *He became my deliverance!*
> *He is my God, I exalt Him:*
> *He is my father's God, and I make Him great!*
> *Yahweh is a true Commander in war:*
> *Yahweh—that is His name!*
> *He has thrown Pharaoh's chariots and armies into the sea:*
> *The elite of his knights are engulfed in the Red Sea!*
> *The abyss covered them,*
> *They sank into the depth like a stone!*
> *Your right hand, Yahweh, showed Its force.*
> *Your right hand, Yahweh, shattered the foes!*
> *In your great Glory, You annihilate Your enemies:*
> *You launch your fury, it consumes them like stubble!*

At the breath of Your nostrils, the waves rose up,
The currents surged like a barrage,
The abyss solidified in the midst of the sea!
The enemy claimed: "I pursue them, I recapture them.
I divide the spoils and my soul is satiated with them.
Let me draw my sword, and my hand will catch them!"
But You blew Your breath, and the sea covered them again:
They slipped like lead into the vast waters!
Who is like You among the gods, Yahweh?
Who is like You—
Incomparable in majesty, fearsome in great deeds,
A Wonder-worker.

(Exodus 15:1–11; incorporated in the *Elohist*)

This unforeseen victory has a bearing far beyond the event itself: it fixes forever the religious vision of Yahweh's devotees, and thus it determines the future development of their religion. In the successful escape, which for Israel drew its importance only from the disproportion of forces and the deliverance granted against all hope to the weak, those believers who followed saw the intervention of Yahweh, as that admirable song still conveys to our senses in spite of the time separating us from what occurred. In some way, they super-imposed on the events in this world a mechanism and a force that were ordered by God: this is what we have called "faith" (page 4).

At one stroke, this supernatural conviction of His involvement here below gave Yahweh his full dimension: seeing the turn of events and twist of fortune whereby, with a sudden gust of wind, the felicitous presence of quicksand, His people were rescued from the Egyptian yoke, the Israelites began to be persuaded that their God had the upper hand over nature and people alike. In nuclear form, here we have the destiny of Yahweh. The "miraculous" departure from Egypt is the first step of a long ascension.

We can sense that the moment was ripe for this faith to be conceived, and, furthermore, instilled in others by Moses the chief, whose spiritual leadership was no less than his worldly leadership and whose course still had far to run. Instead of their returning promptly to Canaan by the shortest route after the unexpected victory, tradition attributes to the fugitives a long experience of wandering in the "desert of Sinai." That is what Moses understood by the words *"When you have brought this people out of Egypt, you will come to worship God here at this mountain,"* the mountain where He had revealed Himself to Moses. The events that had already come to pass were far from sufficient to create between Yahweh and Israel, between Israel and Yahweh, the bonds that Moses was planning to tie between them: he wanted to make of Israel the People of Yahweh, chosen and protected by Him, and of Yahweh the unique God of Israel, the only One who would count in their eyes. For, in his thought—and here the unforeseen strike by Yahweh and the departure from Egypt could only reinforce his conviction—if there were such ties, exclusive ties between them, Yahweh would intervene again to defend His people, in the face of the entire world, and every hope of prosperity and greatness would be permitted under such a "Commander in war."

With this purpose in mind, Moses wanted to return to an old practice, established and in use among the ancient Semites, which would now replace blood relationship with a kinship of the imagination, no less tangible and solid, a community of flesh, of life, and of destiny, simultaneously symbolized and made real by a collection of rites: the ceremony of the Covenant, with a communal meal (and an exchange of blood?) and the swearing of an oath, by each participant, to fulfill their duties toward the others.

This Covenant had to be ratified at the place proper to Yahweh's cult, "on the mountain." And this is the explanation of the long detour of the Israelites.

One tradition, not especially credible, has it that this "mountain" (sometimes called Sinai, sometimes Horeb, in the Bible) is one of the summits of the Sinai peninsula, namely, Jabal Musa. This tradition arose more than a millennium after the events and came to be generally accepted. Much more ancient, and rooted in the collective memory of Israel, is another tradition, which seems to make the first immediate contact of Israel with Yahweh, at the moment of the Covenant, coincide with an altogether anomalous, terrible upheaval of nature. If we put together its various features, beginning with what we are told in the oldest narratives of Exodus, it can scarcely be anything but a volcanic eruption. The mountain was *"encompassed by thunder, lightning, and a great cloud, with sounds like the trumpet,"* the mountain, *"smoking all around, for Yahweh descended in a fire whose smoke rose up as from a furnace, and the whole mountain shook"* (Exodus 19:16 and 18; *Elohist*). This mountain would have to be sought in a region known for volcanic activity in historical times. This is the case with the land of Madian, north of the Hijaz, and a number of ancient biblical references point in the same direction. Surely, the coincidence of Yahweh's personal revelation to His people with this great upheaval struck and marked forever the religious imagination of the Israelites, imposing upon them an idea of a God who is

Master of nature, awesome, who brings devastation, who is irresistible—and He would remain recognizable by those qualities long thereafter.

The Covenant with this God could not but take on even greater importance:

> *Moses came and related to the people all the commandments of Yahweh and all His decisions, and the entire people responded: "All the commandments Yahweh has given we shall follow!" So Moses put into writing all the rules given by Yahweh. Then, early in the morning, he built an altar at the foot of the Mountain. At his order, the young men of Israel sacrificed young bulls in a holocaust, killing them for a sacrificial feast. Then Moses poured half of the blood into basins, and with the other half he sprinkled the altar. And taking the scroll of the Covenant, he read it before the people. And all were repeating: "All that Yahweh has commanded we shall do, we shall obey!" Then Moses took the remaining blood and sprinkled it upon the people: "This," he said, "is the blood of the Covenant that Yahweh has made with you in accordance with these rules!" Then Moses went up the mountain, with Aaron, Hadab, Abihu, and seventy members of the Council of Israel. They saw the God of Israel; at His feet was a pavement of sapphire, like the sky itself. But He did not destroy those privileged ones, who could see God and feast in His presence. (Exodus 24:3–11; Yahwist + Elohist)*

This account was not set down in writing until several centuries later. One can sense this, and many details in it are unlikely (the "young bulls" and the imposing council of seventy in the midst of a desert!). But the essentials breathe authenticity. The shared blood and especially the communal meal are traditional acts that taken together constitute an alliance, or covenant, common among the ancient Semites. Henceforward, Yahweh and His people would find themselves tightly bound, like relatives, owning everything in common, for better or worse. As a people, Israel now belonged to Yahweh, and her political future, linked to her religious life, had entered that supernatural universe perceptible only to faith and enveloping the world here below.

Yet even this still is not the unique, the truly original feature of the charter constitutive of the Israelite people. It still remains for us to speak of the ultimate subject, the contents of the Covenant, the rules on which it was established. In the narrative we have just read, Moses "wrote" them on a "scroll." Since nothing of the sort was present at the time (see note 4 on page 111), this detail may be an anachronism. What is certainly anachronistic is our account's textual reference itself: it refers to the text of Exodus 20:22 through 23:19 (*Elohist*; see page 14 above). This passage has been called the Code of the Covenant; it appears to present the oldest legislative collection preserved in the Bible (see pages 32f. and 45f. below). Because it bears unmistakable markings of a settled life, dedicated to cultivation, we cannot attribute its wording to that sheik of Bedouins in pitiful circumstances, Moses. Most certainly, we shall remain forever ignorant of the text of the Covenant that was actually confirmed "on the mountain." Nevertheless, everything leads us to believe that the essential traits of the Covenant have been preserved by the tradition and that they are well reflected in what is known as the Decalogue:

> —*I, Yahweh, am your God, I, Who have led you out of Egypt, out of the house where you were slaves! You shall have no other gods besides Me!*
>
> —*You shall make no idols in the shape of anything on high in Heaven, or here below on earth, or in the waters below the earth.*[8] *You shall not prostrate before them, or worship them. For I, Yahweh, your God, am an exclusive God!*
>
> —*Do not use the name of Yahweh, your God, to tell a lie.*
>
> —*Do not forget to sanctify the Day of Rest. For six days you may work and accomplish all you have to do. But the seventh day is a holiday reserved for Yahweh, your God.*
>
> —*Honor your father and your mother!*
>
> —*Do not kill anyone!*
>
> —*Do not commit adultery!*

8. The understanding of this passage, and quite a few others of the same sort, quoted from time to time in the present work, presupposes a worldview that is not at all like ours and that rendered the cosmology of the ancient Israelites. The Israelites, very probably dependent on the ancient Mesopotamians, conceived of the universe as follows: an immense hollow sphere, wholly submerged in the "Waters above" of the "Great Abyss," separated from the "Waters below" by the "Vault" of Heaven. These "Waters below" were of two kinds. First were those of the "Sea," which were like the "Waters above" and surrounded the earth completely. Then, the earth, like an enormous circular "island," was itself established and "founded" by means of pedestals below a sheet of fresh water that was coextensive with the earth itself and rose up through the earth's wells and springs. All the way down, so it seems, extended the immense subterranean cavern of Sheol, the Netherworld, the abode of all the spirits of the dead, without distinctions among them. At the Horizon of the Earth, a number of tall mountains formed many "columns" to support the Vault of Heaven. A complete and complex, abundant, and not always logical mythology was grafted upon this schematic "plan." See also pages 150ff. below.

—Do not steal!
—Do not bear false witness against your fellow men!
—Do not covet the house of your fellow man, or his wife, servant,
or servant girl—or anything that belongs to him! (Exodus 20:2–17;
Elohist)

What matters here is not so much what is said word by word as it is the
real substance of these "commandments." When we compare them to axioms
of the other great religions of that time, including the greatest and most
venerable, from Babylon to Egypt—axioms that remain uninsistent and are
more to be inferred—we perceive in the commandments of Israel's Covenant
something purposely "spiritual," profound, sublime, and we are forced to
marvel even more at the genius of Moses. Admittedly, the commandments
do not tell us that Yahweh is the only true God in the absolute sense; however,
He is the only one who matters and who must matter for Israel. The others
exist, but not for Israel. In the eyes of Israel, there is only Yahweh. And
against the customs that were then universal, one must not seek to imagine
or represent this God, to reduce Him to a form. It is enough to know by His
word that, as His name indicates, "He exists," "He is there." One must
honor Him, not only with a portion of one's time, but in the knowledge that
He insists on being served above all else by respect for other people, for their
lives, for their honor and their goods, as though the practice of justice and
fraternity—even though it remains, in the present context, directed only
toward fellow Israelites—were indeed what He demanded above all!

Thus, binding Israel to Yahweh in accordance with the grand and profound idea he had formed of this God and their Covenant, Moses fulfilled
the first part of his mission. But he died—by 1250, according to the historians—
leaving it to his followers to look after the second task: making Israel into a
nation and giving her Palestine as her land.

SETTLING IN PALESTINE AND ITS POLITICAL
CONSEQUENCES

We would be deceived about what happened after Moses' death if we only
read, in its present state, the book that bears the name of his immediate
successor, Joshua. That book presupposes the national unity of the Israelites,
lacking only "The Promised Land," and makes it seem as though they

completed its conquest with drums beating, in stunning advances, the conquerors eliminating the conquered from first to last, and then divided the spoils and established themselves in the others' place like squatters in an emptied location.

In fact, things happened differently, and it is above all the Book of Judges that allows us to understand what took place, so long as we are careful to extract the original elements from the theological frame in which pious compilers embedded them (see page 10 above).

Turning to chapter 5, for example, we find the Song of Deborah,[9] whose language and style easily permit us to link it to those events eleven hundred years before our era, and which is not only one of the greatest poems in the Bible but also one of its most ancient documents. What does the Song of Deborah tell us? Confronting the "Canaanites," who are ensconced in their manors and fortified cities and led by their kings (v. 19), Israel is scattered over the territory and fragmented politically into its dozen "clans," or "tribes," subdivisions characteristic among nomads or seminomads who have become too numerous. The southernmost tribe, Judah, is not mentioned, for it seems to have kept aloof even then; we see only its closest neighbor and ally, the clan of Benjamin (v. 13), abiding in the area of Jerusalem; the tribe of Dan (v. 17), to the west, toward the sea; Ephraim (v. 13), a bit further north; and still further north, Machir (v. 14), another name of Manasseh; and further north, near the Lake of Gennesaret, Issachar (v. 15); further yet, Zebulun (v. 14); and still further, Naphtali (v. 15); then, toward the west of the latter, along the Mediterranean, north of the promontory of Carmel, Asher (v. 17); beyond the Jordan, Reuben (v. 15–16), in the neighborhood of the Dead Sea; a little higher, in the land of Gilead, the tribe of the same name, Gilead, or Gad (v. 17). Such a dispersion implies that, in the peaceful way of their ancestors or perhaps by war and particular conquests, the various Israelite clans had been penetrating the land from the eleventh century on. Another significant passage in Judges (3:5–6) states quite plainly that they lived *"side by side with the Canaanites, marrying their daughters and accepting them as sons-in-law, and worshiping their gods."*

Scattered though they may be, in some way they maintain profound ties. Their consciousness of being part of one people appears principally at a time of danger. When Deborah, herself of the tribe of Ephraim, broadcasts her call to war against the Canaanites (vv. 7, 12), the majority—Ephraim, Benjamin, Machir-Manasseh, Zebulun, and Naphtali (vv. 13–15a, 18)—send their men

---

9. Translated in its entirety and explained on pages 110–18 below.

into battle, under the command of Barak-ben-Abinoam (v. 12), a Naphtalite, although some clans, less bellicose or out of danger—Reuben, Gilead, Dan, and Asher (vv. 15b–17)—turn a deaf ear and keep to themselves at home, out of harm's way (scolded and scoffed at by the poet). Above all, the ethnic bond is redoubled and enforced by the religious communion of the tribes. The whole poem is full of it: they are keenly aware of their one and only Commander in war, who is Yahweh alone. He came from beyond the Midianite desert (vv. 4–5), where He had His traditional abode, to direct the battle in person, for the Canaanites are His enemies inasmuch as they are enemies of the Israelites (v. 31). He intervenes even to give orders to the stars above to attack the foe from their orbits, dashing it with a torrential rain, and to the torrent of the Kishon to swell and sweep away the Canaanite soldiery (vv. 20–21). Thus did the poet stress that nature came to the aid of the Israelites by a welcome tempest and contributed to the rout of their adversaries. It is clear how greatly the faith in Yahweh united all the clans of Israel and imparted to them a considerable will to power through the conviction that, headed by a captain like Yahweh, victory would be theirs in any event.

This enthusiasm, this profound sense of coherence, together with the new and vigorous blood of a race that was already "sure of itself," made Israel a formidable opponent for the Canaanites, who were politically divided, worn out by their mutual struggles, and anemic from the very excellence of their venerable culture. The Israelites had to prevail. Another set of lucky circumstances played in their favor. By the end of the second millennium, the mighty political powers of the Near East found themselves in difficult straits and preoccupied with other problems. They were either moribund, like the Hittites, or enmeshed in their own internal conflicts, like the Egyptians. The Babylonians and Assyrians had forever been vying with them for control over Palestine, that region which was within their reach, forming a bridge between their empires as well as a barrier, opening out on the sea, and attractive as an inexhaustible source of precious materials (such as cedar wood). But at that particular period none of the great powers had the energy or the leisure to keep an eye on the fate of the territory between them.

Helped by their valor, their stubbornness, and their might, the Israelites, finally, in less than two centuries, were given their "Promised Land," there to organize themselves into a unique kingdom, around their capital, Jerusalem, and one sovereign leader, a king, thus welding yet a stronger coalition, with a dwelling place of their own in the assembly of political forces around them.

The second king, David (approximately 1000 B.C.E.), is the one who consummated all their ambitions and carried their achievement furthest. A seductive adventurer and also a very generous man, both chivalrous and Machiavellian, of indomitable courage in war and true wisdom in peace, unyielding to everything except his impetuous passions, including the passions of love, which made him even more human, he had everything necessary to leave of himself forever an unforgettable dream image (see also pages 40, 56, 88)—everything, even unto a sensitive and poetic soul. His fascinating personality reveals itself fully in the admirable lament he composed when he learned of the death in war of his former friend and rival, the first king, Saul, and Saul's son, Jonathan, whom David had loved as a brother:

Alas, the Glory of Israel
Lies swallowed up in these hills!
How have the heroes fallen?
Do not trumpet the news in Gath,
Do not proclaim it in the squares of Ashkelon:
The daughters of the Philistines would be happy for it,
Too exultant—the daughters of the uncircumcised!
O mounts of Gilboa,
No dew, no rain on you,
O treacherous fields!
There the shield of the heroes was soiled,
The shield of Saul, which was not anointed with oil,
But with the blood of the wounded, with the fat of the brave!
O bow of Jonathan,
Which never faltered!
O sword of Saul,
Which never returned unsuccessful!
Saul and Jonathan, the well-loved, our delight,
Were not divided in life or death,
Those, swifter than eagles,
Those, more courageous than lions!
O daughters of Israel,
Shed your tears over Saul,
Him who clothed you with fine scarlet linen,
Who put golden ornaments on your garments!
How have the heroes fallen

In the midst of the battle?
Jonathan, I am sorely afflicted by your death!
I am overcome with misery, my brother Jonathan!
You were my great delight!
Your friendship was marvelous,
More than the love of women!
How have the heroes fallen?
How has the gear of war crumbled?

(2 Samuel 1:21–27)

And so, after long and stubborn endeavors, and peaceful invasions inter-rupted by periods of war and bloodshed, the Israelites finally realized the dream of their ancient patriarch: as the People of Yahweh, they ascended at last to the rank of a nation, implanted on the land of His choice, and they became an autonomous political power.

THE CULTURAL AND RELIGIOUS RESULTS OF THE ESTABLISHMENT IN PALESTINE

For us who in this book focus less on the development of the institutions of the Israelites than on their spiritual trajectory, the stages of this political ascension are not of great interest. On the other hand, a handful of wandering nomads and shepherds does not change into an established nation, urban and just as refined as the kingdoms around, without becoming profoundly affected, transformed in its life and its very ways of thought. With this in mind, it is essential to weigh the accomplishment of the "People of Yahweh."

In the schematic and tendentious presentation the Book of Joshua makes of the Conquest (see pages 26f. above), at least one actual fact becomes evi-dent: the Israelites, having taken the place of the Canaanites in the unchanged framework of life of the latter, would thus have been their true heirs. In fact, when it comes to material and intellectual development, the Israelites indeed received *everything* and learned *everything* from the Canaanites, including their own language.

The nomadic or seminomadic life is a culture, but not a civilization. It is a rude and basic, certainly ascetic way of living, without refinement in any domain one can think of. Moreover, it is almost completely sufficient unto itself and limits as much as possible its relations to the outside world. Apart from the ordinary routines of their daily life, their preoccupation with their flocks, and their confrontations over things and prestige with other nomads or with settled communities that were equipped with more useful goods than they were, the nomadic Israelites lived, turned in on themselves, on a rather pitiful cultural and intellectual wherewithal. They had nothing more to call their own than their oral traditions concerning their ancestors and their visceral bond with that God, Yahweh, whom they must have taken for a sort of supernatural Sheik of their horde.

The Canaanites, settled in Palestine since the middle of the third millennium, had for a long time been leading a truly civilized life, wealthy and open to the world. Attached to their land, they cultivated it and extracted from it all it could give, and for what it lacked, they compensated through an active trade with the countries surrounding them. In so doing, they received ideas as well as goods. They had a complex social and political organization in their little kingdoms, each with its center in a capital: a fortified city where the monarch resided in his palace, with an entire army of officials; and in their temples the gods were surrounded by numerous attendants at their service. The Canaanite customs were polished, refined. In that sign of authentic civilization, they excelled at producing things that had no immediate usefulness: their works of art. They knew how to write; in fact, we owe to them—for the Phoenicians were Canaanites in language, culture, and location—the prodigious simplification in the art of writing that is the alphabet. They had an entire literature,[10] and to the extent that we have been able to retrieve it, we can see the important place of mythology in it, that is to say, in short, the "intellectual" reflection and the "philosophy" of that time. In response to the numerous questions that they asked themselves under these rubrics, they turned to the imagined activity of their gods—and they had many of them, each with his own role and functions, together grouped in a hierarchy resembling the pattern that obtained among people. Quite a few features in their myths were probably not creations of the Canaanites themselves but adapted borrowings from the great civilizations of the Near East, principally Mesopotamia, the oldest and most venerable among them. With Mesopotamia the Canaanites were closely connected as fellow Semites in thought as well as blood.

10. Notably, we have the findings, made since 1928, at Ras-Shamra, the modern name of the ancient city of Ugarit (located on the Mediterranean, close to the modern Syrian city of Latakia). A sizable number of these "Ugaritic Texts" have been translated by A. Caquot and M. Sznycer in the work cited in note 1 above, *Les religions du Proche-Orient asiatique*, 351–458.

The Israelites were just as much Semites as were the Canaanites: their assimilation to the Canaanites went all the more quickly as they found among the Canaanites, now in a perfected form, many elements of which they themselves had merely the germ or the earliest inception. Thus, having entered without much hardship into the inheritance of the Canaanites, they received everything from them—with the exception of their basic trust and faith in Yahweh, with all that that implied, beginning with the Covenant as the essence of their mutual relations.

Once Israel was established in her new life, both elements, the one spiritual and inherited from the Israelites' ancestors, the other cultural and recently acquired, had to find a way to live together and lead her into the future. How did that happen?

In some instances, the two factors were perfectly compatible and formed a syncretism without difficulty, enriching each other.

A first example is in the domain of collective rules of conduct and of "legislation." The social obligations by which the Israelites knew each other as participants in their Alliance with Yahweh appear to be affirmed in the specific clauses of the Covenant. Some maxims are so elementary, judging by their contents preserved in the Decalogue (see page 25 above), that, in broad lines, they seem a simple translation of a fundamental ethical attitude in all things, rather than a precise directory of human conduct. When they had entered into a socially more complex existence, quite differently oriented, the Israelites not only had to learn to reconcile their old principles with a new way of life and the unforeseen situations it brought with it, but, in harmony with every civilization that knew writing, they had to put into some sort of written casuistry the enrichment and manifold increase of their duties. In the ancient Near East, the editing of such "codes" was an ongoing affair, beginning with Mesopotamian times at the end of the third millennium. Although not the slightest Canaanite document of this type has been preserved, the odds are that such documents did exist and that the Israelites did set eyes on them. In proportion as their way of life changed, they must have been guided by these models in rethinking and adapting the old rules of the Covenant. The earliest compilation resulting from such a process that has been preserved in the Bible, incorporated in a late *Elohist* text, may be dated some time between the end of the second millennium and the beginning of the first: the Code of the Covenant (Exodus 20:22–23:19; see pages 24f. above). It will suffice here to give the first lines:

Yahweh said to Moses: This is what you will tell the Israelites:
"You have seen for yourselves how I spoke to you from heaven!
You shall not make deities of silver or gold next to Me.

You shall make Me an altar of earth to sacrifice on, in your
holocausts and your brotherly festive offerings, your small and large
livestock; do this in every place where I shall manifest My presence:
then I shall come to you and I shall bless you.

If you make Me an altar of stone, do not build it of hewn stones,
for by moving your chisel over them, you will profane them." (Exodus
20:22–25)

What a change from the original Decalogue! Certainly, in order to
underline the continuity, the new rules are expressly related to Moses and
placed in the mouth of Yahweh, who would have communicated them as He
did the rules of the Covenant. But the idols of gold and silver, the altars of
piled-up stones, the ritual that one senses has become more complex, with
"holocausts" distinct from "brotherly festive offerings"—all of this obviously
comes from the Canaanites. We know this well from Canaanite literature
and also from the findings of archeologists. Hence we understand that the
religious leaders of Israel were at work adapting the established certainties
of Yahwism to the new cultural facts. The earlier certainties were characterized by a worship reserved for Yahweh alone and by the prohibition of
any image. A new liturgical pattern, unknown until now and obviously an
adaptation from the Canaanite ritual, was indeed accepted. It became part
and parcel of the Israelite customs and became, so to speak, "Yahwized."
The same conclusions would follow from reading the entire remainder of the
code. In passing, we should add that the adoption of Canaanite liturgical
habits will go still further, since this God of the desert, this God of vagabonds
with neither fire nor hearth, who, according to the Code of the Covenant,
still prefers a rude and perishable altar of earth and who in any event does
not want hewn stones, will turn out to be pleased not merely with sacred
places here and there throughout the land but, under the third king, Solomon,
with a "royal chapel" in the capital: a large and superb temple.

There is another area where with equal clarity we can trace a syncretism
of new data with ancient thought. What I have in mind is once again a "philosophy," in the sense of a response through images and myths—in the absence
of concepts and theories, which could not yet be constructed—to the great
and eternal questions that man has always asked about the origin and meaning
of his life.

We do not know to what extent the Israelites, when still nomads, nurtured such interests. All that is evident, as we have seen, is that they attributed to Yahweh a real sovereignty over all events and over nature. To be sure, this could suffice for the still basic set of problems of people too immersed in a rough existence to give themselves over to speculation. But upon their contact with the Canaanites their horizon widened considerably. The Canaanites, like those who had first taught and inspired them, especially the Babylonians, assigned an important place to this "philosophy," both in the questions it raised and in the answers it provided. In order to illuminate the answers, borrowing and speculating anew, they brought an entire mythology into focus. In this mythology their gods functioned as mediators to explain the setting, as well as the course, of the world. Several of these myths in turn gave rise to works of literature (some of which have been preserved for us; see note 10 above). Indubitably, the Israelites became familiar with them at the same time that they were learning to formulate the question "why" about matters on which they apparently had never been in doubt or felt concerned. In this realm too, they felt the need to "Yahwize" things and to bring in their God everywhere that the Canaanites had put their own deities to work. And with the Israelites too, just as with the Canaanites, their concerns gave rise to literary works, from at least the beginning of the first millennium.

The earliest actual literary flight of real breadth is the *Yahwist*, the document whose existence we have spoken of before and whose presence we have underlined in the Hexateuch. This document was not composed before the ninth century (see page 13), but, as we shall understand better later on (page 45), it is right to discuss it at the present place in our remarks.

Perhaps the author of the *Yahwist* made frequent use of the sources he copied, and yet this author, forever unknown, is an independent and powerful writer and thinker. He set out to write a history of his people, but he did so with the twofold vision of the believer, narrating a "theological" history in which all that happens here below is willed and guided by a supernatural Person (see also page 48): the God of Israel, Yahweh, whom he likes to call by the name that is only His. At the same time, in order to encompass His plans from a higher perspective and to show more superbly, in the face of the Canaanite deities, that all had come from Him alone, the Earth and Man, before His sovereignty directed their course, the *Yahwist* takes history from its "absolute" commencement, the moment when its very frame and actors were created—of course by Yahweh Himself:[11]

11. The text that follows is revisited and discussed later, on pages 121ff.

When Yahweh had made the heaven and the earth, no wasteland bush existed yet on the earth, no herb of the field had yet sprung up, because Yahweh had not yet made it rain on the earth and there was no human to work the humus.

So Yahweh made a stream emerge from the earth to water the entire face of the humus. Then Yahweh molded the Human from the clay he drew from the humus and blew the breath of life into his nostrils so as to make him into a living being. Then Yahweh planted a garden in Eden [there] toward the East, and there He placed the Human whom He had molded . . . so that he would till it and protect it. . . .

Then Yahweh said to Himself: "It is not good for the Human to remain all alone! I shall make a fitting companion for him!" And Yahweh molded from soil all the animals of the field and the birds of the sky; then He led them before the Human to see what he would call them. Whatever name he gave to each of them, that would be its name. In this way the Human called out the names of all domestic animals, of all birds in the sky, and of all wild beasts. Still, as to the Human himself, he did not find (among them) a fitting companion. Then Yahweh made a torpor fall upon Man, and he fell asleep. He took a rib from him, and closed up (the empty space, putting) flesh in its place; and of this rib He had taken from the Human he formed Woman, whom He led to the Human, Man. And Man exclaimed: "This time, here is one who is bone of my bone, flesh of my flesh! She will be called Woman [in Hebrew: Ishsha], because she has been drawn from Man [Ish]."

This is the reason why (every) man leaves his father and mother to attach himself to his wife, to form together one single body. (Genesis 2:4b–24, omitting 9–14, 16–17)

Let us set aside for a moment the rigor and abstraction of our rationality and meet again with a mental life that is younger and more ingenuous by three millennia: we find there an authentic endeavor to explain the origins of the universe by means of images that were familiar to the world in which it was born. Within walking distance, one knew the desert landscape, boundless, flat, empty, hostile, lifeless. Without the ability to make use of the abstruse notion of nonbeing, one imagined the earth "before" as a sort of immense desert. It was not uncommon to see those same desolate steppes conquered by agriculture and brought to life by irrigation and by dint of human labor.

One called upon the same agents to give an account of the transformation of an original "nothing" into the state of the true earth as it was meant to be: alive and habitable. And when one invoked the art of the potter for the creation of Man, it was because every day one watched the miraculous change, under the fingers of the artisan, of a formless lump of clay into an almost living figurine. . . . These reasons compel us to see the very beginning of the *Yahwist*'s account as manifestly Canaanite, while we hear in it as well some echoes set off far back in ancient Mesopotamia (see pages 147ff.). However, the *Yahwist* author substituted the one, unique Yahweh for the numerous deities, often in conflict with each other, that the Canaanites and Babylonians dispatched to animate such myths. With a stroke, he made this one Personality, who in the eyes of ancient Israel was only very powerful and capable of effecting natural phenomena, into a cosmic god; by switching scales of measurement altogether, the *Yahwist* enlarged and exalted the sphere of His power and His involvement in the world.

In what follows in the *Yahwist*'s work, placing the same Yahweh at the origin of all that had happened to human beings—the misadventures of the first couple and their offspring (see especially pages 164ff.); the universal punishment of the Flood; the choice of a survivor to found the new humanity after the Flood; the distribution of the races and nations of the world, and the election, among them, of a particular people, also taken from its very beginning, in its first ancestor, Abraham, who leaves his home and is brought to the land that is to become his land (see page 17)—in all of this, the *Yahwist* articulates and at the same time considerably reinforces the power and the superiority of Yahweh, who intervenes in the course of the world after having created it: God of history as well as of nature.

In the domain of "theology," the joining of the ancient experience of the primacy of Yahweh with the Canaanite concerns and explanations for the origin and deeper meaning of things not only proceeded smoothly but resulted in a remarkable enrichment of religious thought.

The fusion that had occurred between the Israelites and the Canaanites did have its dangers. In "social morality" as well as in the deepening of the relationship with Yahweh that we have observed, it gave rise also to grave conflicts, which had an equally serious bearing on the spiritual development of Israel.

The ordinances of the Covenant were adapted to particular life circumstances. It was to nomads that Yahweh gave the order never to harm the neighbor, whether in his life or his goods—in other words, to share a brotherly existence. This was no doubt the rule of conduct for a wandering tribe, a closed community, where collective activity took such precedence as to leave little or nothing for a private life. As with every nomadic tribe, virtually everything was held in common. But the sedentary life, tying people down, divides family units and their interests; and concerns for work and productivity, which now begin to weigh heavy on their minds, inevitably bring disagreement and a growing disequilibrium in the possession of goods and the level of existence. It is among sedentary people that there are rich and poor, wealth at the expense of the poor, creditors and debtors, oppressors and oppressed. Could one have imagined, in the desert, a member of the tribe brought down far enough to cry out: *"I have nothing left but a handful of flour in the jar, and a tiny bit of oil in the jug. With two sticks of wood that I shall pick up, once I have cooked and eaten it all, together with my child, we cannot do anything but die of hunger!"* (1 Kings 17:12)? Or again, *"After the death of my husband, there comes the pawnbroker to take my sons as slaves . . . and I have nothing left in my house!"* (2 Kings 4:1ff.)?

Thus, the progress of Israel in the socioeconomic realm, due to her establishment in the Promised Land, created an accumulation of obstacles to the practice of the great fraternity that Moses had dreamt of and that he laid down as law. That law remained a fundamental precept of Yahwism, but now acquired detailed and various applications throughout new collections of rules (see pages 32f. above). For example, the fundamental precept is applied to a new circumstance where the wording of the Code of the Covenant (see again pages 32f.) anticipates the duty to set free, after six years of servitude, every *Hebrew* slave (Exodus 21:2ff.).

In addition, being in the company of the Canaanites and their gods was not without risks to the very reliance on Yahweh. Yahweh had always held that He was and would forever remain the only God of Israel. To stay attached to Him alone was easy in the desert, when He functioned in the role of Sheik, of Captain, for the tribe in its isolation and its struggle against all others. But once among the Canaanites, learning from them a new way of life, imitating them and all the while trying to take their place, the Israelites were constantly face-to-face with other deities, venerated everywhere in the land, toward whom they could hardly remain indifferent. After all, these gods, and no other gods, were the ones whom the Canaanite devotees had delighted in for centuries. To them was attributed both sovereignty over the land the Canaanites inhabited and the efficacious mysteries needed to make the most of it.

How could one gamble with the harvests by not paying homage, as the Canaanites had done forever, to Dagon, "Grandmaster of Grain and Work, Creator of Wheat and the Plough," to Hadad, "Dispenser of Beneficent Rain," and to Astarte, "Lady of Love," and therefore of "Fecundity and Abundance." Surely, the temptation was strong, and if we keep in mind that even today there are those who give preference to the saints of their parish over God, we can hardly be astonished that three thousand years ago Israelites succumbed to it quickly and in large numbers. We have read earlier (page 27), in the Book of Judges (3:5–6): *"they lived side by side with the Canaanites, . . . worshiping their gods."* From this point of view, the artificial frame of the same book (see page 10 above) is justified and keeps its historical validity when it depicts the historical Conquest as a series of apostasies on the part of Israel in her abandonment of Yahweh for *"the Baals and Astartes"* (Judges 10:6).

Certainly, such abandonment of Yahweh was not the act of the people in its entirety, but of the mass of the more dull-minded and fickle. In response to that considerable mass of humanity, there arose a kind of elite that was fervidly attached to Yahweh, to Yahweh alone, and that forcefully defended His absolute Preeminence, invoking the early Covenant by which Israel unanimously swore to serve none but Him, and the successes experienced by remaining faithful to Him. The Song of Deborah (see pages 107ff.) could well have been one of the first manifestos of these exclusive Yahwists. One need only consider its fundamental content, summed up in the concluding verse:

> *Thus all Your enemies perish, O Yahweh,*
> *But Your friends are like the Sun rising in its glory!*

The significance of this "elite," faithful to the utmost, cannot be over-estimated for the development to come: in their midst would arise the spiritual leaders, the great religious thinkers whom we shall meet, who would guide the entire history and leave their mark on it.

What characterized them, together with their attachment to their God and to His will, was, ever and always, faith, meaning the capacity to see beyond the things that everyone sees to a supernatural order that envelops those things in its midst. In this way they understood that with the Conquest and its benefits, *evil* had entered into the Israelite people, from the standpoint of social life and of faithfulness to Yahweh: moral evil, misconduct, forgetfulness of vows and of the ancient, sacred rules of life.

Could the tremendous problem of Evil indeed have presented itself only then, as if for the first time—but now empirically—to religious thought and aroused it to profound reflection? The *Yahwist*'s account gives us a stunning proof. Going through the first chapters one by one, we realize that the author constructed his narrations upon one idea that he wanted to develop; it was his way of "philosophizing" on history.[12] Each of his stories turns around a wrong act, or an instance of evil conduct, and very often a disastrous situation that results from it: Cain kills his brother and is rejected by everyone around him; Lamech is an invidious brute; the misbehavior of human beings brings on the universal Flood; Ham fails to respect his father and thus is destined to slavery; finally, men, in their megalomania, aspire to build the Tower of Babel and condemn themselves to utter confusion. The misconduct and calamities fan out: from individual cases (Cain, Lamech) they become collective and pass on universally to peoples, henceforward living in isolation, unable to "understand each other," and consequently prepared to oppose and destroy each other. As a matter of fact, here we touch on the reason why God was preparing to choose a particular person, devoted to sanctity and perfection, and selected Abraham.

The *Yahwist* author went still further. He asked himself what might be the origin of this universal evil, "toward which the human heart is inclined from a most tender age" (Genesis 8:21). His idea of God was too elevated for him to held God accountable; therefore evil had been introduced here on earth by man. That is the profound meaning of the famous introductory narrative, belonging to the *Yahwist*, concerning "Original Sin."[13] By means of the myth of the forbidden fruit and the Serpent-tempter—in which the first man, through an act of immoderation, attempting to elevate himself beyond his natural condition and "become equal" to his Creator, disobeys Yahweh and sees himself suddenly reduced to a mortal and miserable state, bringing upon his offspring a double legacy: of inclination toward evil and susceptibility to misfortune—the *Yahwist* searched for a religious, in fact, a "theological," explanation for the universality of moral wrong, misconduct, which brings in its wake physical wrong—that is, pain and misery—as a just punishment.

This myth, this explanation, so admirable in its psychological insight and profundity, is unique in all that we have unearthed of ancient Near Eastern literature (see also page 175 and the note there). It does, however, follow the

12. We shall return to this "philosophy of history" of the *Yahwist* in greater depth. See pages 161ff. and 172ff.

13. Once again, see especially pages 161ff. below.

logic of an ancient conviction that the Semites held in common, which would never cease to be asserted by the faithful of Yahweh, that sovereignty over the domain of justice is a prerogative of the Divinity;[14] every obligation here on earth is sanctioned by God, and each infringement of whatever social command is an attack on His preeminence, a revolt against His will, exposing the culpable to His rage and His vengeance.

Thus we clearly see why the faithful of Yahweh had to look as they did upon the apostasies of their people and their numerous failures in following the rules of the Covenant—not only with sadness, but with a heavy uneasiness. Did they not foretell a redoubled chastisement from their God?

THE FIRST DISTURBANCES AND THE FIRST PROPHETS

And indeed, exactly at that time, after so many victories, after conquests, after glory, misfortune was beginning to establish itself in Israel.

At first, it merely touched upon that national grandeur and prosperity which reached its summit through the great David, whose memory would only be better preserved as a result, all at once as a hero, a sort of saint, the ideal monarch, ruling in a golden age.

In spite of David's brilliance, the number and quality of his enterprises, his administrative feats, and his renown, the reign of his son, Solomon (around 950), already represents a decline, and paves the way to sad disillusionment. From the very beginning of the reign of Solomon's successor, Rehoboam (931–913), the irreparable damage is done: worn down by the fiscal abuse and tyranny of the Southerners of Judah and Benjamin, who since the days of David exerted a high-handed rule over the entire nation, the "Ten Tribes" of the North (see page 26f. above), long allied among themselves, recovered their freedom. From that moment on, there would be two kingdoms: in the North, Israel, first around Tirzah, then Samaria; in the South, Judah, with Jerusalem as its capital.

It is true that neither the one nor the other gave up the sense of a deep solidarity, based on their common origin, their ancient traditions, their kinship in the face of all the other nations, including Semitic peoples, and the destiny by which their Covenant dedicated both of them to Yahweh. Politically, however, they were separate, sometimes allied, sometimes rivals, and even at war.

14. On this subject, see "La naissance du péché," *L'histoire*, no. 100 (May 1987): 40–49.

To face facts, it would have to be evident that hope had faded for the ancient dream, realized for a few decades, of a unified People of Yahweh, mighty and glorious, for the Israelites had only *too well* taken the place of the Canaanites, to the point of assuming even their domestic divisions and weaknesses. Nevertheless, it is possible that this first ominous blow in some way may have passed over those it reached without upsetting them terribly. For a century and a half, through political ups and downs, on parallel paths or in antagonism to each other, life in the two kingdoms seemed to go on unchanged, on that course which was set by the Conquest, of which it merely witnessed the flowering.

Putting aside the two kingdoms' mutual encroachments, as well as the unity they sustained with the preceding epoch, it is more worthwhile to analyze the new moment in the religious history of Israel. For a group of men now becomes prominent who are called to play a very important role in that history: it has become customary to refer to them as the Prophets. They are by no means the sum total of the elite thinkers and the faithful guardians and promoters of the religion of Yahweh, but for centuries they will make up the most active, the most decisive, element.

The social phenomenon of prophecy is not exclusive to Israel. Without leaving the ancient Near East, we can attest that other civilizations, notably Semitic ones, and especially Mesopotamia, have known such "seers," who presented themselves in the name of a deity with whom, it was believed, or they themselves declared, they had a personal communication, transmitting orders or warnings in a vehement and authoritative language, often accompanied by more or less ecstatic manifestations. The Babylonians had undergone a certain rationalizing influence by way of their Sumerian atavism; their religious view was more cosmic than historic, and they do not seem to have set great store by prophesying. The Israelites, however, believed in a God who intervened in history as a matter of course. In addition, marked by their still recent nomadic past, and having remained closer to their Semitic roots, they retained an imaginative, spirited, and impetuous character, perfectly in tune with the wild, uncompromising utterings of the Prophets, their singular and unexpected comportment, and the power of their words.

We see the Prophets play a more and more emphatic social and political role, above all with respect to royalty; indeed, it is quite remarkable with regard to the masters of this world. It will be a Prophet, Nathan by name, who goes to King David after David's adultery with Bathsheba and his criminal elimination of Uriah, the husband of his mistress, and casts at the king the most blood-curdling reproaches: *"Yahweh, the God of Israel, speaks with these words: '. . . Why have you despised Yahweh and done what is to Him a crime? You murdered Uriah, the Hittite! Not only did you take his wife, but you caused him to be killed by the swords of the Ammonites! Therefore, from now on, the sword shall not leave your family. I shall bring up misfortune against you from your own house!' . . . And David answered Nathan: 'I have sinned against Yahweh!' Then Nathan said to David: 'Very well! Yahweh forgives your fault, and you will not die yourself! But since you have grieved, seriously grieved Yahweh by this deed, the child born to you shall die!'"* (2 Samuel 12:7–14).

We can grasp through this example that the Prophets are the voice of Israel's conscience. They defend the moral will of Yahweh, the imperative of Justice spelled out and sworn to in the Covenant. They oppose with great force the wave of iniquity and oppression unleashed by the adoption of the Canaanite way of life (see page 37 above). The Prophets acted on behalf of the fiercely Yahwist elite whose rise we have seen among the Israelites (page 38). They strove to rescue social behavior from decay and exerted themselves to keep intact the ideal of Justice and Fraternity that Moses had set among the rules of the Covenant.

This goal involved an essential innovation. In the name of Yahweh, the Prophets availed themselves of a threat against backsliders to be matched with the promise of recompense for the faithful. This they based on the ancient sentiment (see page 39), which they emphasized and made explicit, according to which Yahweh alone was the author and guardian of right and duty. Entitled as such, in analogy to judges on earth, He was therefore to punish crimes, just as He had promised to reward fidelity to His commandments. This the Prophets introduced as if a rule for the interventions of Yahweh in history. (Later we shall see the great significance of this idea for religious thought: pages 58f., 67f., 80, 90, 95f.) Though arbitrary until then—as in *"I am gracious to whom I want to be gracious and I love whom I want to love"* (Exodus 33:19; Elohist)—Yahweh's interventions became in some manner logical. And, as the Yahwist had already understood very well (pages 39f.), physical evil—misfortune—in turn found an explanation: it could be derived from moral evil, from wickedness, through the intermediation of the just and vengeful will of Yahweh.

The Prophets did more than defend moral principles. Something else, more sacred and basic, was menaced by the new conditions of life (page 38): the exclusive faith in Yahweh was weakened by the allure of alien gods. More of these were added beside the ones inherited from the Canaanites as closer links were formed with neighboring lands like Phoenicia and Syria. The more powerful Northern Kingdom, which was more involved in the international politics of the time, was more exposed to such idolatry. In its territory, the greatest Prophet of the period, Elijah the Tishbite, exercised his calling. He had his work cut out for him, for the king of Israel, Ahab (874–853), who had married the Sidonian Jezebel, ensured together with his wife the worship of the great Phoenician Baal. Elijah left such a vivid memory that after his death his great deeds were collected, as well as those of his major disciple, Elisha, in a sort of hagiographic anthology that was finally incorporated almost completely in the Book of Kings (1 Kings 17 to 2 Kings 10, with interruptions). As in all "lives of saints," there is no lack of legends and miracles, yet through the folklore, the author has rendered the profound truth of the personage: Elijah was an exceptional figure, filled with integrity, obsessed with one *idée fixe*—*"The Living Yahweh is the God of Israel"* (1 Kings 17:1)—a sort of religious agitator who with good right was given the epithet "Troubler of Israel." The author succeeded also in giving an authentic image of his work, which well enables us to understand the prophetic activity of the time.

The most significant Elijah episode is the famous scene where, before *"the whole people"* assembled by Ahab, he contended with

> *four hundred and fifty prophets of Baal, creatures of Jezebel. Addressing himself to the assembled people, he said: "How long will you go on, limping with both feet? If Yahweh is God, follow Him! If it is Baal, follow him!" And the crowd did not utter a word in response. Then, appealing to them again, he continued: "You see me here all alone, in the face of the prophets of Baal, who are four hundred and fifty in number! Give us two young bulls! They will choose one of them, cut it up, place it on the wood, but without putting fire to it. And I shall deal with the other in the same way, without putting fire to it! Then you will call on your god, and I shall call on Yahweh. The god who replies with fire, that is the one who is God!" And the whole people declared themselves in agreement! . . . The prophets of Baal . . . set to work in vain calling Baal, from morning until noon: "O Baal, answer us!" Not the least reply, not the least response . . . ! . . . At noon, Elijah began to mock them: "Cry louder," he said to them. "Certainly, he is a god, but he must be busy, or has business to transact, or he is*

traveling! Or perhaps he has fallen asleep? He must wake up in the end!" . . . [At his turn, when the altar of Yahweh had been prepared and the victim was placed on the wood, Elijah said:] *"Yahweh, God of Abraham, Isaac, and Israel, today it will be known that You are the only God in Israel, and that I am your servant who has always obeyed Your commandments. Answer me, Yahweh, answer me, so that this whole people know that it is You, Yahweh, who is God, You who will turn their hearts!"* And the fire of Yahweh fell and devoured the victim and the wood. . . . Shaking, the entire people fell on their faces and said: "It is Yahweh who is God! It is Yahweh who is God!" After this, Elijah ordered them: "Seize the prophets of Baal, let none of them escape!" And when they had seized them, he took them down to the river bed of the Kishon, and cut their throats on the spot. (1 Kings 18:19–40)

The story itself is less important than the results of the events: Elijah sealed the work of the ancient Prophets. Against all powers and all contrary forces, he brought to triumph for all time to come the conviction that in Israel Yahweh was the only God, in conformity with the ancient Covenant. He discouraged his people not only from all apostasy but even from any serious attempt at syncretism that would have disfigured Yahweh and once again placed His sovereignty in doubt.

Such a victory, with the struggles it involved, did not come about without a thoughtful deepening of the idea of God. Another famous episode of the "Life of Elijah" is instructive on this subject. It is the meeting between the Prophet and Yahweh. To renew himself, the man went on a pilgrimage to the very mountain—here called Horeb (see page 30 above)—where Yahweh had revealed Himself at the moment of the Covenant. As if for him alone, the enormous seismic upheaval of nature that had struck Moses and his companions with terror reoccurred: *"an enormous and terrifying hurricane, which split the mountains and set the rocks flying in torrents,"* then *"an earthquake,"* then the terrific eruption properly called *"the fire."* However, contrary to what had always been associated with the first theophany, *"Yahweh was not in the hurricane, or in the earthquake, or in the fire!"* These were only precursors of His presence. His presence became manifest thereafter: *"in the rustle of a gentle breeze"* (1 Kings 19:1–12). Could one more assuredly emphasize that the idea of Yahweh had changed so much as to be no longer encumbered by any display of manifest and violent terror, and that it emerges anew in the least perceptible and least material appearance one could imagine? Since the Covenant—obviously thanks to Elijah and the first Prophets—such a "spiritualization," something almost like a sublimation, had come about. Thus Yahweh is presented in a different order of grandeur.

The Prophets are not alone responsible for this development. Less conspicuously, in more closed, less turbulent circles, others among the faithful in their own way followed the work of their predecessors (page 38), consolidating and enriching the contents of Yahwism. Although their personalities remain forever inaccessible in anonymity and the passage of time, some of them have left us writings. In fact, the reign of David saw the beginning of an intense and truly literary activity. Eschewing a chronological formalism that could be exacted only in a history capable of recounting each and every event, I have described the *Yahwist* earlier, somewhat in anticipation of the real era of its composition. The reason is that in the *Yahwist* document the entire spiritual and "philosophic" work that issued from the Conquest as such (pages 34ff.) reveals itself so extraordinarily well. With the same intent to draw whole contours (even if their edges touch neighboring realms), I must cite the *Elohist*—which was probably composed in the eighth century (see page 13)—in order to focus on the biblical document that best presents the process initiated by the first Prophets. This is the earliest document where prophets are mentioned (Numbers 12:6), and the text places them on a pedestal, for it counts Abraham among them (Genesis 20:7).

The *Elohist*'s work commences (in chapter 15 of Genesis) not as early in time as that of the *Yahwist*: the history of the world is of little interest to the *Elohist* author; what does concern him is the first chief of his people. He dates the creation of his people to the moment when its first ancestor, Abraham, has just arrived in the land that later will belong to him. It is not that the *Elohist* author ignores all "philosophy" of origins: he does know that the world (in which he explicitly mentions the sea, until then unconsidered in the *Yahwist*) is the work of Yahweh. However, what he knows of the Creation, or at least what he cites, either he himself or others have placed into accord with religious and ritual duty, as if while explaining it to sanctify it with God's guarantee (see also page 10 above): *"Therefore in six days Yahweh made the Heaven, the Earth, and the Sea, and all that they contain; but on the seventh day He rested. This is why Yahweh blessed the seventh day and sanctified it!"* (Exodus 20:11; a gloss?).

Such a way of looking at things bespeaks a certain "juridical" preoccupation. While the *Yahwist* devotes itself almost exclusively to history, it is the

Elohist that augments its Decalogue with the Code of the Covenant, seemingly with the purpose of attaching the (newer) elaborate rules to the Covenant to give greater weight to them.

The trait that makes the *Elohist* author most remarkable is that he carefully avoids everything that would give Yahweh a material and visible shape. Unlike the *Yahwist* author, who is more impulsive and "naive," he never tells of a divine apparition. When He must manifest Himself to the people, Yahweh, according to the *Elohist*, is always replaced by an intermediary, usually His "messenger" (Genesis 48:16, Exodus 23:20, etc.). For instance, in the "Dream of Jacob" (see pages 13f. above), the *Elohist* substitutes a dream for the personal manifestation of Yahweh; and furthermore, in the course of the dream, Jacob sees only the staircase to the House of God, and His servants, that is, His "messengers," coming and going. Such a concern for eliminating all figuration of God is certainly attributable to a more scrupulous and deferential observance of the old precept that forbade every image of Yahweh. Yet the *Elohist* evinces at the same time—as in the meaningful episode where Yahweh did not appear except "in the rustle of a gentle breeze" (see page 36 above)—a more vivid consciousness of God's sublimity and, as it were, a first apprehension of His *spiritual* nature.

By this touch, as well as by his attention to stricter observance, the *Elohist* author confirms the religious progress made in his time, above all thanks to the activity of the first Prophets.

THE FIRST GREAT CATASTROPHES AND THE NEW PROPHETS

In the middle of the eighth century, the formidable menace of Assyria suddenly darkened the political horizon in Palestine.

The inhabitants of Mesopotamia, a land abundant in farming and cattle-raising but completely devoid of certain natural resources, had always been compelled to procure these elsewhere, in places where such materials were most easily at hand. The region bordering on the Mediterranean, with its mountains—Taurus, Amanus, and Lebanon—densely forested, rich in stone and metallic veins, had been since the dawn of time among the principal crossroads of this trade, based on commerce but "prolonged by other means" as soon as the rulers of Mesopotamia felt strong enough for conquest.

Such was the case with Assyria at the time. From the end of the second millennium, Assyria had triumphed over Babylonia, her rival to the south, and had established her dominion over the whole traditional territory of Mesopotamia; then, after overcoming a long period of internal crisis, she once again took to the road toward "the Great Sea," the Mediterranean.

The annals of Assurnasirpal II (885–859), one of the first Assyrian monarchs to launch an attack on the entire northern and western region of the Fertile Crescent, provide an example of the Assyrian conduct in war and treatment of those who resisted:

> *I drew near to the fortified city of Hulai. With the masses of my troops in a furious onset I stormed, I captured the city; six hundred of their warriors I put to the sword; three thousand habitants I took captive I burned with fire; I did not leave a single one among them alive to serve as a hostage. Hulai, their governor, I captured alive. Their corpses I formed into mounds; their young men and maidens I burned in the fire. Hulai, their governor, I flayed, his skin I spread upon the wall of the city Damdammusa; the city I destroyed, I devastated, I burned with fire.*[15]

With such a pitiless disposition of the most powerful military, economic, and political force then in the Near East, it stands to reason that the mere shadow of Assyria, leaning continually further west, had to weigh the region down with unrest, fear, a nameless terror.

Some decided to resist, and to this end formed pathetic coalitions that were sent flying by the first charge of the monster. The more prudent dispatched messages of submission, from as far away as they could, to the appalling conqueror. So doing, they gave up virtually all independence and condemned themselves and their people to misery by agreeing annually to pay to the occupier a devastating percentage of their national revenue.

The work of the invaders was rendered even easier by rivalries and struggles that the multiple little states and kingdoms of Syria, Phoenicia, and Palestine carried on among themselves: Damascus, Hamath, Tyre, and Sidon in the North, and Edom in the far South; Judah and Israel, the most frequent rivals, sometimes allied themselves with the others and sometimes resisted them.

---

15. Reported in col. 1, lines 107ff., of the annals. See D. D. Luckenbill, *Ancient Records of Assyria and Babylonia I* (Chicago: University of Chicago Press, 1926), 146, sec. 445. The scene takes place in upper Syria, in the region of the sources of the Euphrates, in the Bît-Zamani territory. Hullai was its king, and Damdammusa a fortified city.

Under Tiglathphileser III (744–727), contemporary of Kings Uzziah (781–740), Jotham (740–736), and Ahaz (736–716) of Judah, and Menahem (743–738), Pekahiah (738–737), Pekah (737–732), and Hezekiah (732–724) of Israel, Assyria's dominion over all of the North and West of the Fertile Crescent is firmly established. Still, though Judah stays quiet, Hezekiah, king of Israel, has lent his ear to pharaoh's emissaries and counts on support from Egypt in shaking off the unbearable Assyrian yoke. Shalmaneser V of Assyria (726–722) lays siege before Samaria. The city holds out for three years, but is at last taken by Shalmaneser's successor, the great Sargon II (721–705), at the very beginning of his reign. Without destroying the city, the victor returns to the traditional policy of his nation and is satisfied by dispersing the elite of the city—27,900 people, he says, for the most part warriors, artisans, and technicians—throughout his empire, as far as distant Media. He sets a governor over a now decapitated people.

Thus the kingdom of the North has ceased to exist. Only Judah is left to watch over the old endowment, Yahwism.

A new generation of Prophets will draw the lesson of these events on the plane of religion. They preach, they intervene in public life, but in addition to the spoken word and to the examples they set, they proselytize *in writing*. They produce vehement tracts, pamphlets and poems, which their disciples distribute far and wide in order that their influence might spread, and of which the most striking, at least, have been preserved in the Bible, in general under the name of their authors. The oldest, and no doubt the most well known of their time, are Amos, Hosea, Isaiah, and Micah, all dating from the eighth century, from the reign of Jeroboam II of Israel (783–743) to the reign of Hezekiah of Judah (716–687), after the fall of Samaria. Two of these performed their ministry in the Northern Kingdom: Hosea, who was a native there, and Amos, who was from Judah. Isaiah and Micah, also Judaeans, stayed in Jerusalem, but paid as much attention to what happened in Israel as in Judah. This fact is one more proof of the profound unity that continued to attach the two disunited kingdoms.

Like their great predecessors since Moses, these new spiritual masters of the Israelite people have in common a characteristic profound and universal faith: convinced that everything that happens here below is only the visible counterpart to a supernatural history that is guided by Yahweh, they penetrate with this "twofold" vision all that they see around them, and interpret it in this light. This includes even their own personal lives. Thus it is that for Hosea, a deceived and humiliated husband, his disastrous marital experiences (told at the beginning of his book) have made him understand that between Yahweh and His people the same ties were woven of enduring attachment and unalterable love as between himself and his wife, the unfaithful one who is still loved tenderly and passionately:

Denounce, denounce your mother:
She is no longer my wife,
And I am no longer her husband!
May she remove her adulteries from her face,
And her shameless profligacies from her breasts,
Or I shall strip her naked,
And render her as she was born:
I shall change her into a desert,
And make her like an arid land,
I shall make her die of thirst!
I shall not love her children,
For they are the fruit of adultery!
Yes, their mother has been unfaithful,
She who conceived them has covered herself with shame:
"I shall go after my lovers," she said,
"Because they give me my bread and my water,
And my wool and my linen, my oil and my drink!"
She has not understood
That I was the one who gave her
Wheat, wine, virgin oil!
Now I will bar her way with a hedge of thorns
And shut her in with a fence,
So that, running after her lovers,
She may not join them,
And she searches without finding them!
Then she will say: "I shall go back to my first husband,
Because then it was better for me than now!"
And I, here I am, ready to regain her!
I shall restore her in the Desert,
I shall speak to her, heart to heart . . .
There she will again find her youthful yearnings for me,
As when she came up from Egypt!
Yes, on that day—oracle of Yahweh!—
She will call Me again: "My Husband!"

She will not call Me: "My Baal!"
I shall remove the names of the Baals from her mouth!
I shall make you my wife forever.
I shall take you for my wife in all justice and rightfulness,
In tenderness and love.
I shall marry you to Me indissolubly:
Then you will understand who is Yahweh!
    (Hosea 2:4–10, with transposition of 8–9 before 6, 18–19, 21–22)

It will be much later, after a long ripening process, that this new definition, introduced by Hosea, of relations with God on the level of love and erotic attraction, and no longer only fear and reverence, will bear fruit and transform, in Judaism, and especially in Christianity, not only the tone and expressiveness of religious sentiment but the very conception of God.

The Prophets of the eighth century influenced Yahwism considerably by their endeavors to instill in their contemporaries the interpretation that their own faith provided for the great political events. They contemplated and judged those events with a remarkable lucidity, beginning with the Assyrian advances, with their blows inflicted upon prosperity and peace in Israel and Judah and the still heavier perils they brought down on independence and national survival.

In the first place, it went without saying that for the Prophets such misfortunes admitted of one irrefutable explanation: the revenge of Yahweh against His people for disloyalty to the Covenant (see page 36).

If, especially since Elijah (page 44), there was no longer any question of looking elsewhere for a national God, one *did* ask, now and again, whether it would not be beneficial to add a pantheon of foreign deities. Since the installation in Canaan, the latter had never ceased to exert on the crowd an appeal most injurious to the radical will of Yahweh to remain forever the *only* cult object of His people (page 26). In the passage from Hosea just cited, if the unfaithful wife, who is Israel, wants to "follow her lovers," it is because she believes them alone to be capable of furnishing "her bread and her water, her wool and her linen, her oil and her drink," or, in other words, guaranteeing the efficaciousness of work in the field and with the cattle (see page 38).

Even among those who did not feel drawn to foreign deities, there was a pernicious influence those deities were able to exert, obliquely, within Yahwism. Little by little, as we know (pages 33ff.), Yahwism had adopted the Canaanite ceremonial pattern in the splendor of sanctuaries and the wherewithal of the cult, in ceremonial pomp, ostentatiousness, and multiplicity of sacrifices and offerings. For the devotees of other divinities, the religious obligations toward their gods went no further than all that; once the ceremony was completed, they felt entitled to protection and benefits from their sovereigns on high. But for those who kept to the Covenant, all that could amount to no more than some sort of accessory affair. The true observance, demanded by Yahweh and solemnly promised by Israel, lay elsewhere, in recognizing through constant obedience His moral commandments of righteousness, fraternity, and profound devotion.

But what did the Prophets see all around them? Like their predecessors at the time of the entrance into the Promised Land, and indubitably now even more so: extortions, injustice, excesses, and countless crimes:

> *They sell the innocent for silver,*
> *And the destitute for a pair of sandals!*
> *They crush the heads of the poor,*
> *They confine poor wretches to misery!*
> *Son and father sleep with the same girl!*
> *They sprawl next to every altar*
> *On blankets for rent.*
> *In the house of their God they drink*
> *The wine of those they crushed!*
>
> (Amos 2:6ff.)

> *Woe to those who join house to house*
> *And who link one field to the next,*
> *So there is no room anymore*
> *And so that they alone are lodged*
> *In the midst of the land!*
> *Woe to those who get up in the morning*
> *To rush for alcohol,*
> *And who linger until dusk,*
> *Excited by wine!*
> *There is nothing to their carousals but lyres and harps,*
> *Drums and pipes*
> *And drink.*
> *Woe to those who yoke together iniquities as with cattle rope*
> *And misdeeds as a line of chariots!*

Woe to those who say
Of evil, "It is good!" and of good, "It is evil!"
They pretend that darkness is light and light is darkness,
Bitterness sweet and sweetness bitter!
Woe to those who are wise in their own eyes,
To those entitled to an opinion according to themselves!
Woe to the champions in downing wine,
To braggarts at mixing drinks,
Who acquit the wicked for a fee,
But deny justice to the innocent.

(Isaiah 5:8–23)

Side by side with such crimes, in scandalous contradiction to the words of the Covenant, do not this cult and this liturgy—which are not even mentioned by name—seem a monstrous hypocrisy, a perversion of authentic Yahwism, an abomination in Yahweh's sight? What difference could it make if it all were performed in zeal and splendor?

What does the abundance of your sacrifices matter to me,
Says Yahweh!
I am satiated with the holocausts of rams
And the fat of calves;
And the blood of bulls, of lambs and he-goats.
I want no more of it!
When you come to visit Me,
Who has asked you for it?
Do not go on
To crowd My outer sanctuaries,
Or to bring your offerings!
Vain is the smoke of incense!
I am disgusted with it!
New Moon, Sabbath,
The holding of Assemblies—
I cannot stand them anymore,
Neither fasts nor feasts!
And your First-of-the-Month and solemnities—
My soul detests them.
All that is a burden to Me,
And I hate the distress of it!

When you stretch your hands [in prayer],
I shut my eyes before you!
You can pile up your prayers in vain.
I do not listen!
Your hands are bloody!
Wash yourselves, purify yourselves!
Remove the evil from acts you do
Far away from My eyes!
Turn back from doing evil,
And learn to act justly:
Follow what is Right,
Help those who are persecuted,
Render justice to the orphans,
Defend the widows!

(Isaiah 1:11–17)

Thus did the Prophets, diametrically opposed to the multitude, who thought they owed nothing to Yahweh once they had conformed to the rules of the ritual, demonstrate that the veritable Yahwism was absolutely corrupted once a facile, a laughable, liturgical observance, no different from the customs of all idolaters, had been substituted for its moral demands. By this obstinate neglect of the words of the fathers, by this corruption of the Covenant, Israel had aroused the vengeful fury of Yahweh: hence the reason for that invasion of Misfortune, delivered by the irresistible troops of the king of Assur.

Now, if Amos and his companions had stayed with what we hear thus far, they would have done nothing but apply old principles, ones inferred before them (page 42), to a novel situation. But the keenness of their political view, their realism, their competence in analyzing the state of affairs and its probable evolution, brought them to a further stage of lucidity; in the face of the sanctimonious optimism of some and a hope through thick and thin of others, they foresaw and predicted catastrophes, and the events proved them right.

Thus the anger of Yahweh has been
Ignited against His people
And He has raised His hand against them.
He strikes them so as to overturn the mountains.
Their corpses are like refuse in the street!
And yet His furor has not subsided,

And His hand maintains its threat!
He will beckon the distant Nation,
And whistle for them at the other end of the earth!
There they come quickly, quickly!
None of them is fatigued, none stumbles,
None slumbers, none sleeps,
None unhooks his shoulder-belt,
None unlaces his sandals!
Their arrows are sharp,
All their bows bent!
Their horses' hooves are as good as flint,
The wheels of their chariots are like the whirlwind.
They swell into the roars of a lioness,
They roar like a young lion,
Who, growling, snatches his prey,
And carries it away, with none able
To tear it from him!
Then a roar like the sea
Will break over the land.
In vain will people try to find the land.
There will be only black night and anguish,
The light darkened by clouds!

(Isaiah 5:25–30)

Going a step beyond their ancestors, the Prophets of the eighth century were not content to explain misfortune as the just deserts delivered by divine rage (see page 42ff.): they posited *a priori* the necessity for punishment and conceived of Yahweh's Justice as absolute and universal. For them, He was a God who *could not be* unjust; He could not possibly *not* exert His justice everywhere and always.

And furthermore, this same Yahweh, who, in order to effect His design and chastise His people, was able to *"beckon the distant Nation"*—Assyria—and *"whistle for them at the other end of the earth,"* who could command it and move it at His will, must have had full control over that nation, and not only over His own people. And if, moreover, He held in His hands the most immense and formidable empire the world then knew, how much more all the others! Thus, Yahweh appeared to the prophets as the God of the *Universe*. He was not only creator of the earth and its population, as the old *Yahwist* (see pages 35ff.) related; He was not merely able to intervene when the interest of His people was involved, battling and defeating the gods of the other nations: He was the real, the unique, God, not only for Israel but for all the nations, whose deities were idols, *"deceptions,"* as Amos calls them (2:4). Thus it was the Prophets, beginning in the eighth century, who first began to glimpse this principle that was hidden in the very subsoil of their religion (page 26): absolute monotheism, perhaps the most sublime contribution by Israel, her noblest and most admirable contribution to the history of man, for it no doubt is what most surmounts him.

The famous vision that, according to Isaiah, marked the beginning of his prophetic calling may help us see the spirituality, the height of the idea of their God, that those great minds conceived and propagated under the blows of the ordeals sustained by their people:

> *In the year that King Uzziah died (740), I saw the Lord Yahweh on a throne, high and sublime. The train of His garment filled the Temple. Above Him were the Luminous Angels, each with six wings: with two, they kept their face covered, with two, their feet, and with the other two, they flew. In concert, they exclaimed:*
> *"Holy, holy, holy is Yahweh of Hosts,*
> *Whose glory fills the whole earth!"*
>
> (Isaiah 6:1–3)

In Hebrew, the word we translate as "holy," here repeated three times to underline the absolute superlative, approximated the value of "sacred" and "numinous," which, for lack of better terms, we still use at least to suggest the transcendent and supernatural nature of Divinity. Thus, Isaiah, like the other prophets in his time, had an idea that was not all that different from what we think today, almost three thousand years later, of this God who is beyond all there is, separated by His very sublimity, ruling alone and unique over the world in which His glory is reflected everywhere.

This incomparable forward movement in the idea of God is not the only progress we owe to Israel in the realm of religion. She also discovered a purified and more "spiritual" conception of the Covenant.

In the passage of Hosea found on pages 49ff., Yahweh desired to *"restore"* His unfaithful spouse *"in the Desert,"* so that she would retrieve *"her youthful yearnings for me, as when she came up from Egypt."* Then *"I shall make you my wife,"* and this time, *"forever."* And the other Prophets, including Isaiah and Micah—but excepting, perhaps, Amos, who is more pessimistic—will proclaim, each in his own way, the same conviction, that the time of misfortune, destitution, and political insignificance, disentangling Israel from her supererogatory preoccupations, which in the end, since the entry into the Promised Land, had done nothing but distance her from God, will restore her to Him, in the same dispositions of loyalty, trust, and magnanimity that must have inspired the fathers during their long wanderings upon leaving Egypt. Then she would understand all that for centuries the best of her sons had in vain tried to bind on her heart: that the true ritual of Yahweh is the bond of His Covenant—which meant the bond to His person and His will. With a changed heart, the people would then be ready to subscribe in all sincerity to another Covenant—the first having been misunderstood, then broken—which would bind them forever to Yahweh, at last understood (*"You will understand who is Yahweh!"*) and served as He wished to be served.

This call for a new, more moral, more spiritual form of the Covenant constituted an enormous stride forward. True, there had been attached to this call an entire folklore transposed from the glorious times of the Conquest and the first great reign: certain passages in the Prophets make us think they were expecting a sort of new David, who would bring victory to his people, after a lightning intervention by Yahweh, in a "Day" of triumphant battle of the type one knew from earlier times against the Canaanites. These themes are the first results of messianism (see pages 88ff.). But the best of prophetic thought in this domain can be found in an admirable passage of Micah (which a copyist later transposed in part to chapter 2 of Isaiah). In Micah it would seem that this great and noble thought appears for the first time—like a postulate of "monotheism," one that Second Isaiah (see pages 75f.) will push very far—namely, that when Israel has returned to Yahweh, in the era of universal peace that will follow the present time of catastrophe and carnage, Israel herself, in her capacity as Yahweh's people, will be the center of the whole universe, which will draw on her for knowledge of God, submissiveness to His will, and the taste for unending peace:

> *It will happen, in the course of time,*
> *That the Mountain of the Temple of Yahweh*
> *Shall be established above all mountains*
> *And raised above all hills!*
> *All Nations shall flow to it,*
> *And numerous peoples make their way to it, saying:*

Let us go and ascend the mountain of Yahweh,
To the Temple of the God of Jacob,
So that He may teach us His ways
And that we may follow His paths!
From Zion instruction will come forth,
And from Jerusalem the Word of Yahweh!
He will be the judge of the Peoples
And the arbiter of the strongest nations:
All will beat their swords into ploughshares,
And their spears into sickles.
No nation will lift its sword against another,
And never will they learn war any more!

(Micah 4:1–3)

"REFORM"

For a century, after 721, the political history of Judah remained the affair of an insignificant little people, wholly tributary to almighty Assyria, to whose dominion Esarhaddon (680–669) had subjected every land as far as Egypt.

Judah's religious history is denser than its political development. What determined it was twofold. First of all, the fall of Samaria and the dismantling of the Northern Kingdom, which had long and relentlessly been foreseen and foretold by the Prophets, validated the latter and drew attention to their teachings. Certainly, as is always the case, there were those whom no catastrophe could awaken and also those many who always lean toward "idols," in which they fix their hope more and more, rather than incline toward changing their lives. However, around the Prophets and their disciples the number of faithful was growing, persuaded that it was indeed idolatry and infidelity, abuses and failures in keeping the Covenant, that had brought over Israel a deserved chastisement from Yahweh: if Judah did not take an altogether different road and radically change its way of life, it was bound to undergo an identical fate. It goes without saying that this is precisely the threat the Prophets pronounced. Thus a "reform" movement is born.

In addition, since Israel had been spiritually dismantled by the abduction and disappearance of its leaders and masters and, in a manner of speaking, no longer counted for Yahwism, the new movement in Judah—whatever its origins—was purely Judaic, that is, centered in Jerusalem, its Temple, and its

traditions as capital of the formerly united kingdom. It is even probable that
the reform movement began especially among the intellectual elite and the
clergy of that city, in the course of decades of reflection, discussion, and
activity.

Like all disciples and hangers-on, these reformists did not fail to coarsen and
harden to some extent the sublime thought of their teachers. Speaking of the
return to the Covenant, the Prophets had in mind a profound attachment
and a complete submission to the will of Yahweh, whereby Yahweh was taken
as if a living person, a partner, an inspirer. Their followers were mesmerized
by what was most immediate to them: the duties set in laws that the will of
Yahweh entailed—not merely the ancient "commandments" of the Decalogue
(page 25) but the whole long string of specifications that had been added in
the course of centuries, most of which had been committed to writing after
the model of the old Code of the Covenant (page 33). They saw in the Torah
the "doctrine" of Yahweh and, above all, the codification of such instruction
in duties as it implied. In this way, they placed the written Law on the highest
level and began an inclination toward legalism that later on would go very
far, as we shall see.

    We find a similar distortion in the background of another basic idea of the
reform. For reasons that are difficult to unravel but in which indubitably the
interests and privileges of the Jerusalem clergy played a part, the reformers
wanted to enhance the monotheism deduced and taught by the Prophets by
translating this faith in one unique God into a duty to worship Him in one
unique place: the one God of the Universe should have only *one* residence in
the entire world: the Temple of Jerusalem.

    In short, the adepts of this view made of the absolute Justice of Yahweh
that was posited by the Prophets an essential articulation of their own teachings
by reducing it to a sort of theory of retribution. Misunderstanding the freedom
of Yahweh, the inaccessible character of His vision of things, the impenetrable
mystery of His designs, they regarded Him in some way as obliged to reward
His faithful with material fortune—the only way imaginable (see page 96)—
and, by contrast, to punish the infidels with sufferings and deprivation of
worldly goods.

    These basic ideas—while they substantially preserved the prophetic
message, also to some extent hardened, shrunk it, made it deviate from its
course. The reformist partisans, just like their masters, wanted to make their
ideas more effective by committing them to writing, and they did so in two
ways.

At the very beginning, on the "juridical" level of this Law they posited at the base of the new spirituality they wished to draw their brethren into, they edited a sort of directory, in which, in the new spirit, all commandments and obligations of religious and moral life were integrated, considerably developed and subdivided since the Decalogue and the Code of the Covenant. From the reformist point of view, it was no more than a new exposition, a complete reedition and publication of the "thought of Moses," and therefore they placed their account on the lips of Moses. Once again somewhat warping a great idea of the Prophets, they evidently wished to present their manifesto as the original charter of the new Covenant.

This document, "the *Deuteronomist*," has been preserved for us in the body of the Pentateuch, of which it constitutes one of the four principal sources (see page 13). Its name, Deuteronomy, taken from the Greek, meaning "the second Law," which is to say, the final Law, holds like an echo the idea of a new Covenant. By its language, by its vocabulary, and also by its style and rhetoric, the *Deuteronomist* stands out against all the other documents of the Pentateuch. It is not a historical narrative like the *Yahwist* or *Elohist*. It is not a juridical anthology like the Code of the Covenant. It is first and foremost a sort of sermon, a long and fervent exhortation, and therein surfaces the influence of what the Prophets had always been: preachers.

In selections I am going to cite from Deuteronomy, we will recognize the Prophets' teachings, though at times more or less disfigured or warped. The *Deuteronomist* owes to the Prophets, and only to them, this affirmation of monotheism, absolutely categorical for the first time in Israel's history: "*Only Yahweh is God; besides Him, there is none!*" (Deuteronomy 4:35). And we find, if not the tone, at least the teachings of the same Prophets (see pages 50f.) in the following encouragement to fraternity and goodness among Israelites: "*If there is one among you, one of your brethren, who is in need, no matter where in the land that Yahweh, your God, has given to you, do not keep a hard heart and a tight fist before him, your brother in his need. Open your hand wide for him, and lend to him generously to provide what he needs*" (Deuteronomy 15:7ff.).

Let us turn to something that will enable us to gauge the diametrical change in mentality that had come to pass since the time of the Code of the Covenant. According to the code, one could, whenever one wished, enact a ritual to Yahweh "*in every place where He manifested His presence*" (see the text quoted on page 33), provided only that one did not build any altar that was lavish:

When you cross the Jordan and are settled in the land that Yahweh, your God, wants you to own, once He has sheltered you from the enemies around you and established you in safety, then, exclusively to the place that Yahweh, your God, shall choose there as His personal Residence, there you will bring everything that I command you: holocausts and sacrifices, your tithes and offerings, with all the votive gifts that you have reserved for Yahweh. . . . See to it that you do not offer holocausts in any place you would deem good! No! Exclusively at the place Yahweh shall select, in the territory of one of your tribes, there, and nowhere else, you shall be able to offer your holocausts and perform everything I command you. (Deuteronomy 12:10ff.)

The unique locality where it would be permitted to celebrate the cult of Yahweh is not named, but its designation is transparent: certainly it is Jerusalem and its Temple.

Finally, the long catalogue of chapter 28, which spells out, on the one hand, *"all the blessings that will come over you and that you will obtain because you have obeyed the commandments of Yahweh, your God"* (28:2), and, on the other hand, the disasters likewise promised *"if you do not obey the commandments of Yahweh, your God, by observance and practice of all His commandments and all His laws"* (28:15), shows sufficiently how much place was given in this teaching to a theory of retribution, with the inevitable peril of affecting the religious sentiment with the pursuit of a more trivial interest.

The literary activity of the reformers did not limit itself to elaborations in the Book of Deuteronomy. Just as they wished, in that book, to reedit the Law in accord with their ideology, they arranged and recast the history of their people in the same spirit. Their intervention is especially evident in the historical books that follow Deuteronomy: Joshua, Judges, Samuel, and Kings. What they wanted to show above all was how that same Law had governed the conduct of the Israelites after the death of Moses, who had instilled the Law in them. In pursuit of their goal, they did not so much write accounts as rearrange and compile already existing documents, to which they were content to add glosses or words and phrases that expressed their doctrinal preoccupations. For instance, they added an anachronism to the biographical note on King Hezekiah (716–687) of Judah: *"He is the one who abolished the high places, broke the sacred pillars, and cut down the sacred poles, and destroyed the bronze serpent that Moses had made"* (2 Kings 18:4). In their idea, it was unimaginable that this pious king would not have conformed to the Law in the way *they* understood it, and would not have suppressed the ancient cult places for the benefit of the one Temple of Jerusalem.

Likewise, we owe them the "artificial frame" in which the Book of Judges is set (see page 10), through which we view perfectly what they had in mind: while recounting how in the course of that era the Israelites reaped nothing but miseries and defeats from infidelity to their God, only to regain victory and freedom at once on their return to Him, the Deuteronomists were in fact teaching the theorem of retribution, which to them was fundamental. In passing, let it be said that we would be wrong in these matters to accuse the writers of perpetrating falsehood and lies; the ancients did not know our requirements of scientific critique and objectivity, and to them, it seemed perfectly valid to *infer* history from the "philosophy" that is proper to the historian.

While the "impious" kings, like Manasseh (687–642) and Amon (642–640), held sway, the reform movement was not likely to emerge from the obscurity in which it was working itself out. With the devout Josiah (640–609), who ascended the throne at the age of eight, the reformers found their man. The Second Book of Kings (chapters 22–23) would have it that the high priest at that time *"discovered in the Temple of Yahweh the book of the Law"* (2 Kings 22:8). When it was read to the monarch, he was thunderstruck—to such an extent was the abyss clear to him between the conduct of his people and the Law in question. The book, it is evident, was Deuteronomy, and its champions obtained what they wanted: an official renewal of the Covenant in accordance with the literal text of this new Law:

> *The king called up and assembled before him all the Elders of Judah and Jerusalem. Then he went up to the Temple of Yahweh, accompanied by all the Judaeans and Jerusalemites: priests, prophets, with the whole people, from the least to the greatest, and he proclaimed to them the whole content of the Book of the Covenant found in the Temple of Yahweh. Thereupon, standing by the Pillar, he committed himself, by the Covenant established in front of Him, to follow Yahweh and to keep His commandments, His decrees, and His laws with all his heart and soul, so as to carry out the rules of the Covenant inscribed in that Book. And all people declared their adherence to the Covenant.* (2 Kings 23:1–3)

The reform thus worked out, too distant from the ancient customs to be put into action at once, had at least the advantage that it made the great prophetic ideas widely known. However , it had taken away much of their vigor and primary truth by fixing them into laws, and it furnished the Israelites a repose based on a treacherous and dangerous assurance, insofar as they could believe themselves to be on orderly terms with their God and saved if only they contented themselves to observe the letter of His commandments, just as their fathers had done with the rules of His ritual (page 52f.).

THE APPROACHING DISASTER AND JEREMIAH

Indeed, those who followed Josiah and expected the promised reward from Yahweh could have believed for a while that the horizon was clear; in 612, under the onslaught by Babylon, which had finally come out of its lethargy, Nineveh collapsed, heralding the imminent end of the Assyrian oppressor. Nahum 3:1 describes Nineveh as *"city of bloodshed, the impostor, filled with booty, tireless plunderer."*

But the somber years that fate had in store would soon undeceive them.

In 609, in his endeavor to cut off the road against Pharaoh Neco II (610–595), who was hurrying to the aid of the last king of Assur in his last refuge, Josiah was suddenly defeated and killed. That the promoter and standard-bearer of reform, the pious king, faithful to Yahweh during his entire reign, had met a miserable and manifestly "unmerited" end, in place of glory—what a disenchantment and scandal for those who believed in the "blessings" of the *Deuteronomist!*

And yet, it seemed that their confidence, or their stubbornness, did not break. How else to explain their will to resist the new Babylonian oppressors, who were just as ferocious as the Assyrians, whose place they had assumed? The first decade of the sixth century is filled with conspiracies against them, sometimes resulting almost in revolt, all immediately and mercilessly repressed but apparently without discouraging the "patriots." The reasons will soon become clear.

A handful of Prophets, just as clairvoyant, devoid of illusion, and courageous as their great predecessors, at the expense of their tranquillity, their honor, and sometimes their lives, were the only ones who attempted to stop such ill-advised, desperate, and bloody actions. Accused of defeatism and treason, they were treated accordingly. One of these Prophets left an imposing work in writing and, towering over his contemporaries, gives us a true picture of the great religious advance of the era: this Prophet is Jeremiah, one of the purest geniuses of Israelite history.

Continuing the work of Amos, Hosea, Isaiah, and Micah, he pushes their teachings still further. For him, monotheism has such an obvious reality that, fixing his eye on the other deities, he dismisses them as nothing more than the materials of which their images are made (Jeremiah 2:26–28, 16:20–21). The following passage, which stands out in his book, renders his teachings perfectly, even if, as there is some reason to think, it is not by his own hand:

> Do not submit to the customs of the Nations:
> Do not be frightened at Celestial signs.
> Fright glazes the eyes of the Nations when they see them.
> What terrifies them is futile!
> It is nothing but wood cut in the forest
> And the work of the chisel in a sculptor's hands.
> They beautify it with silver and gold
> And strengthen it with nails, hammered in
> To make it solid!
> Such things are a scarecrow in a field of cucumbers, they do not move,
> And they must be carried, for they do not walk!
> Do not be afraid of them: they cannot harm you!
> But you will not draw the least bit of good from them!
> None is like You, Yahweh, in Your grandeur;
> Your person is sublime and sovereign!
> Who would not fear You, King of the Nations,
> With the awe You are entitled to?
> Yes, among the Spirits of the Nations and all their Kings,
> No one is like You!
> In the same way, they are similarly stupefied, crazed!
> The lore of such vanities is worthless!
> But Yahweh is the true God:
> He is the living God and eternal King!
>
> (Jeremiah 10:2–8, 10)

One area of incalculable importance to the development of Yahwism remained until then virtually unsuspected. Here Jeremiah paved wholly new

ways: the domain of *personal* religious life. Jeremiah came to this discovery
(as we shall see) because of that same eye of faith, seeing all in relation to
Yahweh, by which he sought to understand the things he analyzed so lucidly
all around him and also that which he experienced in himself.

We should underline a difference between Jeremiah and the writing Prophets before him: Jeremiah found himself almost constantly exposed to the
incredulity and persecution of his contemporaries. The latter, as we have
suggested, without really changing anything in their lives, had inevitably
retained of Josiah's reform only what pleased them, above all the certainty
expressed so often in the Book of Deuteronomy that they had to preserve in
their capital the one sole authentic residence on earth of Yahweh, King of the
World, unique and omnipotent God. They were quick to consider blows such
as Josiah's death to be accidents without consequence, and remained
convinced that they would have Yahweh on their side in the future; feeling
not the shadow of a doubt, they counted on the final victory and their return
to prosperity and independence. How ever could the Master of all Nations,
the one true God of the Universe, lose face by abandoning His city and His
house to His enemies, no matter how powerful? Here we see the reason why
they defied Babylon and fomented revolts, telling themselves their success had
been promised.

Jeremiah, however, saw clear as daylight, on the one hand, that before the
enormous and relentless oppressor, all his compatriots' assaults would be
shattered, and their revolts only laid the land bare to plunder, enslavement,
and exile; and, on the other hand, that the real moral reform was far from
accomplished and impiety and injustice were multiplying as before. And so
he felt the need—and, moreover, without the slightest hope of success!—
cruelly to undeceive those who surrounded him.

> Hear what Yahweh declares, all of you Judaeans who enter the gates
> of the Temple, who prostrate before Him. Thus speaks Yahweh of
> Hosts, the God of Israel: "Amend your ways and your acts if you
> want Me to stay with you in this Place! Do not put your trust in
> deceitful words: The Temple of Yahweh! The Temple of Yahweh! The
> Temple of Yahweh! . . . You are ready to believe these lies! But in vain!
> So you would steal, kill, commit adultery, perjure yourselves, burn
> incense to Baal, run after foreign gods that you do not know, and,
> after that, come present yourselves to Me, in this House that bears
> My Name, saying: 'Here we are safe!' safe to continue all those
> horrors? Do you take this House for a robbers' den? Nevertheless, I

see clearly what is going on, Yahweh says. Go and consider Shiloh,[16]
which belonged to Me, and where I formerly placed My Name, and
see what I did to it because of the wickedness of My people Israel!
Well! Because you have done all those things, without listening to My
ceaseless warnings, without responding to My appeal—from now on,
says Yahweh, I shall deal with this House that bears My Name, and
on which you rely, this Place that I gave to you, to you as to your
fathers, I shall deal with it as I dealt with Shiloh, and I shall reject you
far from Me, as I rejected all your brothers who made up all the
descendants of Ephraim."

(Jeremiah 7:2–15)

Those who listened to Jeremiah were neither ready nor inclined to accept
such harsh truths. Hence they never ceased to oppose and condemn him.
Rejected in this way, alone against all, Jeremiah turned to Yahweh, making Him
his companion in his isolation, the confidant of his miseries, the refuge from
discouragement and troubles, which he felt the more vividly because of his
tender soul and lively sensibility:

O Yahweh, remember me, come to me
And take vengeance upon my persecutors!
Do not let me die, restrain Your anger!
Know that I bear their contempt for You!
As soon as Your words came, I devoured them:
They were a joy for me and my heart's delight!
For it was Your Name I carried, Yahweh, God of Hosts!
I have never joined the circle of scoffers:
Held back by Your hand, I remained alone,
As you had filled me with protest!
O, why does my suffering never end,
Why is my desperate wound incurable?
Would You be to me like a deceitful wadi
Of whose waters one cannot be sure?

(Jeremiah 15:15–18)

16. In the course of the Conquest (see pages 26ff. above), Shiloh, almost twenty miles north
of Jerusalem, in the highland of Samaria, seems to have played the role of a religious center of
Yahwism and was one of the main centers of Yahweh (see especially the first four chapters of 1
Samuel). Afterward, we no longer hear a word about it; indubitably, the place was taken and
devastated by the Philistines. This brutal elimination accounts for the reference by Jeremiah.

Jeremiah's book is full of these moving interrogations. Sometimes Yahweh responds, which leads to an intimate dialogue:

> *I will make you for this people*
> *An indestructible wall of bronze!*
> *Let them turn against you: they cannot kill you,*
> *For I am with you, to save you*
> *And to set you free, says Yahweh!*
> *I will deliver you from the power of the wicked,*
> *I will take you from the hand of these brutes!*
>
> (Jeremiah 15:20–21)

Thus, Jeremiah is the first to have taken Yahweh truly as partner, interlocutor, companion, to have centered his inner life on Him *as a Person*—and no longer as Sovereign or Chief of his people. On reflection, we can see that this new step had to come in due time, moving Yahwism as if from an external forum to an inward one and to the secret heart. From *one god* among others as He formerly was, with the government of His people as His essential role, having before Him less the "faithful," in the proper sense of the word, than subjects, Yahweh, recognized as universal and transcendent, had turned into *God*. His function was no longer only social but in some way "metaphysical": He no longer occupied Himself only with the destiny of the people but with the destiny of each human being, and from now on everyone could find in Him a true God, suited to fill the heart and enlighten the spirit. As in the philosophers' vocabulary: transcendence and immanence are inseparable. It is Jeremiah who first found a way to understand this, building on Yahweh a truly spiritual and personal life.

Thus we see how, having an idea of relations with Yahweh altogether different from that of his contemporaries, Jeremiah for the first time defined the new Covenant envisioned on a spiritual level and as the very basis of human existence. Only this Covenant, he thought, was in accord with the real will of Yahweh and capable of "saving" His people:

> *"Yahweh declares: The time is coming when I shall establish a new*
> *Covenant with Israel: not like the one I established with their fathers,*
> *when I took them by the hand and pulled them out of Egypt; for that*
> *Covenant they broke so thoroughly that I had to eliminate them, says*
> *Yahweh. Here then is the Covenant that I shall enter into with Israel*
> *after this present time, says Yahweh: I shall place My Law inside them*

and I shall write in the depth of their hearts. That is how I shall be a God for them, and they will be a people for Me. They will no longer have to exhort one another, everyone saying to his neighbor: 'Understand who is Yahweh!' but all will know Me, from the least to the greatest, says Yahweh!" (Jeremiah 31:31–34)

In this passage Jeremiah defines the imperative evolution of Yahwism: what it must become if it is to remain consistent with its premises and not stray from its course. It is only *"after this present time"* that he expects the establishment of the new Covenant—in other words, after the duration of the Exile, whose inescapable advent he constantly announced. Just as in the old account of the *Yahwist* (Genesis 6:5ff.) Yahweh resigned Himself to annihilating the first humanity He had created, which had become corrupt, in order to inaugurate a less treacherous humanity, the ancient Covenant had to disappear, together with the descendants of those who first subscribed to it, then obstinately transgressed it, emptied it of its meaning, and made it worthless, forcing Yahweh to "discard" the people He had chosen for Himself. But in the course of the years of misery, far from their homeland, the new Noahs of this cataclysm, the survivors of Israel and their descendants, would finally reflect and *"understand who is Yahweh"*: how to *"be His people"* would be understood by contact between *everyone* and Him, by *everyone's* attachment above all to His *moral* will, by *everyone's* obedience to His voice. This will, this voice, would no longer present themselves under their obsolete, coarse, formalized appearance, easy to twist and distort, of written laws, like the ones that regulate the behavior of an ordinary sovereign's subjects: they would be engraved in the depth of *each person*, blended together with his own conscience, as if they came from the immediate ties with God, from those heart-to-heart conversations for which Jeremiah set the example. The Yahwism to come would no longer be primarily national, but personal.

Nevertheless, even if Jeremiah, like many of his predecessors (see pages 56f.), does not at all deny it, he does not explicitly attribute to this Yahwism a character that is, in the real sense of the word, universal and accessible to each and every human being *qua* human being. The prophet remains faithful to the old tradition that set forth Israel as the people chosen by Yahweh and associated with Him as no other people had ever been or would ever be. He only removes from this election every interpretation of a primarily nationalistic nature; the elect are to be seen as a spiritual people, composed of individuals of whom each one is in a personal relationship with the God of all.

The "personalization" in the teachings of Jeremiah reaches into another area that is essential to Yahwism: the area of divine Justice. Handed down since the first author-Prophets in the form of an absolute theorem (cf. page 54), Justice had been thought about until then on an almost exclusively national plane, like all relations with Yahweh. In the Book of Deuteronomy, it was still the people of Israel that was the direct object of God's Justice, just as it was the prime partner in the Covenant, and the "blessings" and "curses" that were promised (see page 60) were all collective in nature. But while explaining that the people as such, forgetful for too long of the words of the first Covenant, in effect needed to be punished, the Prophets' teachings had ended up arousing a certain bitterness and an almost rebellious attitude on the part of the faithful who had nothing with which to reproach themselves and yet saw themselves thrown into misery for the expiation of their ancestors' transgressions. They were wont to mutter: *"The fathers ate sour grapes, but their children's teeth are set on edge"* (Jeremiah 31:29; Ezekiel 18:2; see page 80). In Jeremiah's view, such an apparently mistaken application of divine Justice accorded only with the collective and national character of the first Covenant: in the settling of the old debt, the punishment of Israel as a people brings along some innocents. Afterward, things will no longer be the same, but *"Yahweh . . . will pay back each one according to his conduct"* (Jeremiah 17:10): *"After this present time"* (the same expression he uses in the same passage to refer to the beginning of the new Covenant; see page 66), *"people will no longer say: 'The fathers ate sour grapes, but their children's teeth are set on edge!' No! Everyone will die for his own misdeed, and only he who eats sour grapes will have his teeth set on edge"* (Jeremiah 31:29f.).

THE FALL OF JERUSALEM AND THE EXILE

In 598, following a first brief insurrection, which Babylon punished by sending numerous high dignitaries into exile together with Jehoiachin, the latter's successor, the weak Zedekiah (598–587), deaf to the counsel and reproof of Jeremiah, allowed the resistance party to go beyond all measure, and they unleashed another uprising. Then, in 587, as the Prophet had foreseen, the armies of Nebuchadnezzar II (604–562), king of Babylon, attacked, besieged Jerusalem, took it, dismantled it, sacked and burned the Temple, put a great number of dignitaries to the sword, and sent the whole elite of the nation into exile—four thousand six hundred people, according to a list at the end of the Book of Jeremiah (this apparently relates only to heads of families or to adults)—leaving only people of the lower classes, in a country that by and large had been turned into a Babylonian province.

What would come of this terrible ordeal?

The Exile properly so called was to last for almost half a century; then Babylon, in its turn, succumbed (539) to a young power, even more formidable and finally reaching from the Indus to the Nile. This was the dominion of the Persians and Medes, who had united and were led to victory by the founder of the Achaemenian Empire, Cyrus the Great (558–528).

Nothing can render the sufferings endured by the vanquished and their burning hatred against the perpetrator of carnage and humiliation, the terrifying and implacable sovereign of Babylon, as impressively as the virulent celebration of his defeat and death, which the author of the following admirable piece portrays as ignominious. It is included in the Book of Isaiah, the receptacle of so many incomparable masterworks of ancient Hebrew poetry.

"See"—the prophet is deemed to have said—"the day has come on which Yahweh will give you rest from your trouble and your terrors, and the hard servitude forced upon you, and you will intone this verse addressed to the king of Babel":

> There he is, finished, the despot,
> His tyranny, brought to naught,
> The cudgel of the wicked, crushed,
> And so the scepter of the potentates!
> He who beat the peoples in rage,
> Dealing blows without end!
> Who in fury pursued the nations
> In a pitiless pursuit!
> The whole earth is appeased and calm,
> People are delirious with joy!
> Even the cypresses are happy because of you,
> And the cedars of the Lebanon:
> "Now that you have crumbled,
> The woodcutter does not attack us anymore!"
> Sheol,[17] down below, is excited over you
> At the announcement of your arrival:
> Sheol will arouse the shades in your honor,

17. On infernal Sheol, see note 8 above.

Raise former wielders of power,
All the kings of nations,
From their thrones.
All find their voice to tell you:
"You too, reduced to nothing like us,
Turned into one like us!"
Your majesty has gone down to Sheol.
So has the sound of your harps!
Beneath you a bed of rottenness extends;
Worms are your cover!
Well! See how you have fallen from heaven,
O Lucifer, son of Aurora! How you are beaten to the ground,
You subduer of all the nations!
You who said to yourself in your heart:
'I shall climb up to Heaven!
I shall set my throne
Above the stars of God!
I shall take my seat on the Mount-of-the-Council
In the utmost North![18]
I shall scale the tops of the clouds!
I shall be the equal of the Most High!'
Well! There you are, down in Sheol,
Down in the depth of the Pit!"
Those who see you, think about you,
And meditate on your fate:
"Such is the man who turned the earth upside down
And made kingdoms totter;
Who changed the world into a desert,
And uprooted the cities!
The one who never opened the prison of his captives,
Who confined the kings of all the nations!
All of them rest in glory,
Each of them in his tomb:
But see, you are rejected, without a tomb,
Like a loathsome piece of carrion,

18. Here we may be looking at a Mesopotamian tradition (which the cuneiform texts, however, do not yet allow us to confirm), according to which the place of assembly of the gods, their Olympus, and the residence of their sovereign, would be located in the high mountains of the North, the summits of the Caucasus. See also note 26 on page 148.

Covered by the massacred, those pierced by the sword—
Like a trampled corpse!"
Because you have ruined your country,
Killed your people,
Never shall be mentioned any more
The lineage of the Evildoer.
Arrange for his children to be put to death
To pay for the crimes of their father,
For fear that they rise up and reconquer the earth
And overrun the world again!
I shall stand up against them,
Says Yahweh of Hosts,
And I shall exterminate
Babel's name, kith and kin,
Offspring and successor.
I shall make her into a place of hedgehogs:
A swamp,
And I shall sweep her with the broom of annihilation,
Says Yahweh of Hosts!

(Isaiah 14:3–23)

As soon as he emerged victorious, Cyrus, who was justly called "the Great" and who had broader ideas concerning subjected nations than did the Assyrians and Babylonians, issued an edict (538) to give exiles the freedom to return to their homeland and there regroup themselves. But not all took advantage of this gift.

After all, they had for the most part reorganized themselves in Mesopotamia and had been left alone by their masters in enough freedom of communal life and of exchange with their new surroundings that, in short, they had formed the first Jewish colony in the world: perhaps it was not even a ghetto. And yet, thus reunited, with their daily bread assured by their labor or commerce, where would their thoughts turn, if not to their homeland, terrestrial and spiritual?

By the canals of Babylon,
We sat down, weeping
At the memory of Zion!
There were poplars there;
On them we left our lyres hanging,

While they, our captors, asked us for songs,
Our oppressors, for joyfulness:
"Sing one of those songs of Zion for us!"
How to sing a song of Yahweh
In a strange land?
If I forget you, Jerusalem,
Let my right hand vanish!
Let my tongue stick to the roof of my mouth,
If I do not think of you,
If I do not raise Jerusalem any more
To my supreme joy!

(Psalm 137:1–6)

And indeed, their fatherland and their God, for them inextricably united from the beginning, were at the center of their thought, their conversation, their plans.

Like an individual who has experienced a terrible blow and is obsessed by it, mentally going through it over and over, always asking why, they kept returning to the catastrophe that had uprooted them. Why? Why, the people chosen and preferred by the one God of the Universe, who had established His unique dwelling place on earth with them, in the midst of their capital, who at first were victorious and free under His invincible guidance, why had they been ruined in the end and cast into slavery?

In their eyes, which finally opened, only the answer the Prophets offered and repeated to them for so long could account for such a collapse and such a scandal. Consequently, only then did the teachings of the ancient defenders of the grandeur of Yahweh, of the moral and spiritual nature of the Covenant, of divine Justice, which had been incomprehensible for such a long time and had gone over the heads of all, enter their hearts and change them once and for all. Then the Prophets' lessons sank in—later we shall see exactly how. And since the teachings opened a vista on the hope that, after their chastisement, upon their turning back to God, Yahweh would take Israel again under His wing—delivered from humiliation and promised to happiness, having first gone through a period of discouragement and stupefaction under shock, then through a time to understand the sense of what had happened—people turned resolutely toward the future, to prepare all the better for it.

From this new, intense, and prolonged reflection led by "zealots," in Mesopotamia especially, but also in Palestine and perhaps elsewhere, as in

Phoenicia and Egypt, where some little groups had been able to find refuge, a twofold interpretation of a renewed Yahwism would arise. Both parts take up a number of ideas in the heritage that had been elaborated and deepened by the Prophets; but the two explain things very differently: one is inclined to universalize Yahwism, the other to close it in on itself. In the final analysis, and rather quickly, the former would fade before the latter.

SECOND ISAIAH AND THE APOGEE OF YAHWISM

The universalizing tradition is the one we shall consider first, although we know it on the basis of somewhat later documentation. Its most eminent representative is at the same time the last great Prophet, one of the noblest of thinkers and, together with the author of the Book of Job, the most powerful and magnificent poet of the Bible. And yet, we know neither his name nor his person. All that remains is his written work, anonymous, with a voice, style, imagery, ideology, so special that an ageless tradition made him part of the great Isaiah's book, of which his text makes up chapters 40 through 55. Would not this "Second Isaiah," as we call him, have been given that place (see page 14) in order to assign to him the same rank, for lack of better, as the other giant of Prophetism and Yahwism?

Where did he live? We cannot infer it directly from what he wrote. But the period of his activity is clear from the message of freedom that forms the canvas of his book. Throughout the confrontations of nations after the middle of the sixth century, with that political insight we have already admired in his predecessors, he understood that Babylon was lost, that victory would be on the side of the peoples that had come from the East under the leadership of Cyrus, and that this change in world government had to work to the advantage of his imprisoned people, since the new sovereign found himself compelled by a humane and generous disposition. Being a true Prophet, Second Isaiah saw the almighty and profound plans of Yahweh. Those world upheavals expressed Yahweh's desire to save His people, who from now on were forgiven. The Prophet's announcement resembled a renewal of the earliest history, when Israel was pulled out of Egypt: the departure from Babylon would be followed by a crossing in the desert, for the final triumph, toward a new, enormous theophany that this time was to echo in the whole world:

Comfort, comfort My people,
Says your God!
Speak to the heart of Jerusalem
And cry out to her
That her servitude has come to an end,
Her iniquity has been pardoned,
That she has received from the hand of Yahweh
Twice the price of all her debts!
A voice cries out: "In the desert,
Prepare the way of Yahweh!
In the wasteland, draw straight
A highway toward our God!
That every valley be filled up,
Every mountain and hill brought down;
Let tortuous ways be straightened,
Let rocky terrain be leveled:
The Glory of Yahweh will be manifest
And all living beings together
Will see that Yahweh has spoken!"

(Isaiah 40:1–5)

"All living beings together"—this trait is typical: Second Isaiah has a universal spirit. This is clear, first of all, from the profound and sublime idea he has of Yahweh: Second Isaiah is the one who has given absolute monotheism its strongest, highest, and most developed expression, as if he had still better understood what this prodigious discovery of his predecessors harbored. Not only did he ascribe the quality of God to none but Yahweh and ridicule, like Jeremiah, the other divine pretenders, merely fabricated idols, impotent, lifeless; but, perhaps as a result of a distant or not too distant influence of Babylonian speculation, which must have struck the exiles and led them to reflection (see, for instance, pages 155ff.), he put Him always in relation to the Cosmos, suggesting that only the latter was of His stature and His measure. Of this Cosmos, Yahweh is at the same time the Creator, the Preserver, and the unique Ruler:

Who has ever been able to keep the seas in the palm of his hand,
And measured the sky with a span,
And gauged the dust of the earth in a bushel,
And weighed the mountains in scales?

Who would fathom the Spirit of Yahweh?
What human being would exhort His ideas to Him?
Whom would He call in to give Him counsel
And teach Him to render Justice,
Instruct Him to behave wisely?
Before Him, the Nations are a drop from a bucket,
Barely more than a speck of dust on the scales,
Islands are no more than thinly scattered dust!
The Lebanon does not suffice as fuel,
Nor its animals for a holocaust!
All peoples are nothing before Him:
He accounts them as nonexistent and empty!
But to whom would you compare God?
What image would you make for Him to resemble Him?
Didn't you learn? Haven't you heard?
Haven't you been told from the beginning?
Haven't you understood the origin of the World?
It is He who dwells above the Circle of the Earth—
Whose inhabitants are but crickets!—
He stretches the heavens like an awning,
Unfolds them like a tent to live in!
It is He who brings Princes to naught,
And makes the Judges of the Earth vanish:
Scarcely sown, scarcely planted,
Their stalk barely taken root in the soil,
He blows upon them, and they wither,
Carried off by the squall like stubble!
Whom, then, would you compare Me to?
Whom could I be like, says the Holy One.
Raise your eyes,
Look: Who created those Stars?
Who makes their Hosts come out in order?
Who calls them each by their name?

(Isaiah 40:12–18, 21–26)

Second Isaiah does not use this universal perspective, this constant harking to the World, the Nations, the "Islands"[19]—as he likes to say—only for

19. At that time, the horizon had widened toward distant western maritime regions: Cyprus, Crete, and as far as the shores of the Aegean.

Yahweh: he extends it to His people. He has given thought to their sufferings and their exile, and he considers it unworthy of his God's Grandeur to speak of these sufferings (as had always been done before him) only on the level of perfect retributive Justice rendered only with regard to Israel, since God is also the one God of all Nations of the Universe. Most assuredly, Yahweh is essentially Righteous: Second Isaiah does not deny the evidence established by his predecessors. But he has such a high conception of his God that he feels loath to reduce Him as if to one single prerogative applied to one single fraction, even the most excellent one, in His domain. God would not be God if He occupied Himself only with Israel and were Just only for them. Therefore, by putting His people in the pillory of the entire World, as He had done, He must have had another, subtler goal, less fathomable, more worthy of Him than a straightforward chastisement, corrective and vindictive: by means of this unheard-of, terrible example, He wanted, in order to lead all people to Him, to cause them to know His own people as His agent, to authorize His people in their midst as His witness, through the spectacle of a misfortune it had borne so worthily and courageously before all, *in order to atone for their crimes too.* For it would be Israel's mission from now on to spread in the whole world the knowledge of Yahweh, a zeal for Yahweh and all the privileges thereof, which had first been reserved for Israel but which Yahweh, the one universal God, wanted to extend to all people. The only prerogative that remained unquestionably, unshareable, with His people was that of having been chosen by Him as His herald, His deputy, *His servant:*

> *My servant will prosper,*
> *He will be raised up, preeminent!*
> *Though his sight had first frightened the multitudes,*
> *Innumerable peoples will be astonished by it*
> *And before him kings will lose their voice!*
> *They will see what has never been told,*
> *They will avow what has never been heard;*
> *"Shot up before us like a sapling,*
> *Like a root that grew in dry ground,*
> *He had neither beauty nor luster,*
> *No appearance that made him appeal to us:*
> *His face was disfigured, inhuman;*
> *He did not seem a man any more!*
> *Despised, deserted by all,*
> *A man of misery, who knew suffering,*

Like those before whom one covers one's face,
He seemed despicable and disgraced!
And yet, it is our sufferings he bore,
And our miseries that crushed him!
We, we considered him punished,
Beaten, brought low by God:
In fact, he was pierced and injured for our crimes,
Trampled upon for our sins!
On him weighed a chastisement that set us free,
By his wounds we were healed!"
It has pleased Yahweh to overwhelm him with miseries,
But as he gave his life for atonement,
He will obtain offspring and eternal life,
And the goodwill of Yahweh will be realized through him.

(Isaiah 52:13ff.)

Here is My servant. I stand by him.
He is My chosen, whom I favor!
I have breathed My spirit into him,
That he may reveal the Truth to the Nations.
Without crying, without raising his voice,
Without making it resound in the streets,
Without breaking the crushed reed,
Without extinguishing the flickering lamp,
He will disclose Truth to the peoples:
He himself shall not waver or be crushed
As long as the Truth is not established on Earth
And the Isles are hoping for his teachings!

(Isaiah 42:1–4)

Resuming, completing, and pushing much further an idea some old Prophets had already foreseen (Micah, pages 56f.), Second Isaiah shows himself to be a religious thinker of great originality and profundity. He understood not only that "monotheism" implied a total transcendence in God, a separation from all that is created, a setting apart in a supernatural universe, but that the knowledge of God constituted in itself a value that was equally superior to all that exists in the world, and thus gave rise to an order of purely spiritual greatness. Second Isaiah led his people into this order of greatness. Compared to other protagonists in the great jolts of history—Assyrians,

Babylonians, Egyptians, Medes, Persians—the Israelites carried no special weight; and from the point of view of their celebrity among the nations, a frail celebrity, and their grandeur, short-lived, Israel will never be anything but insignificant. But in the spiritual order, dominated by the knowledge of the one true God, by the attachment to His person, no one is greater than Israel. Veritable intermediary between God and human beings, Israel plays for their sake the role that the Prophets used to play for the sake of Israel: receiving the truth from God to pass it on to others. And just as the Prophets suffered in order to teach that truth to their contemporaries—all souls preserve the memory of Jeremiah's example (see pages 63ff.)—Israel is likewise the expiatory victim of the world. With her sufferings, she redeemed not only her own crimes and ignorance but theirs as well: Israel is ready to make them receive what she has to teach them.

What is that message? A person as august as Second Isaiah would hardly trouble himself with details: nowhere in his book will we find meticulous critical remarks about the conduct or the particular precepts required for the relationship with God. Taking over where Jeremiah left off (see pages 66–67), he held a wholly positive view of that relationship (he speaks very little of sins and failures), and a sublime idea: spiritual and somehow mystical. He too believed in a new and definitive Covenant; but, together with Jeremiah, he sees it at work in human conscience; thus it seems that for him the mere act of giving oneself loyally and completely to Yahweh was sufficient—because of this inner contact with Him—to assure rightness and holiness in conduct and, especially, to fill the hearts of men, *of every human being*. For it is *to all—to each and everyone*—that Yahweh addresses Himself when He says in the text of Second Isaiah:

> *O, all of you who are thirsty, come and drink!*
> *Even without money, come!*
> *Buy your bread without untying your purse,*
> *Purchase for nothing your wine and your milk!*
> *Why spend your money on false bread,*
> *And your riches for that which could not satisfy?*
> *Listen to Me, listen to Me: you will have good fare,*
> *You will delight in exquisite foods!*
> *Lend Me your ear: come to Me,*
> *Listen to Me, and your soul will live!*

(Isaiah 55:1–3)

In the main line of the great ancestors since Moses, Second Isaiah pro-posed the highest and most admirable ideal of Yahwism that we have as yet come to know in the Bible. Was it perhaps too high for his contem-poraries? The greatest minds are always condemned to preach in the wilder-ness. What is more or less absorbed of them are only some poorly under-stood or trivial sayings; less precipitous and less vertiginous ways are more popular.

EZEKIEL AND THE FOUNDATION OF JUDAISM

An entirely different concept of Israel's calling and her relations with Yahweh therefore began to assert itself. It may be glimpsed emerging in the course of the Exile in Mesopotamia: through the principal spiritual leaders, who seem to have been more directly in tune with the basic feelings of their flocks, the Exile was instrumental in preparing for it. The new concept was not revo-lutionary like the one Second Isaiah dreamed of, but it was much more closely linked to the recent past and to the explanation the old Prophets and their disciples, the Deuteronomists, had given of that past.

Of these spiritual masters in exile, the most notable, the greatest in his own way, the one who brought the most weight to bear on the new turn in Israel's history, is Ezekiel.

Because at the beginning of his career, in Jerusalem, he joined in with Jeremiah in predicting the catastrophe and the Exile, before finding himself among the deportees, we know that he was living before Second Isaiah, whom in all likelihood he never knew. And in any case, when it comes to spiritual disposition and religious thought, there could hardly be a more glaring contrast than that between these two great men. Ezekiel's vocation typified him: he was a priest, a member of the clergy of Jeru-salem. In spite of the features that connect him with the ancient Prophets, and other features as well—in particular the literary construction and, let us say, the "surrealist" cast of many a theme in his "visions," which make him the first among their epigones (the authors of apocalypses—see page 90), Ezekiel's priestly function separates him strongly from the original, encompassing, and sublime perspective of Second Isaiah, from his universalistic and "metaphysical" spirit. Ezekiel, much more narrowly connected to the compilers of Deuteronomy, is a nationalist and a moralist.

Overall, he is not an innovator, except on one fundamental point: as if to hold on to the promises of Jeremiah (see page 68), he declares here and now and forever that the time of collective responsibility is over, and announces that henceforth everyone must answer for himself before Yahweh; everyone will be judged and rewarded according to his own conduct; everyone holds in his hands his own salvation:

> *"Why do you repeat over and over again that phrase among the Israelites: 'The fathers ate sour grapes, but their children's teeth are set on edge?' As surely as I am alive, says Yahweh, indeed, you shall have no occasion any more to repeat it: each life is Mine, the son's as well as the father's, and only the sinner will be condemned to death."* (Ezekiel 18:2–4)

> *"The innocence of the just will no longer save him when he undertakes a wrong deed, nor shall the crime of the transgressor seal his doom when he turns away from it. I did say to a man who was just: 'You shall remain alive,' but if he relies on his innocence, and commits evil, he shall die of the evil he has done, and that earlier innocence of his will count for nothing.' And, although I did say to an evil man: 'You are condemned to die,' if he turns away from his faults, and does what is lawful and just—if he restores what he has received in pledges, and returns what he has stolen, and makes up for his evil conduct by observing the laws, then the misdeeds he committed will not count in the least. From the moment he observes what is lawful and just, he will live!"* (Ezekiel 23:12–16)

Inasmuch as a great many exiles could feel enmeshed in an unbearable chastisement for wrongdoing for which they did not feel personally responsible, such a perspective offered hope of salvation to each and all. This is the hope Ezekiel tirelessly preached, thus preparing the resurrection of his people. The "vision of the dry bones" is very well known, and it is easy to imagine the courage with which it might fill his listeners:

> *The Power of Yahweh seized me, and on the strength of His Breath let me down in the middle of a plain covered with bones. . . . There was an infinite multitude of them on the soil, all completely desiccated. "Son of man," Yahweh said to me, "could these bones take on life again?" "You know it, You, Lord Yahweh!" I answered. And He*

said: "Then, prophesy over them, and tell them: Dry bones, hear what Yahweh says . . . : I am going to restore Breath in you, and you will take on life again: I shall rearrange tendons on you, I shall cause flesh to grow on you, I shall stretch skin over you again, I shall again put Breath into you—and you shall live again! Then you will understand who I am, I, Yahweh!" So I prophesied, as I had been ordered; and, at the same time, there was a sudden noise and a tumult: the bones came together, and fitted themselves to each other. Before my eyes, tendons covered them again, flesh came upon them, skin stretched over all of it. . . . Then, Breath came back to them, and they revived, they stood on their feet, like an immense army. "Son of man," Yahweh said to me, "these bones are the whole people of Israel!" (Ezekiel 37:1–11)

Ezekiel brought such a message, of resurrection and salvation, only to the Israelites. The rest of mankind is outside his mission and beyond his thought: *"You have been sent not to the other peoples, with their incomprehensible speech and barbaric languages, but only to the House of Israel!"* (Ezekiel 3:5–6).

Those "other peoples," whom Second Isaiah foresaw assembled around Israel and led by her to Yahweh, Ezekiel, as the first writing Prophets had done, regards as enemies of his people and of God. He scarcely mentions them, except to settle their account in a list of calamity oracles (chaps. 25–32). And when he imagines the return of Israel as an independent nation, and Israel's future relations with her neighbors, he resolutely closes any access of the latter to the Temple and the God who resides there, even when those neighbors are living among the Israelites: *"No stranger, uncircumcised in heart and body, shall have the right to enter into My sanctuary!"* (Ezekiel 44:9).

Succumbing to a psychological attitude well known in prisoners, who are driven by it to plan with care not only the freedom of which they dream but details of the setting in which that freedom can be enjoyed, Ezekiel actually designed precise plans for the rebuilding of the Temple, the reconstruction of Jerusalem, and the reorganization of the national territory: the cardinal idea inspiring everything was a fanatic retrenchment, imposed on Israel because of its very prerogative as the people of God.

We have seen how Second Isaiah deduced universalism from transcendence, for the one true God, beyond all and everything, in the final analysis had to be the God of all there is and of all human beings, the magnet of the entire universe. Ezekiel, for his part, was able to see in this high and noble achievement of Israelite thought only a principle of distancing and separation. Precisely because Yahweh is "holy" (see page 55), He remains and must remain separate from everything, unapproachable. He communicates only a little of His "holiness"—like a radiance that becomes dimmer the further removed it is from the hearth—to everything that He has made more particularly His own: the Temple where He resides, with the servants and the accouterments of His cult; Jerusalem, the city where His sanctuary has been established; the territory of which Jerusalem is the capital, and the chosen people who reside there. Everything else is *profane* and must be kept at a distance. The other nations are nothing but the property of God and could not hope to have closer relations with him than a flock of sheep with its shepherd. For them, there is no hope for change in the state of affairs: no salvation as Second Isaiah understood there to be. In opposition to the entire universe, Yahweh, with His people around Him, forms something like a nebula of sanctity, impenetrable and inaccessible.

How does Ezekiel think Israel should manifest her privilege as a sanctified people? By neither more nor less than a return to a total obedience to Yahweh, for it was through her recalcitrance to His will that she was lost. In contrast to Second Isaiah, in whom one would scarcely find even vague allusion to the infidelities that had occurred, Ezekiel, on this point resuming the line of the earlier Prophets, returns to those infidelities over and over. One of his favorite themes is the "immoral history" of his people, wherein he presents the past as a series of treacheries and abandonments, which could only end in grief (chaps. 16, 20, 22, 23, etc.). And this disobedience, conceived in the most traditional sense, related entirely to the religious and ethical rules of the Covenant, to the ancient commandments given by Yahweh to His people, to all that which, since the *Deuteronomist*, had become the Law (see page 62).

> *The word of Yahweh came to me, speaking thus: "Well, son of man, will you decide, finally, will you judge this bloody city, will you uncover all her abominable misdeeds? Tell her: 'O city soaked in blood . . . , by the blood you have shed, you have made yourself guilty! By the idols you have manufactured, you have made yourself unclean! In that way you have come to the end of your term and have caused your end to come upon you: this is why I have made you the disgrace of the nations and the laughingstock of humanity. . . . Among you, parents are scorned! Among you, strangers, your guests, are brutalized!*

Among you, orphans and widows are mistreated! You despised My Sanctuary! You made light of My Sabbaths! Slanderers busy among you caused blood to be shed! With you, sacrilegious meals were held in the hills! Among you, people indulged in debauchery! Among you, even fathers were stripped naked! With you, you fornicated even with women impure in their menstrual period! Yes and, with you, there was also lewdness with your neighbor's wife! And even another who would shamefully defile his daughter-in-law! And even some who violated their own sisters! Among you, it was the custom to assassinate for a bribe! In loans, you took advance pay and committed usury! Rapaciously, you extorted others! And Me, Me you forgot! (Ezekiel 22:1–12)

Do we not have before us a catalogue, presented succinctly, an abridgement of a code, whose main articles Ezekiel sums up to reproach his people for having infringed them? In doing so, they condemned themselves to a misery whose mere memory should suffice to make them behave, from now on, in scrupulous observance of each rule. In contrast to the spiritual and almost "charismatic" conception of relations Second Isaiah discerned with Yahweh, that relationship for Ezekiel is essentially nothing but obedience to the Law. Yahweh does not speak to the heart of His faithful to rule their conduct through the voice of conscience, passionately attached to Him alone: He has already spoken, a long time ago, once and for all; and His words, His commandments, have been collected in the Law.

For Ezekiel, the Law became such a basic and central theme of religious thought that, renewing the work of the Deuteronomists, he, in his turn, with his disciples, wanted to propose a revision of the essential precepts, a compendium, fitting the taste of the day. These form the final chapters (40–48) of his book. And there one turns up a number of traits that betray their time: not only that punctilious separation of the sacred and the profane, of which, as we have seen, Ezekiel made himself the champion, but, for example, the importance from now on in religious experience of repentance and expiation, to which we find corresponding in the liturgy a complete, entirely novel ceremony, in which one can detect traumatic echoes of the Exile and also an influence of the mental habits and the ritual of Babylon.

Most of the works contemporary with Ezekiel and the end of the Exile are marked by the same isolationistic and legalistic preoccupations. They give voice to a religious, juridical strictness, according to which the people of God, wholly closed in on itself, has no other relations with respect to Him than an essential duty of obedience, an exact observance of a written text that is deemed to render the will of that God directly.

Let us call to mind the two most significant works, both anonymous, both of rather unclear origin. One of them, later incorporated into Leviticus, of which it forms chapters 17 through 26, is a simple juridical anthology: a new presentation of the Law, very close in spirit, in the principles it stresses and in tone, to Ezekiel, and where the recently emerged idea of separating the sacred and the profane is fundamental and prominent, following the leitmotiv *"Be holy, because I Myself, Yahweh, your God, am holy!"* (Leviticus 19:2). By convention, the whole text inserted in Leviticus is called the Code of Holiness (see page 14).

The other work is a history of God's people, put back into the history of the world, just as had been done earlier by the *Yahwist* (pages 13, 33f.) and a bit differently by the *Elohist* (pages 13, 45): this is the *Priestly Document* (page 14), which, together with the other two and the *Deuteronomist*, forms the substance of our present Hexateuch. In its vocabulary, its language, and especially its mentality and its vision of things, which assumes and embodies the long development of Israelite thought, this work is extraordinarily marked by its time.

Thus, in its introductory section, the solemn recital of the Creation (Genesis 1–2:4a),[20] which everyone is familiar with, God appears as genuinely unique, universal, beyond all, constituting what seems a separate order, and spiritualized to such an extent that His word is enough to bring about His will, to organize the Cosmos, to produce everything. He literally does not set His hand to the work anymore, in whatever manner, as He does in the *Yahwist* (pages 34ff., 121ff.), and He has nothing to do anymore with the clearing of *one* particular piece of land, or with *one* man whom He would single out from the rest to be somewhat like His peasant, or *one* tree or *one* animal of each kind, or *one* woman—but with universal realities: Chaos, Water, Heaven, and Earth; Light and Darkness, the Stars, botanical and zoological Species, the Human Race. In the articulations of this account, there is an obvious and strong influence of the Babylonian cosmology and cosmogony, which the Jews had learned about, or had come to know better, in exile (see pages 155ff.). However, these borrowed ingredients are transfigured by an ideology that belongs to the Israelites, which took shape little by little in their own thought (as we are seeing) in the course of centuries: the knowledge of the wholly

---

20. Translated and examined in detail on pages 124ff. below.

unique and transcendent character of their God, who has become *the* true and universal God.

Nevertheless, beyond this sublime and immortal vision, is it not evident to one who reads this text to the end, and who pays close attention to all that its authors wished to introduce into it, that the latter, following the *Elohist* (page 45), somehow tried to justify, by means of the very "practice" of God, the seventh-day rest of the Sabbath, which is to say, an institution consecrated by the Law? This is what typifies the *Priestly Document*. No doubt it is a history of Israel. And of course, this history, in its ideology and especially its theology, is up-to-date with developments of the day. However, precisely on this point it bespeaks the new, legalistic spirit that dominated the period and to which historical narration was subject, preferring to tell of those events (real ones or presumed) appropriate to show the divine origin—hence beyond discussion and absolutely obligatory—of stipulations of behavior incorporated in the Law. To cite but one example: what is the purpose, according to the *Priestly Document*, of the enormous and fabulous Flood? As follows: once the survivors had left the ark, "*God blessed Noah and his family, and told them: 'Be fruitful, multiply, and fill the earth. . . . All that moves and has life is there for your nourishment: I grant it to you, just as I gave you the greenery and the plants. Only, you are never to eat of meat that is full of what gives life to it, which is its blood!*" (Genesis 9:1–4).

These commands correspond word for word to the "*law*" that appears in the Code of Holiness: "*Anyone, whether Israelite or stranger living among you, who consumes blood, whatever blood it is, I will turn against him to cut him off from among My people: for it is the blood that gives life to the flesh!*" (Leviticus 17:10f.).

So the *Priestly Document* is much less a history as we understand it, in the sense of a disinterested and objective research into the past, than a sort of apology, under a narrative and historical guise, for everything held to be an essential rule of life for the chosen people and incorporated in the Law, the absolute and definitive communication of God's will to His people. Consequently, this work portrays the religious spirit of its time in its essential components: Israel remains forever the people chosen by God, on condition of total obedience to His will, scrupulously observing the written Law that transmits it.

After the liberating edict by Cyrus the Great (page 71), those who went about the reconstruction of the nation took these elements of isolation and legalism and mixed them into the foundations of the new Israel.

Not all exiles, as we have seen (page 71), returned to their homeland. Many had made a comfortable living for themselves and would have needed a certain heroism to give it up. So the ones who left, in successive groups, over the course of more than a century, were the most fervent, those most attached to their past, at once religious and patriotic. They were also the ones most imbued with the new ideology, which gradually spread and took strong roots: the most resolute led it to victory. That they did not succeed without labor, resistance, and struggle, we know for a fact. In the fifth century, about 430–420, at a point that the mixed-up chronology of our sources does not allow us to ascertain further, the faction of the "zealots" took power. This is how their hegemony in Jerusalem came to be consecrated:

> *At the beginning of the seventh month, the whole people, gathered together to a man on the square opposite the Water Gate, demanded from Ezra the book of the Law of Moses prescribed for Israel. So the priest Ezra produced that Law before the Assembly: men, women, and children old enough to understand . . . and, from early in the morning until noon, he proclaimed it to the people, who were hanging on every word. Ezra, the scholar, standing on a wooden platform made for the occasion, read in a loud voice the book of the Divine Law, which he explained and commented on as he went along, so that what he was reading would be well understood. . . . And all the people were in tears at hearing the Words of the Law. . . . In this manner, every day, from the first to the last, Ezra read the book of the Law during the week the Feast lasted.* (Nehemiah 7:72–8:18)

Just as in an earlier period Josiah had read Deuteronomy, Ezra read the latest edition of the "Law of Moses," revised and augmented according to the view that now prevailed. There is little doubt that what was read corresponds largely to what we call the *Priestly Document* (page 84), to which in the meantime the legislative part, notably the Code of Holiness, had been added. The ceremony just described celebrates a new departure in the religious and national life of Israel, as well as the consecration of its code of conduct as elaborated by the most zealous—or most fanatic?—among the exiles, and then among their descendants, around fundamental principles that narrowed down the essentials of religious practice to a fierce isolationism and a desperate clinging to the letter of the Law.

What is established in this way is less a nation than a religious community. Undoubtedly, individuals of the same race and language are reunited, but are

welded to a religious ideal by their devotion much more than in shared
political ambition or action. We are at a new stage for the faithful of Yahweh,
after a development of three quarters of a millennium since Moses and the
ancient Covenant. It is definitive: nothing substantial will change any more.
The new outlook and the form of life it implied are so different from what
we knew before the Exile that from this point on the term we normally use
is "Judaism" rather than "the religion of Israel" or "Yahwism."

LIFE AND THOUGHT OF ANCIENT JUDAISM

Judaism forms the third period of the biblical era and has continued virtually
changeless; it is still the religion of Yahweh, which it continues without rupture
in a long, slow development. It not only preserved many ancient Yahwist
observances (dietary prohibitions, circumcision, liturgical and moral regula-
tions), but especially, it retained the fundamental idea of the Covenant with
God. However, in the course of time, it transformed that idea profoundly by
a certain shift: attributing primary importance less to Yahweh as such and to
His will than to the codification of that will, to its form in writing for all time,
and to the reduction of all religious commandments to one, namely, the duty
of total obedience to this sacred text, this divine code, the Law.

This is the reason why from now on religious leaders are no longer the
independent, inspired persons whom we have called Prophets. Judaism no
longer knows prophets. We noted earlier the titles given to Ezra, the author
and proclaimer of the reform, who was the true founder of Judaism; he is
priest and *scholar*. This means that he was a member of the clergy, which in
the new community constituted the essential authority and hierarchy, no
longer primarily on the level of politics, but ecclesiastic. At the same time, he
is a "man of the written word": a scholar, scribe, doctor of Law. His authority
does not flow from a private communication with God, some irrational
contact or ecstasy beyond his control, but from his profound knowledge of
a text. Too great for there to be, between Him and the people, an immediate
relation of any sort, God has, so to speak, arranged for a go-between: the
text of the Law. This text comes from Him, who dictated it once and for all;
henceforth it is all His faithful need in order to know what He wants.

Nevertheless, one should not conclude that a doctrine apparently so formal
and monolithic transfixed religious life into a dull ritualism. It is true that the

basic choices have already been made: the religion of Judaism, coming out of an agitated youth lasting for centuries, has about it something of the state of adulthood, in the sense of being stabilized and less open to great changes. Hellenism met with more resistance here than anywhere else in the East, if we reckon from Alexander's conquest in 332; and if this Greek humanism, perhaps the grandest ever conceived, ends up in a syncretization with biblical thought, it happens in Christianity, not in Judaism. No wonder that the history of the developments in Judaism, such as it shows itself in the Bible, can be put together from the texts more rapidly than the history of the previous centuries.

To begin with an altogether peripheral matter: what became, among the Jews before our era, of the "promises" with respect to the chosen people? What became of those promises, which constituted, so to speak, the divine part of the Covenant's contractual pledges?

Two things are clear. First, during the Exile, the most that the fieriest of zealous patriots could hope for was the reestablishment of national independence. Once they were free and back home, they surely had to believe that God had at least kept His "promise" of resurrection. But at the same time, religious individualism had blurred the collective character of the Covenant (see page 90 below), and the many miseries that had been borne had their impact on whatever remained of national ambition. Broken in collisions with enormous empires, these people from now on could see themselves only as a tiny nation, quite incapable of playing a role on its own in a universe whose horizon seemed to grow from day to day. And besides, was not the tendency to consider every stranger an enemy? This xenophobia, this profound feeling of impotence and inferiority, mixed with a nostalgia for the ancient glory and prosperity of the nation, in the happy times of David, and with the promises of victory and salvation made by the ancient Prophets (see pages 56f.), was established and elaborated in an almost doctrinal way according to which in the end God would send his people an even greater king, a true successor of David, "consecrated" like him, one who would impose universal peace and return his people to wealth and luster.

> *Rejoice forever, O daughter of Zion,*
> *Exult, O Daughter of Jerusalem:*
> *Here comes your King!*
> *He is Just and Victorious,*
> *Yet Meek and riding on a donkey,*

A simple jackass, born of a she-ass!
He will abolish the chariots of Ephraim
And the cavalry of Jerusalem;
All weapons of war will be done away with,
And he will declare peace to the Nations!
His sovereignty will spread from one Sea to the other,
And from the Euphrates to the end of the World!

(Zechariah 9:9f.)

This messianism (in Hebrew, the term "messiah," *mashîah*, refers to the king's "consecration"), which for centuries grew richer in folklore, sometimes incorporated other, more squarely xenophobic views of the future: enemies of the chosen people, the other nations were plainly destined to annihilation. This last would arrive through a personal intervention by God, His power made manifest in a cosmic catastrophe, and as in the case of Noah's escape from the Flood, none would remain but the holy and righteous—henceforth ruling over the earth and safe from oppression and want:

The floodgates on high will open up,
And the Earth's foundations will totter,
The World break down utterly
And shake violently,
And collapse disastrously,
And stagger dizzily:
The Earth will be like a drunkard,
And shaken like a hut!
Her breach of trust will weigh heavy upon her:
She will fall and never rise up any more!
And then, on that day,
On high, Yahweh will chastise the host of heaven,
And down here the Kings of the earth:
They will be assembled,
Caught in the Pit,
Fenced in the final Enclosure,
And after many days, punished!
The moon will turn red
And the sun will blanch!
And Yahweh of Hosts will be King

On the Mountain of Zion, in Jerusalem,
His faithful of old witnessing His Glory!

(Isaiah 24:18–23)

Such themes spurred the imagination: messianism as well as eschatological scenes gave birth to an entire literature, of which a good deal was not deemed quite right for admission into the biblical canon but was relegated to the "Apocrypha" and "Pseudepigrapha."[21] Thus a whole original genre was unleashed: apocalyptic writings, made up of grandiose visions, often enigmatic and obscure on purpose, filled with allegory and magniloquence, all turning around the detailed prediction of a universal upset, programmed by God from beginning to end. In the Bible, the Book of Daniel and all of chapters 24 to 27 that were later inserted into Isaiah (of which the passage just cited is an excerpt) are apocalypses, probably composed in the second century B.C.E.

If the national "promises," the only ones imaginable before the Exile (page 68), count for less in Judaism, it is because the latter is based on individual responsibility (page 80). The Jewish people remains the chosen people and, as such, is promised a sublime destiny. But now, on account of His indubitable and unfailing Justice, God must punish the disobedience of each person and reward the submission of each person to His will. Thus the traditional perspective is overturned. The new axiom allowed, and even obliged, everyone to initiate immediate relations with God and to establish upon these a personal spiritual life.

This considerable enrichment in religious potential was expressed especially in two areas in that period: prayer and moral life.

The Book of Psalms is a collection of songs and devout poems of which most may have served an official use in public cult but in which a new personalized spirituality, based on a dialogue with God, found various expression: attach-

21. The "biblical canon" is the official collection of books that are held to be "inspired" and sanctified by God. This list was more lenient among the Jews of Alexandria than those of Palestine, and while the Roman Church inherited the "canon" from the former, Protestantism turned to the latter. The term "apocryphal" is specifically used for those "biblical" works that are excluded from the strict Jewish canon but accepted in the Alexandrian. Other works, of similar inspiration, whether Palestinian or Alexandrian in origin, that have never been accepted in either of the two lists, are called "pseudepigraphic." However, the term "apocryphal" is often used, in the wider sense, for this series of writings as well as the other. The best critical edition of these documents is by R. H. Charles, *The Apocrypha and Pseudepigrapha of the Old Testament*, 2 vols. (Oxford: Clarendon Press, 1913; latest reprint, 1968).

ment to His person, trust in Him, zeal for His cause, resignation to His will, and frequently a true love and, as we would say today, a genuinely mystical essence. Although a number of these compositions may go far back in time—tradition preserved the memory of King David as poet and composer of such hymns (but see also pages 29ff.)—many bear the mark of Judaism; they hardly have an equivalent before the Exile, except in the passages where Jeremiah shows himself as the father of spiritual life (pages 65ff.).

> *How long, Yahweh, will You wholly forget me?*
> *How long will You hide Your face from me?*
> *How long must I expose my soul to pain*
> *And my heart to misery all day long?*
> *Look at me: answer me, Yahweh, O my God!*
> *Let my eyes shine, so that I do not fall asleep and die,*
> *That my enemy may not shout: "I have vanquished him!"*
> *And that my adversary shall not take pleasure in my defeat!*
> *But I trust in Your benevolence,*
> *And quickly my heart will see Your Help coming!*
> *Yes, I sing to Yahweh for all the good He has done to me!*
>
> (Psalm 13)

In this spiritual life, obedience to the will of Yahweh, codified in the Law, is preeminent: it becomes an ideal of life that fills the heart and governs thoughts and deeds. It blends with the search for God, and the Law itself, almost hypostasized, shares in the admiration, enthusiasm, and adoration that His faithful bear toward its Author:

> *I searched for You with my whole heart:*
> *Do not let me stray far from Your Commandments!*
> *I keep Your Words hidden in my heart,*
> *So that I will never sin against You!*
>
> . . . .
>
> *I have never ceased to recite with my lips*
> *All the commandments that came from Your Mouth!*
> *I have taken greater delight in following Your Ordinances*
> *Than in any riches!*
> *I do not wish for anything but to meditate on Your Instructions*
> *And to contemplate Your Rules of Conduct!*
>
> (Psalm 119:10–15)

Because Yahweh's will, since the first Covenant (pages 22ff.), had always given precedence to ethical demands over ritual obligations and had in some way made of a righteous life the essential act of His cult, one can hardly be surprised to see how the preoccupation with the moral order intensified in Judaism as religious life became more a personal concern and divided up into an infinite number of units.

All civilizations have a foundation of traditional axioms that are meant to regulate the comportment of individuals, based on the idea their milieu entertains about the existence and hierarchy of its values. From the dawn of time in the Near East, a land of patriarchal culture, such pronounce-ments took the form of counsels from the mouths of the "fathers," the "ancient ones," who were deemed to present their long and sound experi-ence to their "children." Known in Mesopotamia and Egypt since the early third millennium, collections of those utterances were no doubt also spread in Israel, and it is not impossible that a particular literary activity was devoted to them rather early on, to which we gain testimony, directly or indirectly, in the legend of Solomon, the sage and recipient of wisdom from Yahweh (1 Kings 5:9–14). But especially after the Exile, whole collections of maxims were composed and assembled, sometimes translated almost literally from a foreign original but most often made from scratch and modeled after a clearly Hebraic vision of things. The growing interest in these "Proverbs" clearly emerged from the intensified concern that was felt by all, each on his own account, for leading a life that conformed to the Law: not only devout but honest and in strict compliance with a punctilious moral code. Indubitably, many of the maxims reflected a desire that was down-to-earth for a moderate, prudent, and successful life, with a more or less immediate personal advantage as its main motive. One hardly goes very far, and in any case not very high, by taking exhortations like these to heart:

> *Those who work take command.*
> *The lazy toil.*

(Proverbs 12:24)

> *Simpletons believe all they are told:*
> *The shrewd watch where they go!*

(Proverbs 14:15)

A good reputation is worth more than piled up riches,
And consideration more than hard cash!

(Proverbs 22:1)

The favor of Princes is on those who speak what is right.
They prefer those who express themselves with loyalty!

(Proverbs 16:13)

Other sayings, however, are rooted in something loftier: a truly religious spirit, in search for God, His preeminence, His Will, which are essentially known in the rule of life of every man:

May goodwill and loyalty never leave you: . . .
Inscribe them on the tablet of your soul!
Place your trust in Yahweh with all your heart,
Without relying on your own judgment!
In all you do, think of Him:
He will direct what you undertake!
Be not content with your self-conceit,
But fear Yahweh and guard against evil!

(Proverbs 3:3, 5–7)

Whosoever engages in a close reading of the various collections that together make up the present biblical Book of Proverbs will clearly perceive that in the final analysis they have been laid out like so many pieces of religious casuistry, detailing the line to be followed by every person faithful to the Law, resolved to lead an existence in conformity with it, and, consequently, agreeable to God.

The mode of behavior thus regulated becomes—as elsewhere, and in other times, that of the *honnête homme*, or that of the Hero—an ideal of human life. The word "wisdom," which pointed in Hebrew first of all to a "know-how," a simple technical skill (see also note 26 on page 202), became the term for the art of living and, in accordance with the Law, of course, the supreme virtue. No wonder it was exalted above all human activity, as in the following admirable poem from the Book of Job, where it is placed infinitely higher than the most arduous and most spectacular achievements in what was then the final word in progress: technique in the quest for metals and hard stones:

There are many mines for silver
And places where gold is refined,
Where iron is taken from the earth,
Copper smelted from ore!
Men have put an end to darkness:
Down to the utmost depth, they search
For the dark and gloomy stone!
A people of strangers digs shafts:
Invisible, unsupported,
They swing, lowered far from humans!
The depths of this earth, which yields bread,
Are disjointed in fire:
Its rocks are the dwellings of sapphire
And its soils hold gold!
Along a path that the eagles do not know,
That the vulture's eye could not detect,
And the wild beasts never pace . . .
Men reach for flint,
Uprooting the mountains!
They dig tunnels in rock,
The eye directed toward manifold wonders!
They explore the Source of the rivers!
They bring to light what is hidden!
But Wisdom, where does it come from?
What is the mine of Understanding?
No one knows its course:
It is not found on the earth of men.
The Abyss says: "It is not in me!"
And the Ocean: "Not with me!"
But Elohim knows its path:
He alone knows where it abides!
When He encompassed at a glance all ends of the World,
And considered all that Heaven covers,
When He established the winds' weights
And gauged the Waters by measure,
When He set a limit to the Rain
And made a way for the Thunderbolt,
Then He saw it and valued it,
He created it and pierced it with His sight.

(Job 28:1–14 and 23–27)

Like the Law in another context (see pages 58f., 86), here wisdom is in some way reified: created by God at the very beginning as one of the essential and superior components of the universe. Later, the same thought will be continued even further, when wisdom is made into a personal attribute of God, like Life and the Word, in which He allows His elect among people to participate.

For the Jews, the duties toward the Covenant take on the form of inner life and devotion, on one hand, and, on the other, that of a just life and wisdom. As to the benefits of this manner of contract, established long ago with the people—its very "promises" and "threats," made only more infallible by the centuries-long development of the idea of God linked to His absolute Justice (pages 60, 62)—they too had moved mostly to the level of the individual (see page 90): what in former times Yahweh promised the obedient "House of Israel," prosperity and happiness, and the threats He made in case it was insubordinate, decay and misfortune, everyone had come to take personally and to wait for, or perhaps fear, in accordance with his own conduct.

Happy is the man who has no part in the agreement of the impious,
Nor detains himself on the way of sinners,
Nor has joined the gathering of banterers,
But whose delight is in the Law of Yahweh,
And who recites that Law day and night!
He is like a tree planted by a stream,
That gives its fruit at its time
And whose foliage never withers:
All that he undertakes will succeed!
For the impious, it will not be thus, not at all:
They will be like chaff carried off by the wind!

(Psalm 1:1–4)

Sinners have misfortune at their heels,
But the righteous shall be full of happiness!

(Proverbs 13:21)

The righteous always have enough to eat,
But the belly of the evil ones remains empty

(Proverbs 13:25)

The Book of Psalms and the collections in Proverbs are full of this double certitude: happiness for the just, and ruin for the sinners, both founded on the unequivocally infallible Justice of God and simply carrying over to individuals the "blessings" and "curses" that Deuteronomy had formerly reserved for the Israelite nation (page 60).

Here, however, a serious problem arose. A people of course has a future, and when no hint of realization of the promises was in sight, one could always hope for their fulfillment at some later time. However, an individual has a short life. And according to common opinion at the time, death put an end to everything: afterward, nothing remained of a person but his "shadow," the *nefesh*, an uncertain, spectral transfer of what he had been in life, which, deprived of the vitality and power it formerly possessed, of the blood (see page 85) or divine "breath" imparted to it for a stretch of time (see page 35), was not able to live more than a lusterless, torpid, and, above all, negative existence in the mysterious residence of shades, infernal Sheol. Under these conditions, divine Justice, rewarding the just and punishing the transgressors, at the peril of denying itself—blasphemous and unthinkable eventuality— had inevitably to make itself felt during the brief span of one's life. Of course, in those days, as at present, no one could seriously ascertain any fair balance between moral-religious worthiness and fate, and the fate of libertines could sometimes, perhaps often, look more enviable than that of decent and saintly people.

In postexilic biblical literature there echo again and again passionate discussions concerning this quandary, which threatened one of the most fundamental axioms of religion: the absolute Justice of God. The constantly recurring thesis comes from theologians of the time who stand out by their remarkable intransigence and obstinacy, always insist on their professional prerogative, and, content to ignore objections arising from experience, reaffirm, tooth and nail, the traditional equation of saintliness with happiness and misfortune with impiety. Nevertheless, in more clairvoyant eyes, this was sufficient to ruin the very foundation of Judaism: if God did not treat each man according to his merits, He was not Just, and hence, He was not God.

Two "solutions" were found to this redoubtable problem, and they may be the last great achievements of pre-Christian biblical thought.

The one I shall mention first is in fact the more recent. It was not an inference drawn from the problem posed by the anomalies of divine retribution. It is rather like the natural result, the most exquisite fruit, of postexilic religion and its "mystical" turn toward confidence and love for God (page 90). Within particularly devout spirits, such experience causes intuitions of faith to blossom, as we hear in this psalm:

I bless the Lord who instructs me,
And who, even at night, teaches me humility!
I always place Yahweh before me:
Because He is close to me, I never falter!
Hence my heart is full of joy and my soul in exultation;
Even my body rests in safety:
No, You will not abandon my person to Sheol,
You will not let Your devotee go down into the Pit,
But You will show me the way of Life,
The treasure and joy of Your Presence,
And the sweetness of being with You forever!

(Psalm 16:7–11)

In familiarity with God, faith found the certainty that such an intimate relation *could not* cease at death: indubitably, another life *had to begin* thereafter, at least for the friends of God. And this conception will become even more articulate in the Wisdom of Solomon, in the first century B.C.E.:

The Just are in God's Hand:
They will not be given over to the Great Ordeal!
In the eyes of the senseless, they seem to die:
Their disappearance is deemed catastrophe,
And their departure from us a return to nothingness!
And yet, they are in Peace!
Though in the eyes of men they would seem to have been punished,
Their hope was fulfilled with a life of Immortality!

(Wisdom of Solomon 3:1–4)

If man can achieve immortal life, the unfinished accounts left behind in this world can always be settled later; even if he does not see it happen before his death, a believer will be assured that in the end justice cannot fail to come about. And this solves the problem posed by delays in divine Justice in the course of this life on earth.

In spite of the great career that we know was in store for the doctrine of immortality, the major part it was destined to play, especially in Christianity, one may regard this sort of solution as a bit simplistic and naive. Hidden behind the scandals of retribution is, after all, another, more terrible one: the very existence of Evil. Retribution is but an aspect of divine Justice. It is justified indeed if God rewards the just after their death, when here on earth they have led a life of misery. But why inflict unjustified suffering in the first place? Why would He, who is the Cause of everything, precede the "happy ending" with such painful detours? In the final analysis, how is His absolute Justice reconciled with the existence of undeserved Evil, which, moreover, is ultimately pointless because in the end it is blotted out by the Good? Here is the key problem of every religion that is "metaphysical" and at the same time assumes a personal, free deity. In Judaism in particular, there doubtlessly has never been a more insurmountable and more terrible theological scandal— even if only the greatest spirits perceived it. That Judaism resolved this problem so quickly, and at such depth, cannot but startle us in the history of thought and arouse our surprise and boundless admiration.

The first who saw the problem clearly (no doubt by the middle of the fifth century), is the author of the Book of Job. For this reason one must consider him not only an extraordinary poet but a religious thinker of the very first rank. In his work, he purposely takes as his point of departure a typical case, available to him in a popular story about a man named Job who is undeniably righteous and perfect (God personally testifies to this!) and who nevertheless finds himself cast into the depths of misery. The author sets up a discussion of this predicament between the sufferer and three of his friends. The latter, denoting conformists, stubbornly conclude that Job's ruin is due to immorality, while the victim, who knows his own affairs, cries out his innocence and demands an accounting from God. These vehement and fruitless confrontations lead to nothing; they typify all human discussion. But in the end, God speaks, and it is He who disseminates light. What does He say? We give here only the first verses of His incomparable apostrophe, vivid and magnificent, in which He sums up His own work in creation and the daily rule over the World:[22]

> Then Yahweh, answering Job from the midst of a tempest, said to him:
> "Who is the one who muddles My Plan
> With stupid prattle?
> Gird your loins, like a wrestler:
> I shall question you, and you will teach Me!
> Where were you when I established the Earth?
> Point it out, for you possess omniscience!
> Who set its dimensions, if you know it,

22. For the complete translation of the text of this admirable piece, see pages 129ff.; the question of its fundamental meaning is taken up again on page 182.

Or who stretched the line upon it?
What holds its foundations in place,
Or who laid its cornerstones
While the morning stars were singing in chorus,
And all the Sons-of-Elohim cheered?
Who set a limit to the Sea with two doors,
When it burst forth at its very origin;
When I dressed it with clouds
And swaddled it with fog;
When, to impose its border,
I installed bolts and doors,
And told it: "You will come this far, and no farther!
Here the pride of your waves will break!"

(Job 38:1–11)

The simple and overwhelming truth that follows from His sovereign account, which encompasses all of nature, is that He, the Master of the Universe, transcends human thought so far that before Him, and *no matter what He does*, one can do nothing but fall silent in admiration: the Universe can only be wonderful and perfect, even if, especially if, man cannot comprehend it. All this is certainly in the tradition of that absolute transcendence of God that the Prophets, in particular Second Isaiah (pages 74ff.), had already arrived at. But it had never been this clearly understood and explained in an area that was at the same time so metaphysical and so contrary to the natural tendency of the mind and the heart. Thus a century before Plato, by pure religious intuition, the author of the Book of Job succeeded in truly positing a divine order of things absolutely dissimilar to the human order, and in underlining the final word of all metaphysics and all theology: "I am not in need of a God whom I can understand!"

Even though contemporaries were very far from understanding the Book of Job—the traditional edition bears traces of their clerical, narrow-minded amendments—even though, two or three centuries later, another Jew, the author of the Book of Ecclesiastes (also duly altered and corrected by obtuse and myopic revisionists), already influenced to a certain extent by Hellenism, went still further, in the cool and exact language of philosophy, without any flights of fancy, extending the conclusion about the evil of human suffering to encompass universal evil (see pages 179ff. below)—who cannot see that Job marks one of the highest summits of thought, not only for Israel but for all humanity?

THE TRUE GREATNESS OF WHAT THE BIBLE REPRESENTS

Our admiration can only increase if we consider that the problem of a just divine recompense had already been raised in Babylon, where, beginning at least in the early second millennium, the theme of "the honest man who wished to learn why he was unfortunate" was known. This theme was developed and discussed for a thousand years, inspiring three or four works of a certain weight.[23] In this magnificent civilization, perhaps the first in the world fully to deserve the name, supported by an economic, political, and military power that at times was gigantic, the cultural "inventions" were innumerable for three long millennia: bronze metallurgy, writing, accounting, jurisprudence, systematic "scientific" dealings with the universe, "philosophical" researches (in the form of mythology), mathematics, astronomy, medicine, the first rudiments of a logical epistemology, not to mention infinite successes in every other domain. Nevertheless, in this civilization, the theme of "the honest man who wished to learn why he was unfortunate" was never sized in its amplitude or resolved otherwise than by invoking the inconstancy of the gods or by a fainthearted hope that everything would turn out well. This was in fact a ridiculous reaction, unworthy of great minds, yet, after all, wholly on the level of a religious way of thought that, in spite of evident efforts, in the final analysis never went beyond a commonplace polytheism and anthropomorphism.

And here we have, minute in comparison to colossal Mesopotamia, Israel, who had never counted for much on the political scene; who had never won the great battles; who had always been the debtor, with respect to cultural goods, to her predecessors and neighbors (especially Babylon); who invented nothing, nor left anything technical or scientific to the world—and yet, in less than a thousand years, this very small people succeeded not only in formulating but in solving one of the supreme problems of religious thought, which those powerful and immortal Babylonians had barely caught sight of and, in the end, relinquished! This small number of faithful of an initially obscure God, merely by their attachment to His person and by their faith in Him as their only strength, even without the support of properly rational thought, which only later would impose itself and render arguments and proofs among the Greeks, arrives at an experience of interiorization, an

23. These texts have been translated and explained in "Le Problème du Mal en Mésopotamie ancienne: Prologue a une étude du 'Juste souffrant,'" document 77/7 of *Recherches et documents du Centre Thomas Moore* (L'Arbresle, 1977).

enrichment of religion of such a quality that no one has surpassed it. And willingly or not, we must recognize that the two millennia that have made us who we are have lived off that heritage, and we still live off it—since nothing higher and better has come to light yet in this domain. For Christianity, which remains, until further notice, at the very heart of Western civilization, to this day conquering the globe, has neither added to nor modified anything *essential* about Yahwism or Judaism, whether on the level of theology properly so called or on that of religious behavior; and even when it presents itself from the first as a universal religion of salvation, has it not, above all, desired to realize the sublime ideal proposed by Second Isaiah?

Whether one adheres to the Bible's message, whether one connects it to God or not, it is obvious that the Bible represents one of the most sublime moments of human history. And even if man were still to change much, it would never be possible to expunge from his past this glorious millennium. For who, even after an existence full of agonies, a life called in question more than once, has ever reached the point where he abolished the luminous memories of his childhood?

TWO

BIBLICAL HISTORY AND LITERATURE

The title of these pages, "The Oldest Biblical Poem," could easily perplex someone who maintained that the Bible is a literary monolith. How could there be anything more, or less, "old" in this unique book, of mysterious origin, come to us from the dawn of time, which one would love to imagine was written all at once, in the very state we find it in today?

Reality is at some distance from this postulate devised at a time when history, as a critical and "scientific" recovery of the human past, did not yet exist, when the Bible seemed the oldest book in the world because no other was known to compare it to and the archives of peoples living side by side with the Israelites, but of more venerable antiquity, had not yet been excavated, let alone deciphered.

We now know the Mesopotamians, the Egyptians, the Hittites—to name only the greatest, beginning with the third millennium: the splendors of their history, details of their daily life, the artifacts and masterworks of their craftsmen and artists, and the vast literature that each of them produced. So Israel, the youngest in their midst, even if she may always remain the messenger of God in the view of the believers, is only one ancient people among others; and if faith is always free to regard the Bible as the Holy Book, the source of truth and religious life, the Bible, in its concrete and historical reality, still could not be considered otherwise than as an anthology, through which we have received important pieces of religious literature, worked out by Israel during a thousand years of her history (see also page 5 above).

Properly speaking, this history does not go further back than the end of the second millennium B.C.E. (see pages 16ff. above). It begins with the conquest of the land that was to become Israel's. The Israelites were not the indigenous people of Palestine but its invaders: from about 1200, for a duration of about two centuries, these "Bedouins" (as they really were), in hordes and "tribes," united by the memory of a unique proto-ancestor and by the common faith and devotion to one and the same divine protector, Yahweh, conducted in turn raids, military campaigns, and peaceful penetrations that in the end took the land away from its ancient inhabitants, the small Canaanite kingdoms. By the end of this long-lasting invasion, Israel, now no longer nomadic but settled and "culturally" conquered by her victims, conformed to their model, organized herself like them, adopted the same urbane and agricultural life, supported by some cattle-breeding, some agriculture, and some "industry," and provided herself with one sole chief, a king. Historians assign the time between 1000 and 970 to the first great Israelite monarch: David.

The stability, safety, and prosperity that resulted from this new way of life allowed the blossoming of a literature, in the full sense of the word. It is the literature of which the Bible has preserved so many parts, sometimes intact, sometimes significantly modified, spaced out from the beginning until almost the end of the first millennium.

Within this "biblical" literature, which is almost wholly the work of a sedentary people, at home in their settlements, rather civilized and cultured—at least the elite—there survived nevertheless some traces of the preceding epoch, namely, of nomadic existence and its uncertainties: a struggle for life and endeavors to carve out a territory in a primitive and almost savage period when Israel was no more than an unstable and bellicose horde, barely emerged from the desert and from that special way of life and experience that imposes itself there. Whether this early life was marked by oral compositions passed on by rhapsodists, or there was already literature more or less recorded in writing,[1] it is certain that the Israelites had a "literature," just like the Arabs before Mohammed. As among the latter, this literature had to be rather restricted in its "genres," tending toward poetry, love poetry and especially war poetry, more bare, more vigorous, more impetuous and passionate, not yet imbued by the rational coolness and distance to things that "cultural" progress foists on the minds and hearts of men and on all they do.

THE SONG OF DEBORAH: INTRODUCTION

Hence the major importance, historical as well as aesthetic, of the ancient poem that philologists have long recognized as the oldest work of literature preserved in the Bible. Its archaic language, as removed from classical Hebrew as the English of Chaucer is from that of Milton, and the authenticity of its images show it to be a work contemporary with the events it brings to mind, of about 1100 B.C.E. Moreover, already so rich in splendors, this venerable chant happens to be one of the masterworks of biblical literature.

It is found in the fifth chapter of the Book of Judges, a collection that tells us of the conquest of Canaan by the Israelite tribes. The various successive authors of this composite narration (see pages 10, 26f.) brought together a quantity of materials from various eras, all of it provided by copious tradition concerning the heroic times of Israel. Thus the celebrated Song of Deborah, to which we now turn, was preserved.

Before reading the text, we must pave the way toward understanding by placing the song back in the midst of the events that it evokes (see pages 26ff. above), for it is quite dense and filled with allusions to matters that were contemporary with it; and this is disconcerting to the unprepared reader.

1. This would not have been impossible by the end of the second millennium, more than fifteen hundred years after the invention of writing and its spread throughout the entire ancient Orient and more than two centuries after the refinement of this prodigious invention, namely, the great simplification of writing and reading through the alphabet, which first appeared in Phoenicia, to the north of Palestine proper, probably at the beginning of the fourteenth century B.C.E.

What is told occurs *"in the time of Shamgar, son of Anath"* (v. 6), which is to say, some decades after the Conquest had begun. The Israelite tribes had already infiltrated into the territory of Canaan—most having been there since a time before the "descent into Egypt," and others in addition having come in from the desert south of the Dead Sea—and had made themselves at home here and there: Benjamin (v. 13) as far as the area of Jerusalem, with Dan (v. 17) just west, toward the sea; Ephraim (v. 13) further to the north, and Manasseh, here going by the name Machir (v. 14), still further north; ascending to the height of the lake of Genesareth, Issachar (v. 15); then, higher, Zebulun (v. 14), and still higher, Naphtali (v. 15); to the west of the latter, along the Mediterranean, north of the promontory of Carmel, Asher (v. 17); to the east, beyond the Jordan, Reuben; as far up as the Dead Sea, and a bit higher as well, in the land of Gilead (v. 17), Gad. But the Canaanites, who were still masters of a good part of the country and firmly established in their fortified cities, resisted the march of the invaders as well as they could. Sometimes they launched counterattacks; sometimes they were satisfied to make life impossible for the Israelites with the threat of continuous raids.

Such is the situation as the poem begins, conveying the presentiment of war: Men loosen their hair and let it grow long, in a customary prelude to combat; the people spontaneously become incorporated in the army (v. 2). Let the whole world know, beginning with the heads of nations and the high potentates, that it is all to the glory and honor of Yahweh (v. 3). For God, the Protector and the true Commander in war, is present once again and prepared to save His faithful, as in former days, when the Conquest first began and He moved with them from the South, the land of Seir and Edom, into the midst of the natural disturbances that were the visible sign of His presence and His engagement (vv. 4–5).

And indeed, it was high time, for the ongoing Canaanite oppression prevented free movement (v. 6), forcing peasants to abandon their fields and their necessary work to seek refuge in fortified places (v. 7). As if numbed by this lasting oppression, Israel at first had not reacted: her warriors had stood by; she failed even to make preparations and store up arms (v. 8).

But the change came thus: Deborah, an ancient Joan of Arc, belonging, we believe, to the tribe of Ephraim, which had perhaps been more exposed to oppression, arose to announce a call for insurrection and deliverance (vv. 7 and 12). Henceforth, from one watering place (in other words, from one stopping place) to the next, roads the Israelites had feared to travel would be once more in use, by officers on their harnessed mounts, and foot soldiers (vv. 9–10), in such a multitude and with such excitement as to make one think of the journey to those tumultuous and joyful meetings in which the feasts of Yahweh and His blessings were celebrated (v. 11).

In preaching her message of revolt, and in order to bring an alliance of tribes, Deborah had caused the appointment of a man from Naphtali to commander in chief: Barak Abinoam, perhaps a former prisoner of the Canaanites (v. 12). Some of the tribes reacted courageously; once their elders had deliberated at the gates of the cities, where counsel was held at the time (v. 13), they sent out men, who converged upon the plain where all were to meet. These tribes were Ephraim, Benjamin, Machir (also called Manasseh), Issachar, Zebulun, and Naphtali (vv. 13–15). The last two may have made up the strongest, or the most valorous, contingent; their courage is praised for a second time, at the moment when the clash of arms begins (v. 18).

Other tribes did not respond; their hesitation and interminable discussions led nowhere; they had simply preferred to stay at home in peace: Reuben, Gilead (also known as Gad), Dan, and Asher (vv. 15b–17).

Then came the battle itself. On the bank of the Kishon stream, not far from Taanach and the waters of Megiddo (vv. 19 and 21), which is to say, on the hills (v. 18) and the plain that form the hinterland of modern Haifa, the Israelite alliance met with the army of the confederated Canaanite kings, under the command of Sisera (vv. 26 and 28). Apparently a heavy thunderstorm poured down. A rapid rise of the torrent's waters followed, much to the detriment of the Canaanites, in part swept away by the flood (v. 21), while their horses,[2] abandoned and disoriented, escaped in stampedes (v. 22).

Could it be that fugitives found refuge in the Israelite city of Meroz, which had refused to join the tribal coalition? The allusion made in verse 23 is not clear to us. In any event, Sisera , who had also fled, happens upon an Israelite tent occupied by a woman, Jael. He asks for water. She offers him milk. But while he drinks, this worthy daughter of the warriors of Israel seizes the mallet used to fix tent pins into the ground and batters the skull of the enemy's chief (vv. 24–25).

And even as this is occurring, Sisera's mother, at the family manor, confident in the outcome as all her countrymen surely must have been, grows impatient when he does not return, and does not cease to watch for him through the lattice (v. 28). As if to drive her even deeper into her prideful error and prepare a disillusion all the more cruel, we see her become persuaded that delay can only mean that the plunder will be significant: captives and objects of luxury (vv. 29–30).

---

2. Horses! While the Israelites had only donkeys (see v. 10) and hence found themselves technically inferior to their opponents.

The great victor, the One Triumphant, is Yahweh, who alone can protect His faithful (v. 31).

THE TEXT

We turn to the poem itself, which should now be easier to follow and to which I have added some headings in order to make its progression evident.

I have tried to adhere as closely as possible to the Hebrew text, not only for its meaning, of course, but also, whenever possible, for the order of words, and even to convey something of the rhythm. It is worth pointing out that French and Hebrew,[3] in addition to a syntax that is not all that different, actually have as well a certain prosodic affinity between them: in both, emphasis is marked in the same way by raising the voice; in both, it tends to fall on more or less the same syllables, generally at the end of words; and the length of words in both does not vary too much. Taking into account rhythmic successions (perfectly transferable into French) of "strong" and "weak" measures (see pages 113ff. below), one may indeed attempt straightforwardly in French that which would be completely impossible in classical Greek or Latin: to give rather closely and completely a rendition of a Hebrew poem, including its rhythm. The sole exception to this felicity of translation is the aspect that can properly be called phonetic, for with this element, the attempt at translating becomes complex due to certain circumstances that have altered the meanings. The archaic language of the poem seems to have caused difficulties for later copyists, who did not always understand it very well; hence, when transcribing the text, they accumulated mistakes that the manuscript tradition, once it was written down, preserved. Under peril of leaving a number of verses wholly unintelligible, the translator has to track down those mistakes and, when he can, correct them, at least by conjecture. The results of this operation, which is strictly philological and reserved for specialists, will be worth as much as the translator's reasons for conjecture, which are as a rule no more than hypotheses. It is only fair to warn the reader!

3. [Translator's note: The reader will observe that Professor Bottéro addresses the French reading public in this section. The goals he sets and the result in the "literal" translation that follows can only be approximated in the English rendition of his attempt. However, the typical *dramatic* quality of the classical Hebrew emphasis on what *happens* centers in the finite verb; this characteristic can be rendered comparatively well in English.]

Title	1	*What Deborah and Barak-ben-Abinoam sang on that day:*[4]	*Voici ce que chantèrent Débora et Baraq-ben-Abinoam, ce jour-là:*
Exordium	2	*When hair is unbound, in Israel, Because of the willing engagement of the people, Yahweh be blessed!*	*De l'échevèlement des chevelures, en Israël, Du libre-engagement du peuple, Bénissez Yahvé!*
	3	*Listen, Kings! Lend your ear, O dignitaries! I myself shall sing for Yahweh, Melody after melody for Yahweh, the God of Israel!*	*Écoutez, Rois! Prêtez l'oreille, ô Dignitaires! Moi-même, pour Yahvé, je vais chanter, Moduler pour Yahvé, le Dieu d'Israël*
Recalling the Beginning of the Conquest	4	*Yahweh, at Your leaving from Seir, At Your course from the fields of Edom, The earth staggered, The very heavens shook, Even the clouds turned to water,*	*Yahvé, à Ta sortie de Séïr, À Ton parcours depuis les champs d'Édom, La terre chancela, Même les cieux frémirent, Même les nues se liquéfièrent,*
	5	*The mountains shuddered before Yahweh, Before Yahweh, the God of Israel!*	*Les montagnes tremblèrent devant Yahvé, Devant Yahvé, le Dieu d'Israël!*
Oppression and Inertia of Israel	6	*In the days of Samgar-ben-Anat, Abandoned lay the roads And the travelers Took crooked byways!,*	*Aux jours de Shamgar-ben-Anath, À l'abandon étaient les routes, Et les parcoureurs de chemins Prenaient des sentes tortueuses!*
	7	*Abandoned lay the flat land In Israel, abandoned, Before you stood up, Deborah, Stood up, O Mother of Israel!*	*À l'abandon était le plat-pays, En Israël, à l'abandon, Avant que tu ne fusses debout, Débora, Debout, ô Mère d'Israël!*
	8	*The champions of God kept silence: In five towns, not a shield could be found, Not one lance for forty thousand men in Israel!*	*Restaient cois les champions de Dieu: En cinq villes un bouclier ne se serait trouvé, Une lance pour quarante mille hommes en Israël!*
Preparations for War	9	*My heart rejoins the commanders of Israel, The freely conscripted of the people!*	*Mon cœur rejoint les capitaines d'Israël, Les libres-engagés du peuple!*
	10	*Sitting astride white she-asses, Straddling their rugs. Travelers of the roads sang*	*Des chevaucheurs de blanches ânesses, À califourchon sur leurs tapis, Des parcoureurs de chemins ont chanté,*
	11	*Like playmates, from one watering place to the next, As if to celebrate the blessings of Yahweh, The blessings of His rule in Israel!*	*À la voix des lurons, d'un abreuvoir à l'autre, Comme pour célébrer les bienfaits de Yahvé, Les bienfaits de Son hégémonie en Israël!*
Appeal to Join Together	12	*Awake, awake, Deborah! Awake, awake, intone your song! Courage! To arms! Barak! Catch your captors, O son of Abinoam!*	*Éveille-toi, éveille-toi, Débora! Éveille-toi, éveille-toi, lance ton chant! Courage! Sus! Baraq! Ravis tes ravisseurs, ô fils d'Abinoam!*

4. The title is not part of the poem; it was added later—thereby transforming the heroes of the dithyramb into authors! In the translation of the poem (printed in italics), I used roman print for the few words that I needed to add to the Hebrew in order to present a better rendering of the meaning.

Those Who Joined	13	Then down rushed the people of Yahweh to the Gates,	Alors a dévalé aux Portes le peuple de Yahvé,
		Down they rushed, those champions for Him!	Dévalé pour Lui, tels des braves!
		From Ephraim, set in motion toward the Plain,	D'Éphraïm, on s'est ébranlé vers la Plaine,
		From Benjamin, the people carried along!	Entraînant Benjamin et sa population!
	14	From Machir came the commanders,	Depuis Makir ont dévalé les capitaines,
		And the staff-bearers from Zebulun!	Et depuis Zabulon les porteurs de bâtons!
	15	The chiefs of Issachar are with Deborah,	Les nobles d'Issachar sont avec Débora,
		And Naphtali, in the Plain, rushed after them!	Et Nephtali, en la Plaine, s'est jeté sur ses pas!

Those Who Did Not Join		But, by the brooks of Reuben,	Mais, près des ruisseaux de Ruben,
		What long councils there were!	Qu'il y eut de longues palabres!
	16	Why did you stay, in the midst of sheepfolds?	Pourquoi es-tu resté, au milieu des enclos,
		To listen to the herders' flutes?	À écouter les flûtes des bergers?
		Yes, by the brooks of Reuben,	Oui, près des ruisseaux de Ruben,
		There were long councils!	Il y eut de longues palabres!
	17	Gilead stayed beyond the Jordan.	Galaad au-delà du Jourdain s'est tenu.
		And why did Dan begin to fool about	Et Dan, pourquoi s'est-il mis à hanter
		with boats?	les navires?
		Asher remained on the shore of the Sea:	Asher est resté au rivage de la Mer:
		He stayed along its bays.	Il s'est tenu le long de ses golfes!

The Battle	18	But Zebulun is a people that stakes its life,	Mais Zabulon est un peuple qui méprise sa vie à mort,
		Together with Naphtali, on the heights	Avecque Nephtali, sur les coteaux de la
		of the field!	campagne!
	19	The kings came to do battle,	Ils sont venus, les rois, pour se battre,
		The kings of Canaan, and they battled	Et ils se sont battus, les rois de Canaan,
		Near Taanach, by the Waters of Megiddo,	Lès Taannak, aux Eaux-de-Megiddo,
		But they were deceived in the prize they expected!	Mais sans toucher le profit escompté!
	20	Even from the sky, the stars fought,	Même du ciel se sont battues les étoiles,
		From their orbits, they attacked Sisera:	De leurs orbites, elles ont attaqué Sisera:
	21	The torrent of Kishon carried them all along,	Le torrent du Qishôn les a tous emportés,
		The sacred torrent, the torrent of Kishon,	Le saint torrent, le torrent du Qishôn,
		And the bully's life is gone ...	Et la vie des soudards est partie ...
	22	O! How the horses' hoofs beat the ground,	Oh! qu'ils ont piétiné, les sabots des chevaux,
		And the chargers attacked at a gallop!	Et galopé le grand galop, les coursiers!

Sisera's Death	23	Curse Meroz, says the Messenger of Yahweh,	Maudissez Méroz, dit le Messager-de-Yahvé,
		Curse, curse its inhabitants,	Maudissez, maudissez ses habitants,
		Who did not come to the aid of Yahweh,	Qui ne sont pas venus au secours de Yahvé,
		To Yahweh's aid, with its warriors!	Au secours de Yahvé, avec les braves!
	24	But blessed among women be Jael,	Mais soit bénie entre les femmes Yaël,
		Blessed be she among women of the Tent!	Entre les femmes de la Tente, bénie-soit-elle!
	25	He clamored for water, she gives him milk:	De l'eau il réclamait, du lait elle lui donne:
		In a cup for lords, she offers him cream,	Dans la coupe des chefs, elle offre de la crème,
	26	But she stretches her hand to the tent-pin,	Mais elle envoie sa main vers le piquet,
		Her right hand to the workmen's mallet;	Sa droite vers le maillet des hommes-de-peine.
		She hammers Sisera, she batters his head,	Elle martèle Sisera, elle brise sa tête,
		She pounds and crushes his temple!	Elle lui broie et fracasse la tempe!

27	*He sinks at her feet, demolished, fallen:*	*À ses pieds il s'écroule, il s'abat, il gît:*
	How he sinks down, how he is beaten,	*Tel il s'écroule, tel le voilà abattu,*
	wounded to death!	*navré-à-mort! . . .*

The Scene at Sisera's Manor	28	*Through the window leans Sisera's mother,*	*Par la fenêtre se penche et guette*
		Watching through the lattice:	*La mère de Sisera, à travers le treillis:*
		"Why is his wagon slow to arrive?	*«Pourquoi son char tarde-t-il à venir*
		Why the delay in the pace of his chariots?"	*Pourquoi l'allure de ses chariots traîne-t-elle?»*
	29	*Her most cunning Lady answers,*	*La plus futée de ses Dames lui répond,*
		And she repeats, she herself repeats:	*Et elle-même se répète de qu'elle lui a dit:*
	30	*"Aren't they taking and dividing the spoils?*	*«Ne sont-ils pas à toucher et partager les dépouilles?*
		One, two beautiful girls for every soldier!	*Une beauté, deux beautés pour chaque guerrier!*
		One, two brocades for Sisera!	*Un brocart, deux brocarts pour Sisera!*
		One, two embroideries for my shoulders!"	*Une broderie, deux broderies pour me épaules! » . . .*

Envoy	31	*Thus all Your enemies perish, O Yahweh!*	*Ainsi périssent tous Tes ennemis, ô Yahvé!*
		But Your friends are like the sun rising	*Mais Tes amis sont comme le Soleil se levant*
		in its glory!	*en sa gloire!*

THE POETRY

It would be puerile, if not sheer blasphemy, to build an elaborate exposition—a useless and pedantic "aesthetic commentary"—around this glorious work of art.

But in order to arrive at a fair assessment, it will be useful nonetheless to point out two features that sound forth from this ancient poem and are just as typical and traditional in other sublime Hebrew poetry. I am speaking of the extreme freedom of form and the extraordinary sobriety that strike us in the account of the Song of Deborah as soon as we read it. This is not due to translation, for both features are much more notable in the original. Even if they are not rendered, as inevitably they cannot be, except by approximation, the French allows the two features to stand out as the chief qualities of the work.

The form of the poem seems entirely free from all the conventions that weigh down the creative power of many a poet. Studying its text closely, we discover only two constants, or "laws," on which its poetic character is based; and both are rhythmic in nature.

First of all, there is a certain *tonic rhythm*, made by alternating accented syllables, pronounced with more force, and unaccented syllables. The number of the former, the "strong beats," is constant in a particular verse, that is, within the two hemistichs that normally make up a verse;[5] however, the number of "weak beats" varies:

> *Awake, awake, Deborah!*
>> *Awake, awAKE, intone your SONG!*

(v. 12)

This element at once provides a considerable suppleness and variety.

In addition, we observe that the rhythm is not the same from one verse to another and that it is actually adapted in some way each time to what the text means or suggests, as if the "melody" had to be poetically just as eloquent as the images and the words. The musical force of verse 12, above, an ardent and impatient call for Deborah's intervention to jolt the Israelites out of their pitiful inaction, in contrast to the *lento* of verse 31, which is like the final measures of a chorale, will be sufficient to illustrate this:

> *Thus ALL Your enemies PErish, O YahWEH!*
>> *But Your FRIENDS are like the SUN rising in its GLORy!*

The second poetic "constant" is to be found in the fact that the poem is ruled throughout by a sort of *rhythm of thought*: the two hemistichs that constitute a verse always bear on the same topic and constantly give us two complementary images of it:

> *Listen, Kings!*
>> *Lend your ear, O dignitaries!*
> *I myself shall sing for Yahweh,*
>> *Melody after melody for Yahweh, the God of Israel!*

(v. 3)

Occasionally, the images are contrasts, as in verse 31, quoted previously.

This balancing-out of thought, somehow interlaced with the balance of the rhythm in the melody, is an inexhaustible source of poetry: it continuously brings to mind the richness of things, the impossibility of sounding them in one stroke, encompassing them in one glance, expressing them in one word.

5. In my translation, above, I marked the second hemistich by indenting it; the first one begins at the margin. Sometimes there is a third one, with a different rhythm, which I marked in the same way: for example, "YahWEH be BLESSED," concluding verse 2.

And here again, it is evident that the poet bends the formula of this rhythm of thought to his will, to paint and to evoke a state of mind. So it is, for example, that the poet sometimes duplicates within the parallelism: in verses 4–5, so that the accumulation of the shaking of earth and heaven, the gushing forth of the clouds, and the shudder of the mountains gives rise to terror before these phenomena, which are like the escort and personal guard of Yahweh; and within a single verse, 26b, so that the quick succession of four verbs that depict the death of Sisera renders the effect of a bloodbath and a butchery instantaneously.

Clearly, the poet was familiar with "laws" that ruled the form of his work, but he remained their master, making them a source of inspiration rather than a hindrance to his liberty as an artist.

The other feature with which the poet strikes and still astonishes us is, as I have mentioned, the sobriety, or, more precisely, the amazing conciseness, of his account. He says *nothing* but the essential; he leaves to the reader to understand or sense all the rest. He merely *suggests*, which is the essence of art.

Obviously, the public to which he addressed himself was less in need of explanations than we are, for three long millennia separate us from him. But what I have in mind is not the expression obscure to strangers, such as the "unbound hair" (v. 2) or the proper name of a person or tribe that has been lost in time and must be elucidated for the modern reader before he confronts the ancient text.

I am thinking of the disconcerting brevity of those statements in which one of the essential elements is passed over in silence, because the context makes it sufficiently clear, sooner or later: the name of Sisera is omitted when his personage appears in verse 25; we find it in the middle of verse 26.[6] In verse 21, why would it need to be made clear that it was the Canaanites who were carried off by the Kishon stream? It could only be they, for the Israelites have won. This fact, we should note, is not mentioned anywhere: is it not the very reason for the existence of this victory song?

I think above all of the very succession of ideas and "tableaux" that make up the poem. They are juxtaposed without anything leading from one to the next, so much so that, out of fear of confusion among my readers, I sometimes could not help adding a conjunction or particle to the Hebrew to suppress a hiatus that could not be very well accepted by our taste. After some

6. This procedure of evoking a person or thing first only by a pronoun, or vague appellation, and not mentioning the proper name until a later verse or hemistich is a very old poetic custom that goes back, as far as we know, to the ancient poets of Mesopotamia.

thought, however, it is clear that the order of episodes is regulated and that there is a thread leading through them: it is the contrast, whether latent or manifest, that shifts from one to the other. To the memory of the turmoil of the universe that accompanied the first entrance of Israel into Canaan (vv. 4–5), the present inertia of the people is contrasted: a people abandoned, passive, at the mercy of its enemy (6–8). This sad desperation is now submerged by the hubbub of the combat Deborah has incited with her call (9–11); the author then places in contrast to this his praise of the generous tribes (13–15) and his scorn poured over the cowardly (15b–17). To the selfish peacefulness in which the latter indulge, he contraposes the fracas of the battle (18–22). As foil to the faintheartedness of an entire city, Meroz, he likewise presents the inner strength of a single woman, a "woman of the tent," a nomad, Jael (23ff.), and to the ignominious death of the chief foe (26–27)—killed by a woman!—he opposes the terrible illusion of the Canaanites, their blind faith in their own victory, the greedy wait for loot (28–30). So we see, in spite of the poem's composition in a series of zigzags, that it follows a perfectly mapped route. The author deemed it unnecessary to explain its direction to us: it was enough for him that its direction be enclosed in scenes and stages and be suggested by them.

This kind of vision that places matters in isolation, which the poet has conveyed to us in his work, corresponds entirely to the perspective and the mental habits of the Semites of antiquity and to those of the ancient Hebrews, who were not yet troubled, like ourselves, by a need of abstraction and explanation, of synthesis and exactness in that conceptual analysis of reality which we inherited from the Greeks. The ancient Semitic languages are infinitely more concrete than our language; their grammar virtually ignores, for instance, the refinement of subordinate clauses found in ours; almost everywhere they use simple coordination, characterized by "and . . . , and . . . , and . . ." in places where we need "because . . . , so that . . . , when. . . ."

Inside this psychological and linguistic system, however, we may say that our poet, among all his compatriots whose work we still possess, has gone furthest in that art of reducing the distance between words and things; that concern for expressing only the essential, the real, the manifest; that verbal sobriety and conciseness.

The freedom we have admired in the poet is equally something he inherited from his culture. Classical Hebrew poetry does not know the many demands and importunities that our poetry was long subjected to: the constraint of rhyme and the arithmetic calculations of syllable and verse that ruled our traditional prosody and production of strophes. Classical Hebrew poetry was founded only on the double rhythm of accent and thought, which we described before. However, among the greatest Hebrew poets of the golden age, between the eighth and the fifth century B.C.E., from the first "author-Prophets" to the immortal writer of the Book of Job and including the wonderful Second Isaiah (pages 73f.), perhaps the unknown author to whom we owe the Song of Deborah holds an eminent place for the extraordinary formal independence that—more than all the others—he succeeded in preserving in his work.[7]

The poet's primary qualities: his scorn, or rather his surpassing of all editorial conventions, and the little distance he keeps between things and what he says of them, are powerful factors of poetry. At the same time, the conciseness and the freedom carried to such an extent in the poem evoke both a virtually complete independence and an unrestrained closeness to nature, far from the deformations of "culture," which attributes belonged also to the people of Israel at the moment our unknown author was alive. We cannot stop ourselves from thinking that it is this very archaism that enabled him to compose such a masterpiece.

With its power of unbridled emotion—that ardent, exclusive awe before its God, Yahweh alone; its questionless partiality for its people; that disdain for the peaceful life, for submission, for inaction; that exalted love of battle; that cruelty toward the enemy, and even the kind of sadism with which it goes so far as to imagine in detail the enemy's self-confidence in order to savor his disillusion and fall; with the grandeur of the images that illuminate its recitation: that assembly whom it claims as audience, of all nations of the world, arranged after the order of their kings and dignitaries; that fearful presence of Yahweh, who upsets heaven and earth, who liquefies the skies and makes the mountains sway when He must defend His people; those surges of warriors joining on their way toward the place of carnage; those stars even, high above, turning from their immutable course for a moment to ally themselves with Israel and attack her enemies; that torrent which throws itself into the fray in its turn and engulfs the defeated; and, finally, this people that belongs to Yahweh and raises itself up, as glorious, triumphant, and invincible as the sun—somehow the poem lifts the battle of Taanach to a cosmic, universal, eternal level and transforms it almost before the eyes of its readers into a crucial moment in the history of the world.

7. One might compare the elegy of David on the death of Saul and Jonathan, which is a little more recent, translated on page 29 above.

And yet, it was but a handful of people, microscopic, lost in an out-of-the-way corner of an ancient age, that fought each other in the rain for a patch of ground, without benefiting man and his progress in the least with their ridiculous fuss. They themselves and their tumult would have been buried by the dust of time and forgotten, like countless others, if this immortal song did not bring them back to our memory. Jove dies, the poet's hymn lasts. *Muor Giove, e l'inno del Poeta resta!*

THE TEXTS

A number of passages in the Bible allude to the origins of the world. But four or five in particular seem, so to speak, *professionally* devoted to a more or less systematic account of the cosmogony. It is they we should turn to first, in their entirety and translated as exactly as possible. If we search for elements of a history of cosmogonic thought in Israel, it is important, to the extent we are able, to place these texts in the chronological order of their composition. And this makes it necessary, at least for the first two texts, to add a word of explanation.

The Cosmogony in Genesis

No one will be surprised if we cite first of all the celebrated opening of the Book of Genesis, which our Bibles begin with and which everyone knows— more or less. Many readers of the Bible do not know, however, that these two chapters really contain *two accounts* of the "Creation."

Scholars, drawn to numerous "doublets"—double, and indeed triple, accounts, with various nuances, of the same event—have undertaken systematic investigations into the so-called historical books of the Bible, regarding their vocabulary, their grammar, their style, their ideology.[1] This enterprise, which has gone on for more than two hundred years, has been able to establish that these books, taken together or in isolation, do not come down from one single venue or one single author, but have been compiled from original works. The annals of Israel were not written one time only in the course of the millennium before our era when this people lived: they were the object of several historical and religious syntheses, original ones and ones that were inspired to a greater or lesser extent by each other, in each of which a different author expressed his own point of view and that of his time. Later—indubitably around the fourth century—so that these works, out of devotion, might be preserved, and at the same time to declare their convergence, they were cut to pieces of unequal size, which were then rearranged, as in a kind of rhapsody or mosaic, into a coherent recital. In general, this task was executed with care, so that unsophisticated readers did not notice the handiwork. However, it could not pass the "laboratory" examinations, which, far from demolishing biblical history, somehow, in the final analysis, enriched it throughout, bringing to light several sources where until then only one seemed to have been preserved.

In this manner, in Genesis, three different, originally autonomous narratives of the oldest history of Israel were isolated. One of them is easy to separate from the others: its abstract language, its cold and impersonal style, its ongoing concern for classifications, for precise numbers, for exact dates, its multiple clichés, its particular and, indeed, clerical theological idea of things, and always its rather special vocabulary have long enabled us to view it as one work and relate it to a later period of Israel's history, no doubt after the great Exile, toward the end of the sixth century B.C.E. Anonymous, like almost all writings of the ancient East and of the Bible, it was given the name *Priestly Document*, because it seems to exhibit, in its very makings, a spirit that evokes the clergy at the beginnings of Judaism.

1. See what has already been said on pages 12ff.

What is left after this *Priestly Document* has been set apart is much more difficult to disentangle. Nevertheless, the "doublets," of which there are still many, the vocabulary, as well as a number of recurrent particularities in the language, and certain habitual perceptions of things have permitted us to uncover the compilation of two accounts, both more ancient than the *Priestly Document*, one of which seems to present the religious and historical tradition of the Northern Kingdom, and the other, the Southern Kingdom, in approximately the ninth and eighth centuries. The latter, older, was given the name *Yahwist* by scholars because of its preference for the "proper name" Yahweh for the God of Israel; the former was called the *Elohist*, for it primarily makes use of the more general term *Elohim*, meaning "God."

Judging at least by what has been preserved for us, the *Elohist* commenced its history of Israel only with the story of the first and foremost ancestor, Abraham (Genesis 12ff.).[2] However, the *Yahwist* and the *Priestly Document* took up matters on a grander scale and went back to the very origins of man and the universe. That is why both begin with a cosmogonic exposition.

In any event, the compilers of our Bible chose as the very first subject the cosmogony from the *Priestly Document*, and only then added the one by the *Yahwist*, thus turning around a chronology of composition with which they apparently were not very concerned but which we hold on to.

The Account of the Yahwist

Here then we begin with the oldest Israelite account of the origins of the world and man—the only one that is left from before the great Exile— namely, the first chapter of the *Yahwist* (Genesis 2:4b–25).

The Desert at the Outset	*(4b) When Yahweh had made the heaven and the earth, (5) no wasteland bush existed yet on the earth, and no herb of the field had sprung up yet, because Yahweh had not yet made it rain on the earth and there was no human being to till the humus.*[3]

---

2. Verses 20:8–11 in Exodus, quoted and discussed on page 150 below, show that the *Elohist* author was not unaware of at least certain traditions concerning origins.

3. "Human"–"humus" attempts to render audibly the Hebrew wordplay *Adam–Adama*, which finds its justification in verse 7 ("The Human [being] drawn from the humus") and is reprised several times in the course of the story. See also Ishsha drawn from Ish, in verse 23 below, and the note there.

Water and Man	*(6) So Yahweh made a stream emerge from the earth to water the entire face of the humus. (7) Then Yahweh molded the Human⁴ from clay he drew from the humus and blew the breath of life into his nostrils so as to make him into a living being.*
The First Garden	*(8) Then Yahweh planted a garden in Eden [there] toward the East, and there He placed the Human whom He had molded. (9) Then Yahweh made to sprout forth from the humus all kinds of trees that were pleasant to look upon, and good to eat from, including the Tree-of-Life, in the middle of the Garden, and also the Tree-of-discernment-between-Good-and-Evil.*
The Garden's Hydrography	*(10) Now, a water stream came from Eden to water the Garden. From there, it divided and formed four branches. (11) The first was called Pishon: this is the one that flows around the whole land of Havilah, where gold is found—(12) and the gold of that land is of excellent quality!—and also gum of bdellium and carnelian. (13) The second river was called Gihon: this one encircles the whole land of Cush. (14) The third river was named Tigris and flows before the city of Assur. As to the fourth river, that was the Euphrates.*
Man as "Farmer of God"	*(15) So Yahweh took Man ["the Human"] and placed him in the Garden of Eden, so that he would till it and protect it. (16) And Yahweh gave this commandment to Man: "You can eat from the trees of the Garden as you like, (17) but you shall not eat from the Tree-of-discernment-between-Good-and-Evil. If you eat from it, YOU SHALL DIE!*

4. The Hebrew text and its context make clear that just one "individual of the human race" (the sense of *Adam*, the Hebrew word that is used) is molded from the clay by Yahweh. Thus, as was understood in the ancient versions, *Adam* is a quasi-personal name. One might almost consider translating it as *"TheMan"* to render at the same time this meaning and the ordinary sense of the word.

Man's Companions: the Animals	(18) *Then Yahweh said [to Himself]: "It is not good for the Man to remain all alone! I shall make a fitting companion for him!" (19) And Yahweh molded from humus all the animals of the field and the birds of the sky; then He led them before the Man to see what he would call them. Whatever name he gave to each one, that would be its name. (20) In this way the Human spelled the names of all domestic animals, of all birds in the sky, and of all wild beasts. As for Man himself, however, he did not find [among them] a fitting companion.*
Woman	(21) *Then Yahweh made a torpor fall upon Man, and he fell asleep. He took a rib from him, and closed up [the empty space, putting] flesh in its place; (22) and of this rib He had taken from the Human he formed Woman, whom He led to the Human, Man. (23) And Man exclaimed:*

                                 "*This time, here is one who is bone of my bone, flesh of my flesh!*
                                 "*She will be called Ishsha, because this one has been drawn from Ish.*"[5]
                                 (24) *This is the reason why [every] man leaves his father and mother to cleave to his wife, to form together one single body.*

Primitive State of Man	(25) *And both of them were naked, the man and his wife, but together they did not have the least sense of shame [about it].*

After this narrative comes the first human lapse, which clearly, in the plan of the author, is prepared for by what we have just read (see further pages 164f.).

The Account of the Priestly Document

The other cosmogonic accounts sufficiently complete and coherent in the Bible were all written after the Exile, hence after the first half of the sixth

---

5. *Ish* means "male individual of the human race" (opposed to *Adam*, as *vir* is to *homo* in Latin, *aner* to *anthropos* in Greek). *Ishsha* is the feminine form. This new "wordplay" (see note 3 above: *Adam–Adama*) cannot really be rendered in translation.

century. Let us first turn to the beginning of the *Priestly Document*, which in our traditional Bible keeps close to the cosmogony, discussed above, of the Yahwist (Genesis 1–2:4a).

a. The Initial Chaos	(1) *In the beginning, Elohim created heaven and earth.* (2) *And the earth was desolate and empty: darkness [stretched out] over the abyss and the Breath of Elohim hovered over the waters.*[6]
b. The Light	(3) *Then Elohim said: "Let there be Light!" And there was Light.* (4) *Elohim saw that the Light was something good. Then Elohim separated the Light from the Darkness,* (5) *and Elohim called the Light "Day," and the Darkness He called "Night." Thereupon it became evening, then morning: the first day.*[7]
c. The Separation of the Waters: Heaven	(6) *Then Elohim said: "Let there be a Vault between the Waters so that it divides the Waters in two!" And so it was:* (7) *Elohim established this Vault and separated the Waters below the Vault from the Waters above the Vault.* (8) *Elohim called this Vault "Heaven." And Elohim saw that it was something good. Thereupon it became evening, then morning: the second day.*
d. Separation of Sea and Earth	(9) *Then Elohim said: "Let the Waters below the Heavens be gathered together in one place, that the Dry-Expanse may appear!" And so it was.* (10) *Elohim called the Dry-Expanse "Earth," and the gathering of the Waters He called "Sea." And Elohim saw that it was something good.*
e. Vegetation	(11) *Then Elohim said: "Let the Earth bring forth greenery, plants yielding seed and fruit trees bearing fruit, of every kind, each of them having its own seed in itself, on the earth!" And so it was:* (12) *the Earth*

6. Another possible translation is: "In the beginning of the creation by Elohim of heaven and earth, (2) the earth was desolate and empty." This is perhaps closer to the author's thought.

7. For the ancient Israelites, the day began and ended at sunset.

brought forth greenery, plants bearing seed in themselves, of every kind, and trees bearing fruit, each with its own seed, of every kind. And Elohim saw that it was something good. (13) Thereupon it became evening, then morning: the third day.

f. The Stars

(14) *Then Elohim said: "Let there be lights in the vault of Heaven to divide Day and Night and to serve as signs, for feasts as much as for days and years! (15) And let them serve also, in the Vault of Heaven, as lights to give light on the earth! And so it was: (16) Elohim established the two great lights—the greater to rule over the Day, the lesser to rule over the Night; and also the Stars. (17) Then Elohim distributed them over the Vault of Heaven to light the Earth, (18) to rule over Day and Night and to separate the Light from the Darkness. And Elohim saw that it was something good. (19) Thereupon it became evening, then morning: the fourth day.*

g. Aquatic Animals

(20) *Then Elohim said: "Let the Waters teem with swarms of animals, and may winged animals fly over the Earth, in the face of the Heavenly Vault!" And so it was: (21) Elohim created the gigantic Dragons and all the reptiles with which the waters teem, of every kind, and all the winged birds, of every kind. And Elohim saw that it was something good. (22) After this, Elohim blessed them in these words: "Be fruitful and multiply, until you fill the waters of the Sea! May likewise the birds multiply on the Earth!" (23) Thereupon it became evening, then morning: the fifth day.*

h. Terrestrial Animals

(24) *Then Elohim said: "Let the Earth bring forth animals of every kind: cattle, reptiles, and wild animals of every kind!" And so it was: (25) Elohim made wild animals of every kind, cattle of every kind, and all the reptiles of the soil, of every kind. And Elohim saw that it was something good.*

i. Human Beings

(26) *Finally, Elohim said: "Let us make Mankind in Our image, as a replica of Us, so that they govern the fish of the Sea and the birds of the Sky, the cattle and all the wild animals and all the reptiles that crawl on the Earth!"* (27) *So Elohim created Mankind:*
"He created it in the image of Elohim!
He created them male and female!"
(28) *Then Elohim blessed them in these words: "Be fruitful and multiply: fill the earth and subdue it! Govern the fish of the Sea and the birds of the Sky and all animals that crawl on the Earth!"* (29) *"Now,"* Elohim said again, "I give you all vegetation bearing seed over the whole surface of the Earth, and all trees that bear fruit with seeds: that will be your food. (30) Likewise, I give all greenery of plants to the wild animals, to the birds of the Sky, to all that crawls on the Earth and that has the Breath-of-life."*

j. Completion
of the Creation

(31) *Elohim considered all that He had made and declared that all of it was very good. Thereupon it became evening, then morning: the sixth day. (2:1) [In this way] Heaven, Earth, and everything in them was completed.*

k. The Rest at
the End

(2) *On the seventh day, Elohim, having completed the work He had done, rested that seventh day, from all the work he had accomplished. (3) So Elohim blessed the seventh day and made it sacred: that was the day on which He rested from the work He had accomplished in the Creation.*

l. Conclusion

(4a) *Such is the genealogy of Heaven and Earth when they were created.*

Psalm 104

The two cosmogonic texts that we still wish to read are poems. One is taken from the Book of Job and is approximately a century later than the *Priestly Document* (see pages 129ff. below). The other, one of the songs of which the

Book of Psalms is the canonical collection, is more difficult to date: perhaps it was composed fairly early in the second half of the first millennium B.C.E. In the absence of solid evidence, it may comfortably be assigned to the period immediately after the account of the Priestly Document because it seems to have been written as a kind of poetic and lyrical running commentary on the cosmogonic themes of that account.[8] And then, whereas the extract from the Book of Job will need to be placed in context, the psalm forms a whole in itself:

Introductory	1	*Bless Yahweh, O my soul!*
Invocation		*Yahweh, my God, how great You are!*
		You are wrapped in majesty and luster,
	2	*Clothed with light as with a cloak!*
Heaven		*You stretched the Heavens like a tent,*
	3	*Built Your balcony on the Waters,*
		And made the Cloud into Your Chariot.
		You move on the wings of the wind,
	4	*You have taken the winds as messengers*
		And the flaming fires as slaves!
The Earth	5	*You founded the Earth on its foundations,*
		For ever unshakable.
	6	*The Abyss, like a garment, covered it over,*
		And the Waters stood above the mountains.
	7	*At Your rebuke they fled,*
		They made their escape at Your thunderous Voice!
The Sea	8	*They rose above the mountains, ran down the valleys,*
		To the place You allotted to them.
	9	*[There] You set them an impassable limit,*
		So that they would not return to submerge the Earth.
The Rivers	10	*You have pointed the springs toward the [beds of the] rivers*
		That flow between the hills.
	11	*Thus they water all the animals of the fields:*
		The wild asses quench their thirst in them,

8. Also, some features seem to show an influence of the discourse of Job upon it (see below).

12   *And the birds of Heaven live close to them,*
       They launch their chants from among the boughs.

The Rain   13   *From Your balcony on high, You water the mountains,*
                    And the earth takes abundantly from [Your] celestials
                        skins.

The Plants   14   *[Thus] You make the green herbs sprout for the cattle*
                      And the meadows for man's tame animals;
                      You make bread come from the earth,
              15   *The wine that delights man's heart,*
                      The oil with which You make their face shine,
                      The bread with which You fortify their heart.

The Trees   16   *Even the trees-of-Yahweh are lavished:*
                     Those cedars of Lebanon that You Yourself planted!
             17   *There the sparrows build their nests,*
                     And the storks take shelter at the treetops.

The Mountains   18   *The high mountains are for the mountain goats,*
                         The rocks for the coneys, to find refuge!

Stars, Day   19   *You made the moon, to [mark] the times,*
and Night   *And the sun who knows [the hour of] his setting.*
               20   *You set the darkness—and it is night,*
                      When all the wild animals of the woods prowl,
               21   *[When] the young lions roar after their prey,*
                      Claiming their daily allowance from God.
               22   *But when the sun is up, they retreat*
                      And stretch out in their lairs,
               23   *[While] man sets out to work,*
                      To labor until dusk.

New   24   *How great are Your works, Yahweh!*
Invocation   *You have made all of them with wisdom*
                     And the Earth is filled with Your good things!

Sea and   25   *There is the sea, vast and endless,*
Acquatic   *In which [is concealed] an infinite stirring*
Animals   *Of small and large animals;*

26 *Where ships come and go,*
    And Leviathan, whom You formed to play there for
    You.

Providence   27 *All [beings] hope from You*
    That You give them their food at their time:

              28 *When You give it to them, they gather it.*
    When You open Your hand, they have their fill of
    good things.

              29 *But when You hide Your face, they are seized by*
    anguish,
    When You take back their Breath, they die
    And return to their dust;

              30 *[Whereas] they are created when You send forth Your*
    breath;
    And You renew the face of the earth.

Final   31 *Everlasting Glory for Yahweh!*
Invocation   *May Yahweh rejoice in His works,*

              32 *Before whose eye the earth trembles,*
    At whose touch the mountains smoke!

              33 *I shall chant for Yahweh all my life;*
    Until the end, I shall make music for my God!

              34 *May my devotion be pleasing to Him,*
    As for me, my Joy is in Yahweh!

              35 *May the sinners be annihilated from the earth*
    And may the evildoers no longer live!
    Bless Yahweh, O my soul!"

Yahweh's Discourse in Job

The Book of Job was probably composed in the middle of the fifth century (see page 98 above). It is devoted to the problem of the righteous man's suffering and divine Justice. This theme is first debated between Job, who believes he is afflicted wrongly and who recriminates against God, and his three friends, who defend the traditional thesis in Israel according to which only the sinner and the infidel may, and, indeed, must, be brought to grief by God. Their talk is at cross-purposes and produces no conclusion. And then, all of a sudden, God speaks "from the midst of a tempest"—hence with his whole formidable majesty—which is in some way what gives rise to this upheaval of nature. He does not respond directly to the questions; indeed, He does not answer any question at all: He merely calls up His true role, which places Him infinitely above the human discussion, human problems, human comprehension. This is the passage we shall read: chapter 38. In literal point of fact, only the first eleven verses deal with a cosmogonic theme; God's discourse is interrupted by Job's first avowal of submission, and then it is taken up again—as if God wanted to overwhelm His "recriminator" forever—and for the entire remainder of the discourse, God evokes especially His daily and universal rule over the world of His creation. In this, besides the fact that features relating to the Creation proper are mixed in with others that arise from the notion of Providence (see pages 139ff. below), the close union—already noticeable in Psalm 104—between these two aspects of divine activity is instructive in itself and, in my opinion, contributes to the characterization and definition of Israel's cosmogonic thought. This is the reason why the reader should have the whole of the discourse between Yahweh and Job before his eyes—discourse, moreover, that is one of the most vigorous, one of the most incomparable, poems of the Bible.

Interrogation of Job (chap. 38)	1	*Then Yahweh, answering Job from the midst of a tempest, said to him:*
	2	*"Who is the one who muddles My Plan With stupid prattle?*
	3	*Gird your loins, like a wrestler: I shall question you, and you will teach Me!*
The Earth	4	*Where were you when I established the Earth? Point it out, for you possess omniscience!*
	5	*Who set its dimensions, if you know it, Or who stretched the line upon it?*
	6	*What holds its foundations in place, Or who laid its cornerstones*
	7	*While the morning stars were singing in chorus, And all the Sons-of-Elohim[9] cheered?*
The Sea	8	*Who set a limit to the Sea with two doors, When it burst forth at its very origin;*

9. The "Sons-of-Elohim" are superior beings (what we would call "Angels") at the exclusive service of God, who in some way made up the staff of His celestial court.

9   *When I dressed it with clouds*
     And swaddled it with fog;

10   *When, to impose its border,*
     I installed bolts and doors,

11   *And told it: 'You will come this far, and no farther!*
     Here the pride of your waves will break!'

The Day   12   *Have you given orders to the morning,*
                        Did you tell the dawn what her place was,

                   13   *So that she could lay hold of the world's fringes*
                        And shake off the evildoers,

                   14   *When everything becomes like red clay*
                        And is dyed like a piece of textile,

                   15   *When the evildoers' light is taken away from them*
                        And their menacing arm stopped?

The Abyss   16   *Have you reached the sources of the Sea?*
                        Did you walk at the hidden bottom of the Abyss?

                   17   *Have the gates of Death been uncovered for you?*
                        Have you seen the doorkeepers of the Shade?

                   18   *Have you surveyed the vastness of the World?*
                        Demonstrate if you know all this!

The Light   19   *In what direction does the Light have its dwelling?*
                        And where does the Darkness reside?

                   20   *So that you can take them to their homes*
                        And so that you know the paths of their whereabouts.

                   21   *[All this] you know: you were already born then,*
                        And the number of your days is immense!

The "Waters   22   *Did you reach the storage yards of snow?*
Above"   *Did you see the storage yards of hailstones?*

                   23   *Where I keep the hail and snow for times of agony,*
                        For the days of battle and war?

                   24   *Along what road does the fog disappear,*
                        And the East wind spread out over the earth?

                   25   *Who hollows the trenches for the downpour,*
                        And the ways for the rolling thunder?

26   *Who brings the rain upon the regions without people,*
     Upon the uninhabited deserts?

27   *Who soaks barrenness and desolation with water?*
     Who makes the grass sprout in the steppe?

28   *Is there indeed a father to the rain?*
     Who engenders the dewdrops?

29   *From whose bosom comes the ice?*
     Who generates the hoarfrost of heaven,

30   *When the waters harden like stone*
     And the face of the Abyss turns solid?

The Stars

31   *Can you tie the ropes of the Pleiades*
     Or loosen the cords of Orion?

32   *Cause the corona to appear at its time,*
     Or guide the Great Bear with her little ones?

33   *Do you know the rules of the heavens,*
     And can you apply them on the earth?

**Thunder
and Rain**

34   *Do you lift your voice to the clouds,*
     So that a flood of water comes upon you?

35   *Do you order the lightning bolts on their way,*
     And do they obey, saying: 'Here we are!'?

36   *Who gave wisdom to the ibis?*
     Who gave the rooster its intelligence?

37   *Who counts the clouds wisely,*
     And who bends the celestial waterskins

38   *When lands dissolve into a flow,*
     Only to pile up in hills of mud?

**The Wild
Animals**

39   *Do you chase the prey for the lioness?*
     Do you satisfy the hunger of her cubs,

40   *When they are crouched in their lair*
     Or lying in wait in their thicket?

The Ravens

41   *Who furnishes the portion for the raven,*
     When his nestlings cry for El,[10]
     Tottering for lack of food?

10. See the next note.

Antelope
(chap. 39)

1   *Do you know when the antelope on the cliffs give
     birth?*
  Do you see to the deer's calving?
2   *Do you count the months it will take?*
  Do you know the time of their delivery?
3   *[There they are, who] bow down and drop their
     young,*
  [They] give birth to their brood, in the desert;
4   *Then their fawns, having grown in strength and
     size,*
  Leave and never return to them!

Onagers

5   *Who has set the onager free to go?*
  Who has loosed the fetters of the wild ass,
6   *To which I have given the steppe for home*
  And the salt desert for dwelling place?
7   *It laughs at the throng of the cities,*
  It does not hear the donkey-driver's shouts;
8   *But it ranges the hills, its pasture,*
  Searching after everything green.

Buffalo

9   *Will the buffalo consent in serving you,*
  Or spending the night at your manger?
10 *Will you tie a rope on his neck?*
  Will he follow you and harrow the furrows?
11 *Will you rely on him, on his enormous power,*
  So as to leave your tasks to him?
12 *Will you count on it that he will return,*
  And bring your grain to your threshing floor?

Ostrich

13 *The ostrich's wings flap quickly,*
  With their light plumage and all their pinions,
14 *But she leaves her eggs on the ground,*
  She lets them be hatched in the dust,
15 *Forgetting that they can be crushed by a foot,*
  That a beast of the field may step on them:
16 *She is hard on her chickens, as if they did not belong
     to her,*
  Indifferent at the uselessness of her labor.

17   *Because Eloah[11] kept wisdom from her,*
        And did not endow her with intelligence.
18   *But as soon as she raises herself up and dashes forward,*
        She makes game of the horse and its rider!

Horses

19   *Do you give strength to the horse?*
        Do you cover his neck with his mane?
20   *Do you make him leap like the locust?*
        The glory of his voice inspires fear!
21   *He paws and fumes in the vale,*
        Stamps with impetuous joy,
        He throws himself into the fight!
22   *He makes a mockery of dread, fearless,*
        He does not flee from the point of the sword!
23   *Upon him, the quiver rattles,*
        The lance and spear glitter.
24   *Out of ardor and impatience, he swallows up dirt;*
        At the first trumpet, he will not stay back,
25   *When the trumpet sounds, he neighs:*
        He scents the battle from afar,
        The commanders' shouts and the noise!

Birds of Prey

26   *Would you have thought to feather the hawk*
        So that it could spread its wings to the South?
27   *Does the eagle glide on high at your command,*
        And roost in his space on the summits?
28   *Motionless, he spends the night on his solitary rock,*
        On his lonely peak, his strong castle:
29   *From there, he watches for his victuals,*
        And his eyes search the distance.
30   *His offspring want to sip blood:*
        Where there are corpses, there he is!"

New
Interrogation of
Job (chap. 40)

1   *And Yahweh, questioning Job again, said to him:*
2   *"Will the recriminator of Shadday[12] [now] desist?*
        Will he not give in, the critic of Eloah?"

---

11. *El, Eloah,* and *Shadday* are specifications more or less synonymous with *Elohim* (see page 8). The Book of Job, especially, likes to alternate between these first three and often prefers them to the last.

12. See the previous note.

Response by Job	3	*And Job answers Yahweh:*
	4	*"Yes, I have been thoughtless: how could I argue?*
		I shall lay my hand on my mouth!
	5	*I spoke once: I shall not do it again;*
		Twice: I shall not begin any more!"

Yahweh Speaks Again	6	*But Yahweh speaks again and resumes to Job:*[13]
	8	*"So you truly wanted to annul My right?*
		Put Me in the wrong to justify yourself?
	9	*What you would need is an arm like El's,*
		And a voice, like His, to make it thunder!
	10	*[Now] deck yourself in majesty and grandeur!*
		Dress yourself in splendor and glory!
	11	*Lay open the excesses of your fury!*
		Seek out the haughty, and bring them down!
	12	*Seek out the haughtiest and humble them!*
		Crush the wicked on the spot,
	13	*Bury them in the dust together,*
		Incarcerate each one of them in a hidden place!
	14	*Then, I Myself shall exalt you,*
		For your right hand will have saved you!

The Two Most Extraordinary Beings Created by God:

Behemoth	15	*See, here is Behemoth before you,*
		Who, like the ox, eats grass!
	16	*Look at the strength in his loins*
		And the power of the muscles in his belly!
	17	*He can keep his tail as rigid as a cedar!*
		The tendons of his thighs are interlaced.
	18	*His bones are brass pipes,*
		His frame made of iron bars!
	19	*This was the first work of El,*
		[But] his maker holds the sword over him:
	20	*He deprived him of the mountainous region*
		And all the wild beasts that play there.
	21	*[Thus] he rests sprawled under the papyrus,*
		In the shelter of the reeds and the marsh,

13. The traditional Hebrew text that here, at verse 7, repeats verse 38:3 seems in need of relief from this superfluous repetition. (See also note 16 below, on 38:3a and 4.)

22   *Covered in the shade of the lotus,*
      Surrounded by the willows of the valley.

23   *If the stream rages, it does not move him:*
      Impassible when the Jordan would leap to his mouth!

24   *Who could catch him with a hook,*
      Or pierce his nose with a gaff?

Leviathan   25   *Would you fish for Leviathan with a fishing line?*
                   And would you suppress his tongue with a string?

26   *Could you stick a rush through his nose?*
      Could you drive a hook through his jaw?

27   *Will he beseech you at length?*
      Will he speak friendly words to you?

28   *Make a contract with you?*
      Will you take him as a servant for life?

29   *Could you play with him as with a sparrow?*
      Hold on to him for your little girls?

30   *Could your partners trade him for you*
      And retail him to merchants?

31   *Could you fill his skin with arrows*
      And his head with harpoon holes?

32   *If you lay your hand on him,*
      Think of the carnage: you would not return from it!

(chap. 41)   1   *Your impertinence would be undone:*
                   Merely seeing him, you would fall to the ground!

2   *He is so cruel that no one dares stir him up,*
     That no one can stand before him.

3   *Who has affronted him without harm?*
     No one under the whole sky!

4   *I shall not pass in silence over his members,*
     I shall speak of his incomparable strength.

5   *Who could lift the seam of his garment?*
     Who could get through his double armor?

6   *Who could open the doors of his mouth?*
     His teeth are surrounded by terror!

7   *His back is shields aligned with each other;*
     The joints are sealed with flint.

8   *They are so close together*
     That the wind cannot pass between them!

9   *Each one cleaves to the others:*
     Inseparably, they clasp each other.

10   *His snorting makes the light sparkle.*
     His eyes are like the eyelids of the early morning.

11   *From his mouth come torches*
     And sprays of fire shoot out.

12   *A fume escapes from his nostrils,*
     As from a heated, bubbling kettle!

13   *His breath kindles coals,*
     A flame comes out of his mouth!

14   *His neck is full of power,*
     And terror jumps before him!

15   *The folds of his flesh cling together;*
     If one presses it—it does not give way!

16   *His heart is as hard as a stone,*
     Hard like the lower millstone![14]

18   *The sword does not avail against his armor,*
     Neither do lance, dart, or arrow!

19   *To him, iron is straw,*
     And brass, moldered wood!

20   *The son-of-the-bow*[15] *does not send him flying!*
     Slingstones, to him, are flimsy chaff!

21   *The pike seems a trifle to him!*
     And the javelin's vibration makes him laugh!

22   *His underside has keen-edged shards:*
     It presses in the mud like a harrow.

17   *When he darts forward, the tides tremble,*
     The waves turn back.

23   *He makes the deep boil like a pot,*
     He transforms the lake into an ointment-burner!

24   *Behind him is a track of light:*
     As if the Abyss had white hair!

25   *He has no equal on earth:*
     He was created fearless.

26   *He is the one whom the proudest fear.*
     He is the king of all ferocious animals!"

14. Verse 17 of the Hebrew text seems to have been moved from another location in this text: probably between 22 and 23, where I have reinserted it.

15. Idiomatic expression, referring to "arrow."

Second	1	*Then Job responded to Yahweh:*
Response by	2	*"I know that You are almighty,*
Job		*That for You no plan is unrealizable!*
(chap. 42)	3	*[. . .] Yes, I held forth, without understanding,*
		On marvels that are beyond me and that I am ignorant about[16] *[. . .]*
	5	*I had heard of you and learned about you [only] by hearsay,*
		But now my eyes have seen You.
	6	*Therefore I sink down and repent,*
		In dust and ashes!"

THE IDEAS

THE THEOLOGICAL COSMOGONY

What is striking first of all, when we read these texts, is the theological character of the cosmogony as it appears in the Bible: "theological" meaning that it is derived in some way from a certain conception of the divine or, at least, brought into agreement with it.

Characteristics of This Theological Cosmogony

The essential theses of this theology, the *ideas* that make up the undeniable originality of the biblical cosmogony when we place it beside cosmologies that were contemporary, are, overall, that the universe has a cause that is personal, distinct, and independent from itself; that this cause is unique; and that this same cause continues, ever more, to preside with the same efficacy in the course of the world.

PERSONALITY OF THE CREATOR

All texts agree on this point: whether they call the cause by the "proper name" Yahweh (*Yahwist*; Psalm 104; Job) or by Elohim ("God") (*Priestly Document*) or its equivalents (Job), they present as origin of the cosmos a

16. As in 40:7 (see note 13 above), the traditional text has repetitions probably not attributable to the author: the beginning of verse 3 approximately repeats 38:2, and verse 4 combines parts of 33:31 and 38:3.

Creator: that is to say, an autonomous personality. Nothing tells us that creation had been an obligatory and inevitable work: on the contrary, everything shows us that the maker of the world freely conceived the plan and executed it. In the account of the *Yahwist*, we see Him deliberating the creation of the animals in order to provide company for man: *"I shall make a fitting companion for him!"* (Genesis 2:18). Likewise, in the *Priestly Document*, God decides, finally, to make men: *"Let us make Mankind in Our image, as a replica of Us"* (Genesis 1:26). And this Creator, as such, has manifestly no other relations to the universe than those that relate cause to effect.

UNIQUENESS OF THE CREATOR

The same texts are also in agreement affirming the uniqueness of this cause and this Creator. All the "works" through which the world comes into being and is populated relate to Him alone: heavens, earth, sea, light, stars, plants, animals, and man—all owe their origin to Him. If a passage in Job (38:7) assumes there are spectators to the Great Work: the "morning stars" of the dawn of the world and the celestial court of the "Sons-of-Elohim," these beings, which also owe their existence to God, as we know from elsewhere, are there only to "applaud" the wonders He accomplishes and to "chant" the glory of the Creator. In this context, the use of the first-person plural of *"Let us make Mankind in Our image, as a replica of Us,"* in the *Priestly Document* (Genesis 1:26)[17] could be none other than the "majestic plural," still used today in our languages by the great dignitaries of this world, the leaders of nations. The proper name Elohim, moreover, referring to God in classical Hebrew, is itself a plural, yet constantly used for one single, unique God. Hence one could hardly invoke the passage to suggest a plurality of creators in biblical theology.

CONTINUITY BETWEEN CREATION AND RULE OVER THE COSMOS

In Job, the *continuity* between God's activity in the Creation and in the subsequent course of the world appears more vividly than anywhere else. Immediately after the account of the formation of the earth and the sea (38:4–11), God depicts His daily work in nature: He is the one who makes the dawn break (12ff.) and disposes the light of the day and the nocturnal darkness; He regulates rain, snow, hail, rime, and frost, thunder and wind

17. Likewise, according to the Greek version of the Septuagint and the Latin of the Vulgate, Yahweh would have spoken in the first-person plural in the text of the *Yahwist*, Genesis 2:18, at the moment He decided to create the animals. Perhaps this is no more than a reminiscence of 1:26, which may be attributed to some compiler or copyist?

(22–30 and 34–38), sets the celestial mechanics of the constellations in motion (31ff.), and takes care of the wild animals, those which cannot expect from man either their daily food or help in their reproduction (39ff.). And in these very descriptions of God's daily handiwork in the functions of nature, there appear numerous features that relate more directly, indeed exclusively, to the original constitution of that nature, and hence to the cosmogony. For example, if God "knows in what region" light and darkness "dwell" (38:19ff.), it is because He is the author of their primordial "separation" (cf. Genesis 1:4), and hence assigned to each its own residence. The "trenches" that guide the rain above the regions where it must fall (Job 38:25) have their source in the immense reservoir of the "Waters Above," which was one of the first results of the orderly arrangement of the original Chaos (Genesis 1:7). And then God formed the great reserves of snow and hail (Job 38:22), on which he has drawn, ever since, when necessary. In the very long passage dedicated to the animals, the emphasis falls especially on their originality in each case, their conduct and their surprising or unexpected habits: the meteorological "intelligence" of the ibis and the rooster (38:36), the stupidity of the ostrich (39:13ff.), the stubborn independence of the onager (5ff.), the untamable nature of the buffalo (9ff.), the impetuosity and marvelous courage of the horse (19ff.), the solitary and cruel instincts of the raven (26ff.), ever so many traits inexplicable if one does not connect them with a definitive "plan,"[18] infinitely wise and complex, brought into being by God, at the very Creation, in the prototypes of these animals. The description of the two "ogres," Behemoth and Leviathan (40:15ff.), seems to be centered likewise in their exceptional constitution: in other words, in their creation. Everything that is said about them is intended to arouse astonishment and admiration before the inventiveness, the sagacity, and the power of their maker.

In a briefer compass and conceived differently from the discourse of Job, Psalm 104 shows the same continuity between the making of the universe and its day-to-day governing: to the formation of the earth and sea (5–9) is linked the irrigation of the land by rivers and rain (10–13), and its ever recurring result, the abundance of nutritious plants (14ff.). And so forth.

If the matter does not appear equally clearly in the prose accounts of the *Yahwist* and the *Priestly Document*, that is because I have quoted them here without their subsequent context, namely, that later history for which their cosmogonic introduction is only a preparation and in which, at every moment, the intervention and action of the same God break in. Thus, in the *Yahwist*,

18. See page 145 below.

the prohibition against eating from the Tree-of-discernment-between-Good-and-Evil (Genesis 2:16ff.) leads into the story of man's first disobedience, source of all the others, which will force God to intervene so frequently to resume, correct, and safeguard his work.

CREATION WITHIN THE WHOLE RANGE OF DIVINE ACTIVITY

To sum up, in the theology of the Bible, the cosmogony is only the first act, setting on stage the actors in the *history*, and there is only one single unchanging Director, who is responsible for the entire piece. In creating each prototype, He has infused into the actor the role that he must play forever, he himself and each of his descendants; and each has now only to perform his own part under the permanent management and eternal supervision of the same Director. He has done for each thing that which He did for the sea in the Job narration: having brought it forth from Chaos and given it form, He imposed its unbreakable limits and gave to it His unchanging "law" (Job 38:8–11; cf. Psalm 104:9). We find the equivalent of this in Jeremiah (33:25), at the end of the seventh century B.C.E.:

> *Did I not create the Day and the Night?*
> *Did I not establish the laws of Heaven and Earth?*

And later, no doubt after the Exile, in Psalm 148:

> 5   *Let all these beings praise the name of Yahweh!*
> *He gave a command and they were created,*
> 6   *He established them forever, forever,*
> *He gave them a law they do not transgress!*

Still later, at the beginning of the second century B.C.E., in Ecclesiasticus, or the Wisdom of Jesus the son of Sirach (chap. 16):

> 26   *When in the beginning God created His works,*
> *As soon as He had made [them], He determined their elements.*
> 27   *He set His works in order forever:*
> *From their origins to their generations,*
> 28   *They suffer neither hunger nor fatigue*
> *And never cease to accomplish their work.*
> 29   *None has ever offended the other,*
> *Never do they disobey His commandments*

It follows that creation, in the Bible, is not an act apart from all the rest, completed once and for all and unrepeatable. It is indeed only a "beginning" (Genesis 1:1, and see Ecclesiasticus 16:26; cf. also Proverbs 8:23), signifying that the course of the world, directed by the same God, encompasses other, uniform moments. Thus, for example, the Flood (Genesis 6:5, 9:7) is presented explicitly, especially by the *Priestly Document*, as a new creation of the world, a divine will to begin everything anew (6:7): return to the watery Chaos (see page 150 below) by mixing the Waters "above" with the Waters "below" (7:11); the earth entirely covered anew by the waters (7:18–20); a new separation of the Waters "above" and those "below" (8:2), then of water and earth (8:3ff); a new forthcoming of all the animals, species after species (8:15–19); again the commandment to be fruitful and multiply and again a mutual distribution of creatures to provide food for one another (9:1ff.). And certain "miraculous" interventions by God in the course of things, sudden changes He brings about in the order of nature, likewise closely resemble His creative activity. So it is when, in Isaiah 41, God makes the following promises to those returning from the great Exile, at the moment when they will go back through the desert before reentering Palestine:

> 18 I shall make rivers rise from sand-hills,
> And springs between the narrow passes.
> I shall transform the desert into ponds,
> Dry land into fountains.
> 19 I shall put cedars in the desert,
> Acacias, myrtle, olive trees;
> I shall put juniper trees in the barren plain,
> The sycamore and cypress, all together.[19]

And in Isaiah 13, God threatens to crush Babylon through an unprecedented catastrophe, a cosmic upheaval:

> 10 The heavens and their constellations
> Will no longer give light:
> The sun will be in darkness from the daybreak on,
> The moon will no longer shed its brightness.[20]

---

19. See note 30 below. On the date of "Second-Isaiah," from which this piece comes, see below.

20. This passage is neither by Isaiah himself nor by "Second-Isaiah," but by an author who must have been writing toward the end of the Exile; see pages 69f. above.

Cosmogony and Monotheism

These theological teachings concerning the origins and course of the universe owe their characteristics and their coherence, and, in the final analysis, their very existence, to the fact that they carried into the cosmogonic province the fundamental axiom of the religion of Israel—absolute monotheism.

> *Before Me, no God had been formed,*
> *After Me, there will never be another!*
> *I, I [alone], I am Yahweh*
> *I [alone] am God.*
> *I am He, I, since the beginning!*

This declaration (Isaiah 43:10–13) comes to us from one of the greatest Israelite writers, whose work tradition annexed to that of the Prophet Isaiah (second half of the eighth century) and who, for that reason, is called among specialists "Second-Isaiah," for lack of more knowledge about his person (see pages 73ff. above). He wrote toward the middle of the sixth century, to announce the end of the Exile. However, the idea of monotheism, so vigorously expressed in his text, in fact precedes him. Virtually complete in the thought of Moses, the founder of the religion of Israel, it began to take form in the early first millennium. The Yahwist author sketched it, as we have seen, when he recognized as the sole creator Yahweh, the one and only God.

Later, especially through the great Prophets, the concept of monotheism would be affirmed more strongly, purified, and finally completed in its inevitable conclusion, where it emerges into transcendence, the radical distinction, the total difference between God and the universe. Through this shift, the cosmogonic theology of the Bible, already completed in its essential elements from the time of the Yahwist, reaches its highest point and greatest profundity.

THE PERSON OF THE CREATOR

Let us compare the portrayals of the very person of God the Creator given by the account preceding the Exile and by the *Priestly Document*. In the *Yahwist*, the Creator attends to *one* corner of the garden, with *one* stream—though a large one!—*one* man, whom He considers more or less His farmer, one animal of each kind, one woman; these are the modest beginnings of a cosmos in whose functioning we sense that man will have his role and it will not be a minor one (see the opening of the *Yahwist*'s account in Genesis 2:4b–5). In the *Priestly Document*, the same Creator is presented only in the face of universal realities: Water, Earth, Heavens, Light, Darkness, Stars, botanical and zoological Species, the Human Race. And when His work is complete, we see, above all, that in essence the continuation of the universe will not be more than a matter of number and the multiplication of individuals (Genesis 1:22 and 28).

Psalm 104, with its luminous images, brings out even more the splendor and excellence of the Maker of the Universe. But in the entire Bible, it is perhaps the discussion between God and Job, especially in its context, that gives us the highest, the strongest, expression of the sense of the absolute transcendence of the one God, the Creator. If God deigns to speak in the face of the questions of Job, who *wants to know* why God, by His authority, makes him suffer when he is innocent, in the face of the three friends' vapid theorem that God is *obliged* to mistreat the sinner and gratify the just man, He does so to crush those human claims. He does not argue: He is satisfied to recall His unique, inimitable, fearful, and incomprehensible work, in the formation and course of the universe. Without His even bothering to explain, this work places Him so far above the entire cosmos and His very masterwork, the human spirit, that it leaves to the latter but one attitude to adopt before Him: the admission of radical ignorance, final powerlessness to understand this sublimity, adoration, and submission to His will.

THE WAY OF CREATIVE ACTIVITY

The same sense of transcendence similarly shaped another trait of the cosmogony in the Bible: the very manner in which God's creative act was conceived. In the account of the *Yahwist*, it still appears rather material and anthropomorphic, even though the author seems to remain conscious of the figurative character of the terms he uses. God, in a manner of speaking, has to trouble Himself: like a well-sinker, He "causes a stream to emerge from the earth"; like a gardener, He plants "a garden of trees"; like a potter "molding from clay," He makes the body of man and, later, those of his companions, and He "blows into the nostrils" of these figurines "the breath of life" that will make them into "living beings." These images, taken from activities of human beings, appear also elsewhere, even among more recent biblical writings, where their poetic character is often quite clear: when God "counts the dimensions" of the earth and "stretches the line upon it," in the manner of architects and masons (Psalm 104:5; Job 38:4–6), these metaphors are meant no more literally than when He "barricades the sea" or "dresses it with clouds" or "swaddles it with fog" (Job 38:8ff.), or when He "stretches the heavens" like the Bedouin stretches his tent (Psalm 104:2). The obvious care the *Priestly Document* takes to avoid such expressions is significant. In that account, we might say, God does not really *act:* he only *speaks*, and everything is realized at once, everything appears, everything "is created"[21] in conformity with the commandment that is uttered.

Whatever the original meaning—in Mesopotamia? in Egypt?—of this idea of the "efficacious divine word,"[22] we cannot doubt that it is applied to the cosmogony in the account of the *Priestly Document* to emphasize the transcendence of the Author of the Universe by spiritualizing His activity still more.

Israel will go even further in this desire to raise up the Creator and His Creation; beyond the word, which in a sense is still material, Israel will go all the way to the concept this word makes concrete; it will go to the mental "plane" (already in Job 38:2), to divine ideas, wonderfully encompassing, admirable, infallible, which, in their entirety, will be given the name of Divine Wisdom (see pages 93ff. above). In one of the most recent cosmogonic passages of the Bible, taken from a part of the Book of Proverbs that is probably later than the sixth century, this supernatural wisdom, preceding all the work of God, is presented as the ultimate power governing the Creator's activity as a whole (Proverbs 8):

22   *Yahweh created me at the beginning of His works,*
      prior to (everything) He made, since the beginning!
23   *Since Eternity, I was established,*
      From the beginning, before the origins of the Earth:
24   *When the Abyss did not exist, I was brought forth,*
      When there were neither springs nor the sources of the Seas;
25   *Before the mountains were set,*
      Before the hills, I was brought forth!
26   *There was no earth yet, no land,*
      Nor even the elements of the dust of the world.

21. Here the *Priestly Document* uses the verb *bara*, reserved specifically for the activity, above all creative activity, of God and never used to describe human action.

22. The "efficacious word" whose very expression brings about what it says is not attested in ancient Mesopotamia, except in the area of "Magic"—but there it occurs abundantly. There is no dependable testimony that it was used in Creation mythology, in spite of a passage in the *Enuma elish* where by a mere commandment Marduk causes a constellation to appear and to disappear in order to show his sovereign power (tablet IV:20ff.). On the other hand, the theologians of ancient Egypt did make use of the procedure in creation: see *Sources orientales I: La naissance du monde* (cited on page ix), 40.

27   *When He formed the Heavens, I was there,*
     When He drew a circle on the face of the Abyss;
28   *When he sent forth the clouds, on high,*
     When he set the bounds for the sources of the Abyss;
29   *When he imposed on the Sea its limits*
     Whose line the waters will never trespass;
     When he established the foundation of the Earth,
30   *I was at his side, inseparably . . .*

THE UNDERLYING MYTHOLOGICAL COSMOGONIES

From the ninth and eighth centuries onward, the Israelite thinkers were constructing their "theology" of Creation. In the course of this work, more often than not, they impregnated with their own religious mentality and ideology an array of cosmogonic views furnished to them by traditions different from theirs and anterior or exterior to their own time and world.

We are familiar with the fact that in the ancient Near East, well before Israel and Israel's religion of Yahweh, questions were raised concerning the origins of the world and man, and attempts made to answer them; in these attempts, each people and each time followed its own religious view of things. In this way, quite a few cosmogonic "systems" came into being,[23] each of them possessing authority in the eyes of its adherents, just like the biblical "system" in the eyes of the faithful of Yahweh.

All these cosmogonies were *mythological* in nature. In other words, they were worked out on the basis of a thought that had not yet led to the inference of pure ideas or learned to construct formal reasoning, but instead found its way through images and series of imaginations, searching much less for the objective and verifiable origins of a given fact than for a sequence of events, reconstructed more or less by inspiration, that sufficed to account for it (see also, on this subject, pages 171ff.).

Some of these "systems," advanced by civilizations, like Mesopotamia, that had considerable importance and a wide diffusion in the Near East, or simply elaborated by people who happened to be neighbors of Israel, were known to Israel. And if we analyze the cosmogonic texts of the Bible, setting aside the theology that accompanies them, we rediscover traces of those

23. In order to acquire some notion of the cosmogonic "systems" of Mesopotamia, the reader may refer, for instance, to J. Bottéro, "Les mythes cosmogoniques mineurs," chap. 7 in *Mythes et rites de Babylone* (Paris: Champion, 1985), 279–328.

mythological cosmogonies, whether as vestiges of earlier beliefs or as undergirding for ideas that are special to the religion of Yahweh.

The Account of the Yahwist

COSMOGONY PROPER

The sequence of "well-considered images" that in the *Yahwist's* account (see pages 121ff. above) describes the origins of the universe brings home the following main points: *before,*[24] a waste land, without vegetation; *afterward,* the same earth, provided with herbs, both wild ("thickets") and usable (the "green herbs"), and then with fruit trees (Genesis 2:5, 8). The passage from one state to the next is caused by the addition of two new elements to the virgin soil: the water that makes it fertile, and man, who clears the fallow land and tills it (2:5–7).

The fundamental "image" that regulates the elaboration of this cosmogony is that of the *cultivated desert,* brought into being by wells (the "stream emerging from the earth," of v. 6) and by the mediation of peasants. This would be the thinking of people accustomed to seeing the desert recede before human clearing and irrigation. Palestine itself, especially in its southern and eastern regions, where steppe and cultivated land are side by side, the latter steadily replacing the former, may well have been the original homeland of such a cosmogonic myth, where—significant omission!—the sea plays no role whatsoever. (The sea is not mentioned, nor are fish, in the enumeration of animals molded by Yahweh in Genesis 2:19ff.). It might even be that the authors of the myth were ancient nomads or seminomads, if the Garden, "[there] toward the East," planted with trees (2:8ff.), likely in true desert, evokes, as well it may, a sort of oasis, with its "stream emerging from the earth" to irrigate it.

However, placing the First Garden "[there] toward the East" might have another meaning and point not to the Syro-Arabian desert but, further, to Mesopotamia. The passage in Genesis 2:10–14, which gives the location of Eden with precision, would confirm this interpretation. Not everything is

---

24. My preferred translation for Genesis 2:4b—"when Yahweh had made"—presupposes an earlier, initial act, the "making" of heaven and earth, in other words, the establishment of what was, in the eyes of the Yahwist, only the frame of the universe. Since the author had no special light to shed on that first establishment or did not consider it useful to insist on it, he left it vague, using the very general verb "to make."

clear in the passage, but if the first two "streams," Pishon and Gihon,[25] are unknown, the other two, Tigris and Euphrates, leave us with no doubt at all. The "geography" thus sketched may come into focus if we suppose that Eden is placed in the mountainous region to the north of Mesopotamia, at the source of the two rivers[26] that form its boundaries, and, on the other side, if we imagine the Pishon and Gihon as two arms of an immense flow of water encircling the earth, whose center would be the aforementioned Mesopotamia.[27] This rudimentary and, indeed, mythological "geography" would have some features relating to Mesopotamia, to the extent that—as we are frequently told—the inhabitants really did conceive of their country as the center of the world, whereby they saw the earth surrounded by water (salt water, to be sure, and not the fresh water of the rivers!) and here and there saw the tall mountains to the utmost north as the dwelling place of the great gods (see note 18 on page 70).

It has long been remarked that omitting the passage in question, Genesis 2:10–14, does not spoil what follows in the story, and hence, the passage has the character of an insert. If this is a correct hypothesis, we may have evidence of two different traditions in the cosmogony of the *Yahwist*: one, probably Palestinian, dealing with the origins of the world; the other, Mesopotamian, dealing with the geographic setting of these origins and with the cosmological concept of the earth as an island surrounded by the universal Ocean—a feature that in turn could be reminiscent of the Mesopotamian cosmogony proper (which nevertheless does not function as such in the *Yahwist*'s account).

ANTHROPOGONY AND ZOOGONY

The origin of anthropogonic and zoogonic myths in the *Yahwist* is less transparent. The Creator makes man and animal from clay and then animates

---

25. Their names mean, respectively, "the rushing one" and "the one bursting forth" and seem made up.

26. A Canaanite tradition, probably borrowed from Mesopotamia (see A. Caquot, "La naissance du monde selon Canaan," in *Sources orientales I: La naissance du monde*, 179), places El, the chief god, "at the confluence of the two rivers, at the source of the two abysses." Thus the two "cosmic rivers," the two masses of water that surround the universe and the earth, have a "common source": a point where they meet. And there the chief god resides, no doubt with his court. See note 18 on page 70.

27. Hawila, on one side, is southern Arabia, and Kush, on the other, would be the Caucasus region. (There is another "Kush," which designates Ethiopia.) Hence Pishon and Gihon, conceived as the two frontiers of earth, might represent the seas that form the boundaries of these territories. Since the earth is entirely surrounded by water (see page 152 below), there is a point where the two seas that each delimit half of the island meet. There as well the two great rivers begin, the only ones that count for the authors of the "myth," the Tigris and the Euphrates.

them by the breath that He blows into their nostrils (Genesis 2:7 and 19). This mythological reminder of the potter's craft and of molders of statuettes relates to Mesopotamian legend,[28] but it may just as well have been the conception of anyone familiar with ceramic craftsmen at work, especially, of course, at a time and place where clay was the principal material for many everyday utensils. The choice of man's "rib," enigmatic by contrast, as point of departure for the creation of the first woman, "mother of all who are alive" (Genesis 3:20), may perhaps be explained if—as has long been observed—one brings to mind a "word play" in Sumerian between "rib" and "life," both pronounced in the same way as *til* or *ti*, and both written in the same "ideogram." Hence we might have another reminder of Mesopotamia; and yet, to my knowledge, in Mesopotamia we have not discovered an anthropogonic myth that is based on this homonym.

Likewise, we are not aware of any story from Mesopotamia or other lands in the ancient Near East that would rank the creation of people and animals in the same order as the *Yahwist:* first of all, man—one single individual (see page 122 above)—created in some way as God's farmer, "in order to till and protect the garden" (Genesis 2:7 and 15); thereafter, the various animals, in order to find for man a "suitable companion" (2:18ff.); and then in the end, this search for the perfect companion, leading God to take that companion, in the form of woman, from man's very flesh. Some features of this myth do have a certain correspondence here and there to Mesopotamian anthropogony, according to which man had been created "for service to the gods" and "to complete the creation."[29] But the similarities do not seem typical enough, and for the time being it would not be possible to show anything more than vague reminiscences of Mesopotamian myths in the anthropogony and zoogony of the *Yahwist*.

The same assessment, indeed, should be made with respect to the whole of the *Yahwist*'s mythology of Creation:[30] especially if we consider 2:10–14 as a later addition, that mythology seems quite original, probably autochthonous, and not dependent on Mesopotamia except in a few scattered and uncertain data.

28. See, for instance, the passage quoted below (page 171) from *Atrahasis* (the "exceeding wise one"), where the human prototype is made from clay moistened by the blood of a god.

29. See J. Bottéro, *La religion babylonienne* (Paris: Presses Universitaires de France, 1952), 86ff.; see especially "Les mythes cosmogoniques mineurs" (cited in note 23 above), 193ff. and 321: III/2.

30. In contrast to the cosmogony of the *Priestly Document* (see pages 152ff. above), that of the *Yahwist* seems isolated within the Bible. Perhaps, nevertheless, some passages, such as Isaiah 41:18–19 (quoted on page 142 above), were more or less inspired by it.

Postexilic Cosmogonies

After the Exile, things change. We shall not analyze the accounts in Psalm 104 and the discourse of Yahweh in Job, where the inventions of poetry verge on the mythological imagination and even supplant it. It will be more profitable to focus on the *Priestly Document*, which is also more exclusively and deliberately cosmogonic.

CHRONOLOGICAL FRAME

Let us first address the chronological frame of Creation in this account: the seven days taken by God to accomplish his Great Work. This is obviously a feature conceived in Israel. One of the basic precepts of the religion of Yahweh provided for the seven-day rhythm in time: six days dedicated to work, and the seventh to rest and cult (see, for instance, Exodus 20:8–10; see also page 25 above). The author of the myth sought to found this obligation on what God did in person, to give it more absolute, more cosmic, validity. This is the reason why he divided the creative work, which really encompasses *eight* essential moments (see pages 124ff., subtitles *b–i*, above), into six days, followed by "God's rest," the seventh. The idea is older than the *Priestly Document*: it already occurs in the *Elohist*, in Exodus 20:11 (see note 2 above): *"In six days Yahweh made the heavens, the earth, and all that they contain: but on the seventh day, he rested. Therefore Yahweh blessed the seventh day and made it into something sacred."*

THE COSMOGONY

Once removed from this framework, the cosmogony, zoogony, and anthropogony of the Priestly Document, where the three are much more tightly organized than in the Yahwist, take on an altogether different appearance than they have in the latter work.

The point of departure is no longer the desert earth in need of fertilization, but an immeasurable Chaos that is first to be put in order and then furnished. And this Chaos consists not of land but of *water*. In Genesis 1:2, the earth, "desolate and empty," is not understood as "earth," properly so called, which will appear only later (9–10), under the name "the dry expanse," but as "universe": and the only element of this universe is the boundless and dark watery abyss, with the wind, the "Breath-of-God," sign of His presence and instrument of His power, hovering over it. Psalm 104 refers to the same Chaos, and speaks of the same "earth":

6   *The Abyss, like a garment, covered it over,*
     And the Waters stood above the mountains.

We have already observed (pages 139ff. above) that the Flood, the Creation renewed, likewise begins with a return to the watery Chaos.[31]

As soon as the light appears (Genesis 1:3ff.)—a condition indispensable for all establishment of order—everything will arise from this abyss, this primordial mixture of waters. The first act is precisely the "separation of the Waters" into those "above" and those "below," by means of a vault in between, which assures between them an empty space, the location of our universe (1:6ff.). Then follows a new separation, between the watery element, assigned from now on to a definite place, the sea, and the dry element, which will form the earth, properly so called.

Thus the tripartite structure of the universe is established: the heavens, the earth, and the sea. All that remains is to provide these divisions each with its terrain. First comes vegetation (1:2f.), presented as a complement and completion of the earth part. Only thereafter is the proper population of the three spheres of the universe settled: the stars for the heavens (14f.); the aquatic animals for the sea (20f.); and in the end, for the earth, the terrestrial animals (24f.) and then people, the rulers of the entire creation and representatives of God here below (26f.).

THE MYTHOLOGICAL CHARACTER OF THIS COSMOGONY

Here we have a seemingly logical sequence or, at least, one that demonstrates a certain orderly vision of the universe. It is, nevertheless, without any possible mythological controversy. For instance, it is purely "imaginative" to conceive of the stars as the population of the heavens. And what manner of classifying living species here below! By means of totally fantastic criteria, we have vegetation as a kind of fur upon the earth, and the aquatic animals—fish and birds!—of a wholly different origin than the terrestrial animals, quadrupeds and reptiles and so forth.

Furthermore, if we go back to the anterior division of the universe into its essential parts, we easily see that it presupposes a *cosmology* that is perfectly

---

31. The same idea of a universal watery element already present at the Creation was held in mind, for instance, by the author of the second letter of Saint Peter, when he wrote at the end of the first or the beginning of the second century and spoke of those *"scoffers who pretend not to know that long ago there existed the heavens and the earth, which emerged from the middle of the water and by means of the water, at the commandment of God"* (3:5).

spatial and perfectly imaginative. The universe is thought to be formed of an immense aquatic space (the "Waters above and below"), inside of which a solid vault, the sky, holds the framework of the world (see also note 8 on page 25). The latter contains a dry part (the earth) and a liquid part (the sea). Other passages in the Bible are fundamentally in agreement with this description and articulate it further. For example, according to Proverbs 8:27 (see page 145 above) and Job 26:10 (see page 153 below), the world is circular, since the dome of the sky—supported by "the columns" of the mountains—cuts "a circle on the face of the Abyss" out of the waters below. Hence the earth is immersed in the waters below, into which it is pushed, and yet is held by means of "foundations" (see the texts quoted from Job 38:6 and Psalm 104:5). Finally, if we look closely at the discourse in Job (38:4–11; cf. also Psalm 104:5–9), we find that all is presented as if the sea threatened the earth and sought to submerge it completely: so coasts and shores, "barriers" set by God to "break the pride of the waves," form a continuous line, and the earth is conceived as an island in the middle of the sea.

Let us go still further back, beyond the casting of the universe, to the starting point of the whole Creation, the very origin of things, the abyss-chaos and its first subjugation and orderly arrangement. In the account of the *Priestly Document*, that first orderly arrangement comes about without discord or resistance: God utters a command and the mass of the abyss is separated in two by the appearance of the vault (Genesis 1:6ff.). But Psalm 104:7 has already assumed a kind of struggle between God and the abyss, as it speaks of God's "rebuke" and his "thunderous voice," which cause the universal waters to retreat. And in the discourse of Job (38:8–10), there is collision between Creator and sea, evoked by the furious "bursting forth" of the waves, which must be stopped by a barricade, a border, "bolts and doors," and to which God dictates His law in the end, as victor to the vanquished:

> *You will come this far, and no farther!*
> *Here the pride of your waves will break!*

And finally, we find interspersed through various postexilic books of the Bible—Second-Isaiah, Job, and the Psalms—and in contexts that are cosmogonic in form, a number of strokes that are even more explicitly mythological:

> 9   *Awake! Awake! Clothe yourself with power,*
> *Arm of Yahweh!*
> *Awake, as before*

In ancient times!
Was it not You who cleaved Rahab,
Who pierced the Dragon?
10 *Was it not You who drained the Sea,*
The Waters of the Great Abyss?

(Isaiah 51)

10 *He drew a Circle on the surface of the Waters,*
Marking the confines of Light and Darkness!
11 *The foundations of the Sky reel,*
Terrified by His threats!
12 *With [all] His force, He defeated the Sea:*
By His understanding, He vanquished Rahab!
13 *His breath made the Heavens bright,*
His hand pierced the deceitful Serpent!

(Job 26)

13 *It is You who cleaved the Sea by Your power,*
And smashed the heads of the Dragon on the Waters!
14 *You who shattered the heads of Leviathan*
To feed him as food to the sharks of the Sea!
15 *You broke open the sources, the torrents,*
And drained the inexhaustible streams!
16 *Yours is the Day, yours also the Night!*
You established the Light and the sun!
17 *You determined all limits of the Earth!*
You formed summer and winter!

(Psalm 74)

10 *You vanquished the pride of the Sea!*
You calmed its surging waves!
11 *You trampled Rahab like a dead body*
And scattered Your enemies with an irresistible arm!
12 *Yours are the Heavens, Yours also the Earth:*
You established the World and all that is in it!

(Psalm 89)

These texts clearly place at the beginnings of the universe a formidable struggle between the Creator and the gigantic power of the mass of the

Waters, the Great Abyss that seems to be embodied in an enormous monster bearing various mysterious names: Rahab, Leviathan, the Dragon (*Tannim*), the deceitful Serpent.[32] One might even say that there were two ogres at the same time: the Sea and Rahab (Psalm 89 and Job 26), the Dragon and Leviathan (Psalm 74), Rahab and the Dragon (Isaiah 51), given as obvious equivalents, the former for the Sea, the latter for the Great Abyss. The same two terrible beings occur again in the second part of the discourse between Yahweh and Job, under the names Leviathan (see above) and Behemoth, which means "the beast." To describe them, the poet borrows real features from two animals that would seem the most formidable in the zoological realm he knows: the hippopotamus for Behemoth, and the crocodile for Leviathan. But looking at the texts, we conclude that the poet's conception was determined above all by the memory of the two primordial giants Yahweh had to vanquish: it would seem that His superiority over them, more than over the world and its inhabitants (first discourse: chapters 38–39), was the strongest proof of His sublimity and transcendence. The poet made these even greater by making the two monsters no longer Yahweh's adversaries but His *creatures*. This is what we find again, distinctly, in the fourth book of Esdras [= 2 Esdras 6:47–52—Trans.], a Jewish work of the end of the first millennium B.C.E. that is part of the "Pseudepigrapha," very close to the Bible in tone and thought but not received in the canon of sacred books (see note 21 on page 90):

(6:47) *On the fifth day [of the Creation], You ordered the Seventh-part-of-the-world, where [by Your commandment] the Waters [below] had been brought together to produce animals, winged animals and fish. (48) And thus it happened: The speechless and lifeless water brought forth those animals, in accordance with the divine order, so that on this subject the peoples tell of Your wonders. (49) At that time, you set two living beings aside that you had named, the one Behemoth, the other Leviathan.*

(50) *You separated one from the other, for the Seventh-part-of-the-world, where the water was collected, could not contain them [both].*

---

32. *Rahab* means "tumult," "tempest." It has not been possible to determine with precision the etymological sense of *Leviathan* and *Tannim*, or *Tannin*. In any case, the latter seems also, in other contexts, to point to a sort of reptile (hence the frequent translation "Dragon"). If this is the primary sense of the word, and if we take into consideration the term "tortuous Serpent," it does seem that the mythical monsters of the Beginnings were imagined in the shape of snakes and dragons. Indubitably, this is how it was in Mesopotamia.

> (51) *To Behemoth, You gave as dwelling place one of the [six] parts-of-the-world that had been drained on the third day [of the Creation]: the one where a thousand mountains are found.*[33] (52) *You gave to Leviathan [as abode] the Seventh-part-of-the-world, the liquid-part [=the Sea]. You preserved them to serve as pasture for those whom You want and at the moment You want.*

This piece,[34] taken from a sort of amplified repetition of the account of Creation in Genesis 1, helps us gain a better understanding of a passage in the latter: when creating the sea animals, God begins with the "Dragons" (21) (*Tanninim*, plural of *Tannin*, one of the names of the primordial monsters: see above). Hence, like Job (and see also Psalm 104:26), the *Priestly Document* has changed the monsters, which other texts describe as vanquished adversaries of God at the origin of the world, into mere *creatures*.

THE BEGINNING OF THIS MYTHOLOGY

If the mythological character of these features underlying the cosmogony of the *Priestly Document* (and its other biblical parallels) cannot be denied, neither can we hesitate to name the place of origin of such a mythology: it is Mesopotamia. Only the *order of populating* the universe that is followed in Genesis 1 has no conclusive correspondence in the literature of that country, and hence may be attributed to the Israelite thinkers, unless we find evidence to the contrary.

The *cosmology* presupposed by the biblical ordering of the regions of the universe is essentially identical with the cosmology that absorbed the sages of Mesopotamia, well before Israel existed and began to think and write.

Above all, the *first act of the Creation* translates literally the mythology of origins that we find elaborated in the celebrated Babylonian "Epic of Creation," the *Enuma Elish*.[35] Like this poem, the postexilic biblical texts, properly studied and analyzed, begin the Creation with a colossal struggle between the creator God (Marduk in Mesopotamia, Yahweh in Israel) and an immense watery Chaos, where two monstrous masses are mingled together. In Mesopotamia, we have *Tiamat*, the cosmic Ocean, and *Apsu*, the terrestrial Ocean. The names used by Israel are different, and further, they vary, as we have seen,

33. The tradition differs on this point in Job 40:20.

34. See also another "pseudepigraph," the Ethiopic Book of Enoch, 60:7–9.

35. Following the translation by R. Labat, pages 36–70 in the work cited in note 1 on page ix above, the latest complete translation of this poem, "L'épopée de la Création: Présentation et traduction intégrale," is found in *Recherches et documents du Centre Thomas More*, no. 23:29–60. Detailed commentary in J. Bottéro, *Mythes et rites de Babylone*, 113–62.

from one tradition to another. But the first of the two aquatic masses is several times called "Abyss," our translation of the Hebrew *Tehom*, which is perhaps a proper name but linguistically identical with *Tiamat*; and the term *Apsu* is visible in the Hebrew expression *Aphsei-'Erets*, "the Limits of the Earth" (Deuteronomy 33:17, etc.), which marks the earth's boundaries and at the same time the shores of that terrestrial Ocean which surrounds it (see page 152 above). The separation of the watery mass into the "Waters above" and those "below," according to the *Priestly Document*, brings to mind the separation of *Tiamat*'s body into two halves, of which one becomes heaven and the other, earth. And even the choice of the verb "to split," or "to cleave," in Isaiah 2:9 and Job 26:12, to denote the act through which the creator God prevails over the cosmic monster, bespeaks a circumstance in the Babylonian epic whereby the "dead body of Tiamat" (cf. the "dead body of Rahab" in Psalm 89:11) is "divided in two" by Marduk (tablet 4, 135ff.).[36]

It would be superfluous to push this comparison further in all its details; the point is made by what has already been shown. The Babylonian epic, whose cosmogonic mythology, at least in its essential features, must have guided the cosmology of the *Priestly Document*, Isaiah, Job, and the psalms we have quoted, seems to have been composed in the last quarter of the second millennium B.C.E. The biblical works just mentioned are all later than the great Exile of Israel in Mesopotamia. It is not difficult to see in which direction the borrowing took place.

Did it occur suddenly? Or did the Mesopotamian myths spread from Babylon to Israel only by way of intermediary stages, losing a little or being somewhat changed at each step? This is not an easy question. The possibility of a direct knowledge in Palestine of the Mesopotamian myths cannot be discarded if we keep in mind, for instance, that by the middle of the second millennium, other Babylonian works, such as the Epic of Gilgamesh and treatises on divination and astrology, were read in cuneiform texts, and some were being translated and adapted in the language of the land in Syria, Asia Minor, and Egypt. But neither can we reject the possibility of an indirect transmission, when we think, for example, of Syria and Phoenicia, whose cosmogonic myths, for what little we know of them, still yield traits that are obviously borrowed from Mesopotamia and that we rediscover in the Bible: Baal's battle against the Sea, and probably too the residence of the creator God at the junction of "the two arms of an immense flow of water encircling the earth" (see note 26 on page 148 above).

36. See also Job 40:19 and page 135 above. However, the text in Job is corrupt and difficult, and the translation I have adopted is uncertain.

In any case, we cannot help being struck by the fact that all the biblical texts that reflect the Babylonian cosmogonic mythology most directly were composed *after* the Exile; by contrast, the *Yahwist*'s mythic cosmogony, the only one that has been preserved from an earlier time, is presented in an altogether different way, on a theme of which the essence is almost certainly from an indigenous source, and the Mesopotamian borrowings in it are either quite restricted (the "geography of Eden": see pages 147ff. above) or vague and uncertain (see page 150 above), while, in any case, not a single one of them can definitely be said to betray the mythology proper of the *Enuma Elish*. Under these circumstances, we can hardly avoid concluding that the Mesopotamian cosmogony, little known or poorly known in Israel before the Exile—at least on the basis of the documents—became known, or was brought for the first time to Israel's attention, and came to be held in high regard and adopted to some extent only when Israel's thinkers were brought into immediate contact with Mesopotamia, in Mesopotamia itself.

MYTHOLOGY AND THEOLOGY

Thus mythology and theology show themselves to the historian as two successive stages of cosmogonic thought in Israel. There exists at the same time a certain continuity and a certain discontinuity between the two. We should try to define this more precisely.

The *continuity* is manifest because in full-blown Israelite theological systematics, in the Yahwist's account as well as that of the *Priestly Document* and all the other passages relating to the origin of the world and man, we can locate myths of which we know today that they were worked out in altogether different theological systems.

The Israelite thinkers preserved and integrated in their own cosmogony an entire apparatus of "calculated imaginings" that were foreign to the Yahwist religion.

A number of these vestiges seem to have served above all to stimulate the poetic verve of the biblical authors: Second-Isaiah and the authors of Job and the Psalms in particular. As well, the poets often appeal to folklore—which is to say, commonly held superstitions and beliefs. It is perfectly possible that what held an absolute validity in the mind of the crowd was nothing but metaphor in the view of these great spirits. Subsequent annals of the Bible are instructive if we bring to mind the turmoil and struggles that have stirred the faithful for whom it remained "the Sacred Book"—particularly at the moment when the developmental sciences, beginning with geology and anthropology, were introduced and made their first strides—for then we shall begin properly to assess the importance of the cosmological myths and images for the ancient faithful of Yahweh. The value they have held over more than two millennia and until this day is a matter not only of simple folk but sometimes of the learned, and even of the greatest minds.[37]

Hence, regarding the biblical authors we may also raise the question whether they were not just as attached to the cosmogonic "images" that flowed from their pens as to the "religious ideas" they transmitted. Who will tell us, for instance, in what measure the author of the *Yahwist*, despite the lofty idea he had attained of his God, did not also esteem straightforwardly, or at least obscurely, things that for us could only be metaphor, such as the "molding" of man and the animals from clay.

There are instances where the reliance of biblical writers on the mythological system they adopted goes further and reaches the domain of "religious ideas" proper. Thus the concept of Creation *ex nihilo*, properly so called, though worked out later, does not appear in the Bible itself.[38] God organizes an immeasurable Chaos, transforms it, furnishes it, yet the Chaos itself already existed "in the beginning," and nowhere do we hear it said with certainty that God was its Maker and might have pulled it out of some absolute, anterior nothingness.[39] Here we see an effect of the way in which the cosmogonic problem is posed in the mythology of Mesopotamia, where only the process of becoming is envisaged, and not the absolute origin of existing beings.

Nevertheless, we must recognize that this matter is exceptional and that in the realm of primary ideas in cosmogony, a *discontinuity* is much more evident between the theology of Israel and that which the earlier myths transmitted.

The divergence between theologies is less noticeable in the account of the *Yahwist*, no doubt because in that account we do not know the underlying myths in their own context and also because the Israelite "system," though

37. See, for example, the works by A. Houtin, *La question biblique chez les catholiques de France au XIX siècle* (Paris, 1902), and *La question biblique au XX siècle* (Paris: É. Nourry, 1906).

38. The first biblical passage that speaks of creation *ex nihilo* occurs in the Second Book of Maccabees: "*Direct your eyes, my child, I ask you, toward the Sky and the Earth, consider all that is therein, and recognize that God has not made them by beginning with something preexistent; and thus it was with the human race*" (7:28). But this "Apocryphal" book was composed in Greek, in fully Hellenistic times, and the influence of Greek thought and Greek questions inevitably makes itself felt.

39. In Genesis 2:4b (see note 24 above) the verb "to make" is too vague to allow precise conclusions.

already fixed in its essential features, was not yet fully developed there (see pages 147ff. above). But if we look not for the similarities but for the differences—for instance, between the Babylonian version of the cosmogony according to the *Enuma Elish* and the version of the *Priestly Document* and other postexilic biblical writings—the triumph of Israel's theology seems dazzling.

The accounts of the *Enuma Elish* and other Mesopotamian cosmogonies are laden with polytheism and anthropomorphism: divine battles abound, and envy and fear, greed and selfishness, savagery, and every human vice drives the actions of families of gods at the very origin of our world, and—an affair of even graver significance—in these accounts cosmogony begins with the theology that *the becoming of the gods is comprised within that of the universe* and the gods are an integral part of the cosmos.

These features are gone in the Bible: the only God there is the Creator; and the primordial deities that formed the "prime matter" of the world have lost their divine character and retained only their gigantic and monstrous aspect. The Demiurge no longer has defects. He is infinitely perfect and just, and He evinces the need to create the universe neither due to envy nor due to necessity. Although Job, Second-Isaiah, and the Psalms still maintain traces of His "battle" against the primordial monster of Chaos, the *Priestly Document* suppresses it and "spiritualizes" the divine action by the mediation of the "efficacious word" alone; it preserves "in the beginning" only an impersonal Chaos, transforming (like Job and Psalm 104) into *mere creatures* the formidable beings that had hypostasized the primordial struggle; above all, the *Creator is no longer part of the cosmos*. He is no longer subject to the process of becoming, which from now on is reserved for the world. There is no longer *one single universe*, holding all that exists in the grip of its laws, but two irreducible spheres, the Creator and the creation.

Here, it seems to me, is a transformation with incalculable bearing, the summit of the Israelite cosmogonic system. To be sure, it is not wholly completed in the Bible, which in the final analysis only presents the point of departure, the essential intuitive vision. But whatever one thinks of its objective consequences, one must recognize that it represents, in the realm of metaphysics, one of the highest conquests of the human spirit and, in the realm of religion, a wonderful deepening.

Christianity has always deemed the text from Genesis 2:25
through Genesis 3 the foundation of its cardinal doctrine
of redemption, and indeed this story has made much ink
and much blood flow for two thousand years. How should
we judge it, purely and simply on the plane of history—
the history of religion, to be sure, that is to say, treating it
in its own, irreducible sphere? (For whoever would pro-
fess, as I have heard at one time and another, that religion
is merely "an aspect of economics" would do well to close
these pages without further ado and devote himself exclusively to the study of economics.)

THE CONTEXT

The ancient history of Israel up to its settlement in the land of the Canaanites, as it is presented in the initial part of our Bible, known as the Hexateuch (see page 12), falls into seven parts:

a) From the origins of the world to the origins of Israel: Genesis 1–11
b) From the origins of Israel to its stay in Egypt: Genesis 12–50
c) Formation of the people of Israel: Exodus
d) Israel's basic charter: Leviticus
e) Israel's departure from the Sinai for the Conquest of Palestine: Numbers
f) The final teachings of Moses, and his death, before the Conquest: Deuteronomy
g) The Conquest: Joshua

The first part of this entire collection, Genesis, chapters 1 through 11, is the context of the episode of "Original Sin."

These eleven chapters, like the rest of the Hexateuch, are not the work of one single writer. They are an interweaving (see pages 12ff.) of two "sacred histories," independent to begin with, that the final compilers preserved together, devoutly mixing pieces, as for a mosaic, into a coherent account. (It is what the apologist Tatian would do, in the second century C.E., with the text of the four Gospels, in his *Diatessaron*, "Four-in-One.") Each work has its characteristic language, style, preoccupations, and ideology, and, a bit like geological strata, the two histories can be recognized separately. The more recent one dates from the Exile or immediately thereafter (see page 84), which is to say, around the fifth century B.C.E. The clergy seems to have had a strong hand in it, and thus, for lack of further knowledge concerning its authors, it is has been given the name *Priestly Document*. The other, less learned, less rigid, less sophisticated, but perhaps the more authentically religious, is three or four centuries older and is known as the *Yahwist* (see pages 34ff.).

Chapters 2 (beginning with v. 4b: see pages 121ff.) and 3 of Genesis, which tell the origin of the world and of people and the joys and sorrow of the first couple, make up the introduction to the *Yahwist*. It then follows with the history of Cain and Abel (chap. 4) and the causes of the Flood (6:1–8); a part of the narrative of that cataclysm (6:9ff., interspersed with passages from the *Priestly Document*); the end of the Flood (8:8–12 and 20–22); the story of

Ham's misdeed (9:18–27); a large portion of the catalogue of the descendants of Noah (10:8–30, with some additions from the *Priestly Document*); and the history of the Tower of Babel (11:1–9). Thereafter, with the origins of Abraham (11:28–32 together with 12:1–4a), the second part of his work begins.

When we read this account from beginning to end, we quickly discern that its author built the episodes around one central idea that he wished to make the most of. Each passage recounts, all at once, an evil action, or misbehavior, and a miserable condition that results from it. Cain kills his brother and immediately is cursed, hunted down, condemned to a miserable wandering. The brutish Lamech enters the narration. Accordingly, humanity grows worse *"in malice and obstinately perverse inclinations,"* which provokes the Flood. That completed, Ham, son of Noah, fails gravely in showing respect for his father and is cursed in his offspring, who will be doomed to enslavement. Afterward, people, more and more overcome by megalomania, go so far as to want to erect *"a Tower that reaches to Heaven,"* and, their languages having suddenly multiplied, are no longer able to understand each other. . . . So we see that misconduct and the disappointment resulting from it spread out as time progresses: we move from individuals (Cain and Lamech) to nations, and to the human species and the universality of peoples, henceforth incapable of mutual understanding, ready to do harm, ready, in fact, to kill each other. And precisely this—here is what the *Yahwist* wants to bring out— will make God decide to prepare for Himself "a separate, special people," reserved to Him alone, irreproachable, in the person of the first Father of Israel: Abraham.

The *Yahwist* author's purpose stands in even starker relief if we set his text side by side with the account of the *Priestly Document*, which is preoccupied above all else with rankings and classifications, chronologies and sequences, ticking them off in the precise, successive division in days of the Creator's work (Genesis 1–2; see pages 123ff. above) and, beyond that, for example, in the lists of chapters 5 and 11ff. The *Priestly Document* is much less troubled about human evil. The election of Israel, which, for the *Yahwist*, is brought about by the problem of evil, is, for the *Priestly Document*, prefigured as far back in time as possible: at the conclusion of the Flood, God makes a *covenant* (see page 85) with Noah (11:1–17), and even earlier, with the first people He created (1:28–30). Before such serenity, the preoccupations of the *Yahwist* author, of an altogether different order, burst forth all the stronger: that profound conviction of our evil inclination and our miserable condition that obviously results from it. In his eyes, the earliest records of mankind show above all the growth of evil: both moral evil and the evil of unhappiness, its consequence.

We should bear this in mind when we read the text of the account of the "Original Sin."

THE ACCOUNT OF THE "ORIGINAL SIN"

Here, then, is a very literal translation of the account given in our Hebrew bibles. It takes up immediately following what we have read above (pages 121ff.) of the Yahwist history of Creation.

Primitive State of the First Couple	*(2:25) And both of them were naked, the man and his wife, but mutually they did not have the least sense of shame [about it].*
The Serpent Tempts Woman	*(3:1) But the Serpent, most cunning of all the wild animals Yahweh had made, said to the Woman: "Did God say: 'You shall not eat from any of the Garden's trees?'" (2) And the Woman answered the Serpent: "We can eat fruit from all the Garden's trees; (3) only of the fruit from the tree in the middle of the Garden God told us: 'You shall not eat from it! You shall not touch it! Otherwise, you will die!'" (4) And the Serpent replied to the Woman: "Not so! You will not die at all! (5) Only, God knows well that when you eat from it, your eyes will open and you will be like God, able to distinguish Good and Evil!"*
Woman Succumbs	*(6) And the Woman, seeing that [that] tree was pleasing to eat from and appealing to see, and advantageous for becoming [more] intelligent, took from its fruit, and ate from it; she also gave from it to her husband, who was with her, and he ate from it.*
The Results of the Error	*(7) From that moment, their eyes opened up, and they knew that they were naked: hence they fixed fig leaves together to make loincloths for themselves. (8) Then*

*they heard the sound [of the steps] of Yahweh-Elohim,
Who was walking in the Garden in the evening breeze:
and Man and his wife hid themselves among the trees
of the Garden. (9) But Yahweh-Elohim summoned
Man: "Where are you?" He said to him. (10) And he
answered: "I heard the sound [of] Your [steps] in the
Garden, and I was afraid, because I am naked. Therefore I hid!" (11) "But," He answered [him], "who told
you that you were naked? Can you have eaten from
[this] Tree of which I had forbidden you to eat?" (12)
And Man answered: "The Woman You placed next to
me, she [is the one who] gave me from the Tree [of
which] I ate!" (13) Then Yahweh-Elohim said to the
Woman: "What did you do?" And then the Woman:
"It is the Serpent [who] enticed me," said she, "and I
ate!"*

The Punishment

(14) *And Yahweh-Elohim said to the Serpent:
"Because you did that:
Be cursed among all animals and wild beasts!
You shall move on your belly,
And the earth will feed you
All the days of your life.
(15) I will establish hostility between you and woman,
Between your offspring and hers:
They shall strike at your head,
And you, you shall strike at their heel!"
(16) Then He said to Woman:
"I shall increase your pain in labor:
In travail you shall bring your children into the world!
Your desire shall carry you to your man,
But he shall oppress you!"
(17) Then He said to Man: "Because you listened to
the call of your wife and ate from the Tree of which I
had commanded: 'Don't eat of it!'
Let the earth be cursed because of you:
[Only] in exhausting toil shall you draw food from it,
All the days of your life.
(18) It will bring forth only thorns and thistles.*

*And you shall have for food [nothing but] the herb of
the field.
(19) You shall [not] eat bread [but] by the sweat of
your face,
Until your return to the Earth,
Because from the Earth you were drawn!
Yes! You are clay, and you will be clay again!"
(20) Then Man gave his wife the name Hawwa: for she
is the Mother of all the Living [Haw]. (21) And Yahweh-
Elohim made garments of skin and clothed them.*

The First Couple
Expelled from
the Garden

*(22) Then Yahweh-Elohim said [to Himself]: "So Man
has become like one of Us in matters of discernment of
Good and Evil. Let him not go further, and take, in
addition, from the Tree-of-Life, eat from it and live
forever!" (23) Therefore He drove him out of the
Garden of Eden, to till the earth from which he was
made. (24) And having expelled Man, he placed the
Cherubim and the Flame-of-the-burning-Sword on the
East of the Garden of Eden to guard the way toward
the Tree-of-Life.*

The opening part of the *Priestly Document* finishes with the first half of
verse 2:4: *"Such are the generations of Heaven and Earth when they were
created."* ("Generations" is a frequently recurring expression in the *Document*—in Genesis 5:1; 6:9; 10:1; 11:10, 27, etc.—and can be understood as
"chronicles" or "charts.") At that point the compilers brought in the text
of the *Yahwist*, which is recognizable by its language, its vocabulary (for
instance, it uses the Hebrew verb *'asa*, "to make," where the *Priestly Document* prefers *bara*—see note 21 on page 145), its lively narrative style, its
anthropomorphic, good-natured, almost intimate way of bringing God on
the scene.

The *Priestly Document* narrates just the Creation; the *Yahwist*, on the
other hand, develops in its sequence a double history: that of Creation and
that of "Paradise," the theater of man's first gambols. I have stated before
(pages 120ff.) where the two accounts of Creation differ. If we carefully study
the text and its unfolding, we soon understand how secondary this episode
of Creation is in the *Yahwist* author's eyes. In contrast to the author of the

Priestly Document, he shows no interest at all in the universe in itself: sky and earth, light and darkness, the sea (which he does not even mention: see page 121) and the stars, the assemblage of living beings. . . . The only thing that holds his attention is, by all evidence, the first human couple: he would even have it that the animals are created in order to make this couple complete, a goal the Creator does not actually reach until the end, when He forms woman. And the *Yahwist* author neither looks upon nor treats these two complementary beings as part of the cosmos, but rather considers them for what they are and what they do as actors of a particular drama that he wants to acquaint us with in what follows. In short, the *Yahwist* account of the Creation has virtually no *raison d'être* except to produce the two protagonists of the "Paradise" story.

This story, to which the *Priestly Document* makes no allusion at all and which the *Yahwist* sews and enmeshes into the history of Creation, was, in all likelihood, independent in origin. For one thing, the central theme of the "test" (here the prohibition against touching the fruit of a certain tree) must inevitably be seen as an independent theme that does not apply to the first man only: it reappears, for instance, within the confines of the Bible itself, in the story of Job. But above all, between the two joined accounts are dissonances that could not be explained if the accounts were one whole at the outset or were compositions worked out in balance with each other. Most probably, the Creation story implies that man was placed in the world as he is and always has been: a mortal, ordained to toil; and woman, by nature subject to the pain of childbirth. (Of course, the *Priestly Document* does not dream of actually alluding to these axioms.) The "Paradise" story, however, had to present these particularities as later misfortunes, the result of divine punishment. Likewise, this history must have presupposed the existence of other animals and even other human beings: this is why in 2:15 man is placed in God's Garden "to guard it"; but the fusion with the Creation story is brought about in such a way as to make the generation of animals (and *a fortiori* other people) an event subsequent to the appointing of the Garden. Thus 2:15 becomes unintelligible: guarding against *whom?*

If the *Yahwist* author deliberately added the story of Paradise to the story of Creation, he did so because in his eyes it presented something of major significance. What this episode recounts is clear to every reader of the text. But what is its authentic meaning, the meaning its author wished to convey?

THE SIGNIFICANCE OF THE STORY OF THE "ORIGINAL SIN"

To arrive at that authentic meaning of the "Original Sin" narration, we must see it in the setting of the *Yahwist* as an entire work. (That work has been summarized above.) If human vicissitudes until Abraham, in accordance with the *Yahwist* author's thinking, are above all characterized by the development of human perversion and the disasters it brought with it, it becomes obvious that the *Yahwist*'s prologue, 2:4b–3, aims principally to underline the point of departure and the origin of this fatal propensity toward evil, and how man, from the beginning of his history, found himself inclined to vice and hence doomed to misfortune. This is the reason why the *Yahwist* combined the story of "Original Sin" with the story of beginnings.

How does the *Yahwist* present the human condition at the end of chapter 3? From that moment on, man *"knows Good and Evil."* This is to say that he knows evil also, in addition to the good. Upon leaving the hands of his Creator, he knew nothing but the good—as the *Priestly Code*, for its part, emphasizes, thereby rendering a cardinal maxim of the religion of Israel: at the moment when the Creator has accomplished his work, *"all"* the content of this work *"was good," "every thing"* was *"a good thing!"* (1:4, 8, 10, 12, 18, 21, 25; and, finally, in verse 31, where *"all was very good!"*). But in the ancient Semitic languages, unlike our own, the term "knowledge" never designates a purely objective operation of the mind; the heart is always involved, and knowledge always implies both participation in its object and power over it. Consequently, for man, "knowing evil" is, at the same time, becoming conscious of vicious instincts that emerge in him and, under their influence, being inclined to do evil; it is like what we call a "bad streak" in a spoiled child; it is not only the ability to do evil but having a weakness for misconduct and finding oneself leaning toward it. Thus, by the end of chapter 3, man has acquired troubling and wicked impulses to which henceforth he will more easily give in. This is the reason *he is "afraid"* at that indecent display—shocking, and always prohibited in Semitic tradition, especially in Israel—that came with nudity: from now on, he senses it as potentially evil and shameful.

Besides all this, he is unhappy. Now the most normal acts of his life, such as eating and procreating, are indissolubly accompanied by pain and trouble; he finds woman (in a land that considered her a simple "property" of her husband) tyrannized by the man toward whom her heart goes out. And finally, now man and woman both are handed over to a miserable existence that ends in death. As we understand all too well, reading what is related in the *Yahwist*, and as each of us knows on his own, this portrait of our first parents is the portrait of all their descendants: they are our precedent, their destiny the blueprint of ours, and we receive by birth the same malediction that befell them, just as we receive their ease in doing wrong.

To a mind both supremely religious and supremely clear-sighted, to the mind of the *Yahwist* author, this distressing state of affairs posed an inevitable problem: how did man arrive at the condition in which he finds himself? Was he like this *ab origine*, or did he *become* this way? And in the latter case, by whose doing?

That he might have been like this from the beginning, no one faithful to Yahweh could have professed: God would not have been Himself had He not created everything "good, very good," and irreproachable. Man, who was born faultless, now finding himself in his perverted state, doomed to misfortune, could only have entered into this condition on his own. This is what the *Yahwist* author wants us to learn when he tells the story of the "Original Sin": how, by an act of hubris, excess, in presumptuous desire to surmount his own destiny and *"become like God"* (particularly unforgivable excess in the eyes of an ancient Semite, who held a vivid sense of distance between the divine and the human),[1] man lost his original innocence, became laden with wrong instincts and a propensity to give in to them, and, in chastisement for this premier deviation from his real nature, entered upon a distressing and painful existence.

It was to explain this passage from a flawless, halcyon state (see the opening of chap. 2) to the malign, misfortunate condition that is always ours (the end of chap. 3 and the entire history that follows) that the *Yahwist* placed at the very beginning of his work, and combined with the recital of Creation itself, the misadventure of the "Original Sin."

THE IMPORTANCE OF THIS HISTORY

In what order of truth does this history belong? For if we take it just as it is written, it consists of deeds reported, of events communicated to us. Could we consider it in the way it has been taught for a very long time—and as

---

1. It has often been asked whether the "First Sin" has something to do with sexual life and its taboos: an altogether absurd question! See, on this topic, "Le premier couple," *L'histoire*, January 1984, 38–41.

many still accept it—as *historical* in the proper sense of the word, which refers to circumstances that truly and really came about as we are told?

We are required to go beyond the obvious answer to this question.

An instant of sober reflection of course makes it clear that the account of the *Yahwist*, the story of Creation as well as of the "Original Sin," could not have anything *historical* about it. But beyond this, neither can we resort to the notion of a "primitive tradition" come to us in the *Yahwist*'s account. Some have done just that. But we really cannot seriously join in their opinion either, for after all, if the author of the *Yahwist* is to be a historian, then, keeping to the conditions *sine qua non* of history, his data concerning events he relates would have to come ultimately from witnesses (whether immediate eyewitnesses or not), and we are speaking of events that would have occurred at the very scene of humanity's origin; so, given the million years or so that anthropologists can no longer do without as the time-span of our race, we would need an intrepidity, a naiveté that is given only to the insane or to those who are hallucinating, if we wished to avail ourselves of the idea of *historical* truth handed down through the *Yahwist*.

There has also been talk, in connection with these early chapters of the Bible, of a "popular history," without anyone actually defining this genre of literature or this type of knowledge but with an agreement, no doubt, that some sort of authentic residue persists within the seismic tangle of detail. This is but a way of sidestepping the problem. To the extent any such "popular history" is taken as *history*, no matter how indirectly or with how many reservations, the baleful question of testimony and authentication will present itself once more.

And let us not leave unmentioned another apologia for the historical truth of Genesis chapters 2 and 3. It was once a convention, and is still to be found, outliving its usefulness wheresoever. According to it, the author of those chapters was the beneficiary—for want of human witness—of a divine "revelation." In one way of looking at the world such recourse is normal and inevitable: it is, one might say, a matter of temperament. That devotees might appeal to such an expedient, with that mixture of faith and credulity that is special to them, may pass. But obviously, no one of sober mind could take refuge in it if he wished to stay in objective reality and be grounded in knowledge and understanding.

Hence we have to renounce every claim of historicity in the accounts of Creation and "Paradise" and turn elsewhere. One of my old teachers often said that we do not know our own house as long as we do not leave it. So let us stick our nose outside for a moment and, to stay with the natural milieu of the Bible—which is the ancient Near East—cast a glance at the vast religious literature of Mesopotamia. Here are some verses from a celebrated account of the origins of the world and of people, *The Poem of the Supersage* (*Atrahasis* I, 204ff.; see note 1 on page 4 above):

> *Then the god Enki opened his mouth*
> *And spoke to the Great-gods:*
> *"A god will be sacrificed . . .*
> *And with his flesh and blood*
> *The goddess Nintu will intermix clay:*
> *In this way a union will be made of god and man*
> *Joined in the clay [of the human prototype]"*[2]

The narrative then tells us how this plan is carried out, step by step, giving birth to the human species.

Although in context and style the *event*—the event of man's creation—is presented after the manner of history, no one would take this account as actually historical. Beyond the word-by-word narration, we soon see a more profound teaching, one of a different order, which we understand without difficulty if only we read it as it should be read: the author explains to us very well indeed how, in spite of our body of "clay"—miserable and defective— we have by our origin something superior in our matter, something, in short, of the "divine." This account is not a history; it is what is known as *myth*.

A myth is an account created to respond to the great questions people always pose when they reflect on their origins, on the purpose and the fate of our universe and our human race, and on the great riddlesome phenomena that show themselves to us everywhere. If I am asked what a thunderstorm is, I will invoke humidity, cloud formation, the rapid ascension of clouds, their simultaneous electric and pluviometric charge, and other abstractions. A Loreto, an Indian of Peru, will answer the same question this way: "The thunderstorm is a giant, who has legs that are longer than his body, his shape tall and thin, with ears like a vampire's: the lightning is the movement of his ears. The rumbling of the thunder is the force of his feet when he runs from side to side. He causes the thunderstorm when he fishes for the boa, which is his food and which he calls eel. Then he takes enormous strides, and that is why the thunder sounds from one side to the other" (De Wavrin, *Moeurs et coutumes des Indiens de l'Amérique du Sud*, 615 n). Did the narrator or

---

2. The complete text of this translated passage can be found in *Lorsque les dieux faisaient l'homme*, 537.

his informants *see* the giant in question, who is so meticulously described? Obviously not! They have never ascertained his existence or observed his movements: all that has been said, they infer, they deduce. For, having no cognizance of free causes outside the human realm, they cannot conceive of thunderstorm, which rumbles wherever and whenever, other than as if provoked by a human agent. And given the enormity of the phenomenon, they are forced to posit a "giant" who is commensurate. And so forth. By means of "calculated imaginings" they construct their tale on the very data of the problem they attempt to solve, like the writers of fables, who, imagining their little legends, do their calculating in view of the morality that they want to inculcate into them.

Hence, a myth, at least at the moment of its birth, is not a gratuitous story, pure fantasy meant just for the sake of pleasure or art or entertainment: it is the response to a question, the solution to a problem; it is always an *explanation*—in short, it depends upon "philosophy," if that is understood as the proceedings our mind follows (to the extent that in order to ask and answer, we do not place ourselves in the orbit of "science") when it "seeks to know" and to unravel the great interrogations that rise up in us before the world and ourselves. This kinship between myth and philosophy is so natural, so clear, that the first philosophy of our world, worked out by the Greeks, is famously the direct descendant of Greek mythology. In their mythological theogonies, of which the paradigm is Hesiod's, in the eighth century B.C.E., we can already see, not only the great questions and the essential problems that will occupy all later Greek philosophers, but even the general spirit within which they will each give their responses: integral unity of the universe, divine and human; oneness of all things in principle; the fundamental importance of the process of becoming, while the absolute origin is not even considered. The first Greek philosophers still preserved, each in his system, elements that were really of a mythical nature, to which they seem to begin to attach a universal and abstract validity: the Water of Thales; the Chaos of Anaximander; the Air of Anaximenes; the Love and Hate in Empedocles . . . and even Plato would compose myths to serve as a vehicle, when dialectical explanations must have seemed insufficient or too complicated to lay out clearly.

If I insist on the proximity of myth and "philosophy"—without denying the profound divergencies and the different mental levels on which they function—it is because their convergencies enable us to comprehend what the truth of myth consists in, or rather in what order of knowledge we should look for this truth.

It is not the order of history; that is a settled case. Myth is not in the least the statement of a witness or his interpreter; its purpose is by no means to inform us of a recorded event as such or to attest to it. It follows that its truth is not to be sought in the congruity between the events it tells of and a series of extranormal occurrences it may enumerate. There has never been a giant who set off the tumult of thunderstorm while fishing for his enormous eel, and there has never been a council of gods to arrange for the fabrication of man from a lump of clay soaked in divine blood. The sequence of occurrences reported by the mythical recital is, in the language of logicians, accidental to the truth of myth: that truth is elsewhere.

In the thought process of its authors, myth intends to materialize intuitions, conjectures, ideas, which by themselves are unembodied and conceptual. Its goal is to outfit them palpably, visibly, with movement and drama, in order to communicate them in the realm of the imagination, and not in the abstract. It does not give statements of provable fact, but explanations that proceed by a story to suggest a sequence of happenings and circumstances, producing the state of matters in question, which yields enough sense to satisfy our desire to know: it is a "likely story," as Plato wrote (*Timaeus* 29d). Because the author of *Atrahasis* was convinced there existed in man, beyond the terrestrial and perishable body, something higher, something that went beyond his natural condition, he wove his own story of the blood of a god that had hardened along with the clay (see page 171 above). Taken literally, it is a narration we have before us; but in reality, the narration, the story, is the *bearer* of an interpretation of the world. Incapable as yet of abstract and scientific thought, given entirely to the power of their imagination, and having no other medium to enlighten themselves by than the concrete, the individualized, and the fictitious, the authors of myths made use of the means at their disposal to conceive imaginary scenes that fit the data that perplexed them—as we have seen in examples already cited—and to shed light on their uncertitude. As to the stories they told, they did not pretend that anyone in the world had "verified" them, whether by sight or by hearsay, as would the author of an authentic historical account; their only thought was that without the story they told, or something like it, the question that was posed would remain unanswered.

This, I trust, will explain why I spoke of "deduction" and of "philosophy," contraposing them to attestation and history. In *that* order of truth, the truth of a myth can be grasped: it is a matter of knowledge, not as the situation and its events have been accurately presented, as we like to have it, but as the *idea*, materialized and conveyed to our imagination by that state of affairs and that sequence of scenes, gives an adequate account of the problem that is posed. On the level of history, the Babylonian myth of the creation of man does not have any claim to truth; however, "philosophically " speaking, it is correct, to the extent that the intuition it clothes and carries across is true—at least in the eyes of its authors and listeners—to the extent that man, when compared to the other livings beings, indeed contains concealed in himself, by nature, something superior and sublime, bringing him closer to the "gods" (as those were imagined at the time).

To return, in a final assessment, to the account of "Original Sin," it is perfectly clear that we find ourselves face-to-face with a true myth. On the one hand, we are under the obligation to exclude all historicity from it. On the other hand, it was written in a time and a cultural milieu where appeal to myth was universally accepted. In the absence of conceptual tools, there could not possibly be any other recourse but "calculated imaginings" to respond to such high and universal questions.

It follows that the explanation of the perverted and unfortunate human state as a result of the first couple's ancient refusal to obey God, such as the *Yahwist* author places at the outset of his first account, is mythological. This means that the author's mindfulness does not bear so much on the minutiae of the narrative, in its story line and details, which in that case he would have proved and guaranteed authentic, as on the vision of things, the teachings, the *idea* of which this story is the vehicle. This explanation is not historical in nature, like an attribution of a war to the economic, ideological, and political events that preceded and unleashed it. It is to be argued that our explanation is metaphysical in nature, inasmuch as only the reasoning mind is at work in it, without any concern for experience and verification. More precisely yet, let us say it is of a *religious* nature, for our explanation first appeals to a supernatural world that is thought to animate ours—a little like a way of accounting for a war by attributing it to an altogether different series of causes: forgetfulness or disdain for the priority of the divine; forgetfulness of solidarity among people that must prevail over private interests; forgetfulness of the detachment from the material goods of this world; or forgetfulness of forgiveness of offenses. . . .

The *Yahwist* author's profound religious conviction conveyed in the story of "Original Sin" is that, if people are what they are, are as we know them from the dawn of time—inclined toward evil and burdened with troubles—it is all through their own fault, and not by the will of their Creator or as a result of the conditions in which they were brought forth; that the fault consisted from the beginning in prideful disobedience, man's excess in wanting to go beyond his natural condition—which is present, in fact, at the root of every revolt against the established order; and that this same sin, the cause of all evil, must go back to the very origin of our kind: no, certainly not at his first appearance, because man could first appear from the hands of his Maker only perfectly made and irreproachable, healthy and happy, but since it appears universal, inveterate, and rooted in each of us as if inherited in our nature, we must attribute it to the very first representatives of our line. For it is beyond doubt, in the account of the *Yahwist*, that the actors in the drama are indeed the *first human couple* created by God, our prototypes and original parents.

So he told his story to show how he saw and felt that fundamental "fault," in the tonality of myth and in "calculated imagination" rather than inaccessible abstraction and theory. This is how he gave his interpretation of our natural shortcomings and evil; he knit the myth of "Paradise" and the original "Fall" into his myth of Creation.

Did he, in his meditation, create this added myth by himself, or did he borrow it from elsewhere? We know nothing about that. Some problems that scholars have singled out in the text (and that it would be tedious to discuss in the present context) allow us to suppose that the *Yahwist* author might have used an existing story, adapting it to his own views—just as the author of Job went ahead to find a story, one that was current in his time (see page 98), and adjust it to his views. This much is certain: to this day, no one has convincingly shown the least trace of a comparable account, even in the inexhaustible mythological treasures of ancient Mesopotamia,[3] by which the *Yahwist* author or his predecessors could have been inspired—even in the way the authors of the *exordium* to the *Priestly Document* borrowed something, no matter how indirectly, from the Babylonian cosmogonies (see pages 155ff.). One should not conclude that nothing of the kind will ever be found. Here and now, however, it is incumbent on us to recognize in the author of the *Yahwist*, whether or not he borrowed anything from anywhere, an originality that we already recognized in his version of the origins of the world and the Creation (pages 148ff.).

If he borrowed a myth, was it because he considered its text veracious—or, let us say, "historically" true? To my mind, this question, which I have heard more than once, is completely useless. First of all, because there is not

---

3. Although some authors have referred in this sense either to the legend of Adapa or to the anthropogenic section of "The Epic of Creation" (6, 11–34), they are mistaken. See "Les présumés parallèles mésopotamiens du 'péché originel' biblique," pp. 10–16 of "Le péché en Mésopotamie ancienne," in *Recherches et documents du Centre Thomas More*, no. 43 (1984), 1–16.

a soul who could answer it with any certainty. But above all, because the answer would in effect be of no interest. Whatever his personal adherence may have been, it is at least certain that the *Yahwist* author related this story much less (if at all) for its narrative contents than for its explanatory power. Such is the case with all myths.

If he placed this myth at the opening of his work, it was because he could use it to frame his characteristic "philosophy of history." For (as has no doubt become clear) at least in the first part of his book, and in spite of outer appearances, the *Yahwist* author is much less a "chronicler" than—in his way and with the means at hand—what we would call a "philosopher of history" or, still more accurately, a "theologian of history." He searches less for authentic details in the unfolding of the past than for the crucial moments on the religious level. His temperament seeks, in history, the trajectory and the great supernatural forces that guide it, imperceptible to the vulgar or nonreligious or those ignorant of the God of Israel, but which a Yahweh faithful whose spirit is subtle and penetrating can see behind the moving puppetlike beings that fill the world.

As the first writer of a religious history of his people (see pages 34ff.), the *Yahwist* author perfectly represents the height to which profound faith in Yahweh could lift the best minds of Israel in his time (see page 38): not only that they took Him for their only God well before any accession of a pure and absolute monotheism; not only that they conferred on Him a role that was already cosmic (see page 36)—over nature and people, whose Creator they knew Him to be; but that their sense of His perfection would not let them see in Him the first source of the evil they experienced here below. From the "physical" evils, the pain and trouble strewn through our life, to the most cruel and irremediable of all, death, it was He, certainly, who assigned these to people, but in just punishment for the moral evil they hastened to introduce as soon as they were placed in the world: *they alone did that, on their own account.* As much later the author of Ecclesiastes (pages 179ff.) would write: *"And I reached this conclusion: God made human beings straight, but they are the ones who looked for all kinds of perversion!"* (7:29; see page 195). Yahweh would not have been Himself if His own Justice had not compelled Him to punish misconduct.

The story of the "Original Sin" makes it all plain. By means of faith and veneration for his God, the *Yahwist* author reflected and became the first to understand what history demonstrated, and continues to demonstrate, every day, in cruel and unbearable fashion: man is responsible for his own misery. And he surely knows it; surely he must guard against these fatal ways; but he falls again and again, does not wait to plunge again into adversity and despair, as if some ancient atavism of weakness and propensity to do evil inclined him always to it, without ever allowing him to find a remedy in himself against this native weakness. Thus, well beyond the word-for-word story of the Garden—the forbidden fruit, the Serpent-tempter, the woman who succumbs, the man who follows her example—here is the profound and eternal truth the ancient *Yahwist* author discovered and passed on to us. And who would contradict him?

THE PROBLEM OF EVIL IN ISRAEL

Ecclesiastes is an obscure and difficult book; it is perhaps
the most enigmatic book of the entire Hebrew Bible. The
Jews themselves have held this impression for a long time:
according to the Talmud (Shabbath 30b), *"The Sages
wanted to hide the book of Qoheleth because its words
dispute each other."*[1]

   Ordinarily, the modern reader does not lend a great deal
of importance to it. Perhaps that is because, under the
influence of the work's leitmotiv—"all is vanity!"—he

1. Qoheleth is the Hebrew name of the Book of Ecclesiastes; see page 183.

glimpses the text through an indistinct feeling of universal pessimism, which is enough for him. It could also be, if he is a believer, that he has made it a habit to regard the "Holy Books," above all the nonhistorical books, as a collection of infallible pronouncements, in each of which by itself he may find the greatest spiritual benefit but which in their entirety do not interest him at all.

And yet, each book has a meaning *in its entirety*, a sense that is much more important than that of the propositions of which it consists, for it alone can reveal to us the real and definitive message of the author. And in the case of Ecclesiastes, the message is of considerable value, for the book, I think, deals with the problem of evil, which everyone knows is fundamental in the realm of religious psychology and the history of religions.

To gain an understanding of the book, it is first necessary to recall the way in which this problem presented itself to the Israelites and the reactions it provoked from them. It is quite a history, and a long one, and in order to follow it, as with any other process, we must start from the beginning. So although it is always dangerous to schematize history, where everything lies in details and nuances, let us proceed with a brief summary.

To religious minds, the recognition of evil may pose two distinct intellectual problems. The first is relatively simple: *What is its origin?* The second is formidable: *How can we reconcile it with the existence of God?*

At first, the Israelites asked themselves only the first question, and the definitive answer was given by the *Yahwist* author in Genesis 2:4b–3 (see pages 164ff.). For him, the "physical" evil—

"You shall [not] eat bread [but] by the sweat of your face,
Until your return to the Earth,"

(3:19)

"In travail you shall bring your children into the world!
Your desire shall carry you to your man,
But he shall oppress you!"

(3:16)

—and the "moral" evil, all the distorted instincts and their results, so powerfully evoked in the line *"From that moment, their eyes opened up, and they knew that they were naked"* (3:7)—both are explained by the transgression of the first man, who set into motion in human nature, upon receiving a divine punishment, that loss of balance from which all our evils proceed. This idea, as we know, is always part of Christian ideology.

However, this idea leaves unanswered the second and terrible question: how could God want, or permit, the existence of evil?

It required centuries for the Israelites to be able to formulate this question in all its ramifications.

For a long time, they perceived only the aspect of divine Justice, which brought retribution and was vengeful in nature, and they only asked themselves how it could be God's will that a just person be miserable and an impious one prosper.

The conviction of the absolute Justice of Yahweh had been introduced into the religious ideology of Israel by the teachings of the Prophets, codified in Deuteronomy, in precisely this form of reward and retribution. After Amos, Hosea, and Isaiah, there could be no more conception of personal saintliness or personal rebellion against the Law (except in the sense that happiness or unhappiness would follow), for the principle of divine Justice was formulated in these Prophets, and in the *Deuteronomist*, for the *people* of Israel *as such*, which, at the time, was the immediate subject of the Covenant with Yahweh and the religion founded on the Covenant (see pages 53ff. above).

With the Exile, however, the people had ceased to exist in that way, and the collective nature of Israelite religion had become individual (see page 80). *"You shall not say any more: 'The fathers ate sour grapes, but their children's teeth are set on edge!' In the future, only the sinner himself shall die!"* (Jeremiah 31:29, and Ezekiel 18:2–4).

A transposition of such magnitude from the social to the personal realm could only pose the mighty problem of the relations between moral integrity and destiny. When it was a question of the entire nation, there was no real difficulty in maintaining that without fail God would provide happiness if it obeyed him and unhappiness if it did not. For a people has a future, and it is always possible to hope for the fulfillment of promises. But an individual's life is short. And in the view of the Israelites of the time, as we know, death meant the end of everything: after that, nothing remained but the *nefesh*, a dubious and shadowy ghostlike remainder of all a person had been in his life, but which, now in the Sheol of the netherworld, deprived of the vitality and the power that was given to an individual by the *ruah*, the divine "Breath" lent to him, could lead but a lusterless existence, numb and, most especially, negative.

Hence a new expectation arose: that divine Justice reward the good and punish the impious during the brief span of their lives.

Here the difficulties began. For at that time, as in ours, no one could give credence to a constant and absolute parallel between moral or religious values and human fates, and the lot of miscreants, unbelievers, and libertines could sometimes—nay, often!—appear more enviable than that of honest and saintly folks.

Quite a few echoes of discussions on this subject are preserved in the biblical literature after the Exile, especially in the Psalms, the Book of Proverbs, and the prophetic writings. The thesis that keeps coming back is that of the "theologians" of the period, who obstinately held to the traditional equation that sanctity equals happiness (and vice versa) and misery equals impiety (and vice versa). Even in the time of Christ, a question like that in John 9:2— *"Master, who sinned, he or his parents, so that he was born blind?"*—shows us the persistency of this theorem.

The only one who saw the problem clearly was the author of the Book of Job (see page 98 above), who, on this ground, deserves to be considered a religious thinker of the very first rank (see page 99). In his work, he begins with a typical case, taken from a story that was current, of a man who is undeniably just and perfect (God himself states it!) and who nevertheless finds himself in the worst straits. We are presented with the sufferer and his three friends as they argue the situation. The friends, representing all conformists, conclude that Job's downfall must be due to immorality, while Job in his misery, knowing he is blameless, cries out his innocence and calls on God to account for the sufferings he undergoes. These vehement and wearisome confrontations—like all human discussion—lead nowhere. But in the end, God speaks, and it is He who shows the situation in its true light. He confines Himself, in a splendid, powerful speech, to some glimpses of His work as Creator and Preserver of the World. But this truth, simple and overwhelming, emerges: that He, the Master of the Universe, is so far beyond human thought that before Him, and *whatever He does*, one can only fall silent and marvel: what He does can only be admired, even, and above all, when human beings cannot understand it.

Basically, a century before Plato and through pure religious intuition, the author of Job posited an order of things absolutely separate from the human, in the absolute transcendence of God: "I am not in need of a God whom I comprehend!" His contemporaries were very far from understanding him; the edition of his text that we have seems to bear traces of their clerical and narrow-minded revisions. But in spite of what they may have done to it, there is no other Israelite religious "solution" to the problem they and he were facing.

It seems to me that, as it happens, the author of Ecclesiastes took up this idea again, to apply it not only to the problem of human fate and suffering but to that of evil in all its ramifications. Doing so, he became the first in Israel to raise that issue and solve it.

THE BOOK OF ECCLESIASTES

Before reading the book of this author from the point of view I have raised, let us attempt, insofar as we can, to portray him and make him accessible.

The language of Ecclesiastes is filled with Aramaisms, and it is only by approximately five hundred years before our era that Aramaic began to spread through the Near East, gradually superseding Akkadian in the East and Hebrew in the West. By this criterion alone, although it is neither the only one nor the most vital, we are able to date the composition of Ecclesiastes as considerably late in the postexilic period, at least two centuries later than Job. Perhaps it was written by 250 B.C.E., and perhaps even more recently.

The work appears to be attributed to Solomon—*"The words of the Qoheleth, son of David, king in Jerusalem"* (1:1)—but when we look closely, we find it is no more by Solomon than the *Phaedo* or the *Timaeus* are by Socrates. As Plato uses Socrates, our author, by a literary fiction, places his own ideas in the mouth of Solomon, whom he calls "the Qoheleth," which means something like "Head of the (Learned) Assembly," "Teacher," or even "Professor." For Solomon, as he was imagined at that time, fit the project of our author very well. Tradition had made Solomon, who in reality was not all that interesting, at one and the same time into the paradigm of great kings and fortunate mortals and the sage of sages. This is the personage whom our author presents as the bearer of a judgment on life and the universe: who else could speak with such experience and authority? For the rest, the author is careful to underscore the literary fiction by occasionally bringing out his own presence with a discreet *"so says Qoheleth"* (1:2; 7:27; 12:8; see also the end: 12:9ff.).

He gives no other detail about himself, and we shall no doubt be forever ignorant of his identity.

The fact remains, nevertheless, that upon reading his book, we feel greatly tempted, first of all, to attribute to him a remarkable obscurity of mind, for the absence of order in the propositions that are brought together is evident at a glance. This is the greatest difficulty in the work: the Jews themselves, as we have mentioned, remained perplexed at its "contradictions."

Especially from chapter 4 onward, the line of thought is subject to surprising jumps. For instance, in the midst of bitter reflections on the established

powers (4:13–16 and 5:7), why do we suddenly find counsel on proper deport-
ment in the Temple? In the course of a metaphysical flight on divine omnipo-
tence (4:10–13 and 7:13), why a series of warnings of this caliber: *A good
reputation is better than a good ointment?*

One is reminded, strictly speaking, of a collection of *proverbs* (as we find
in the canonical book by that name, or in Ecclesiasticus, known as the
Wisdom of Jesus the Son of Sirach). But after each "break," one rediscovers
the thread, the same words, the turns of phrase, the ideas. We are forced to
acknowledge that there is one plan and a consistent text. Only, this text has
interruptions, and, curiously, the interruptions are sentences in verse form
(like the classical Hebrew proverbs), while the rest is mostly in prose.

Another major difficulty is that four or five passages (all in prose) explicitly
contradict the plainest affirmations made by the book, and exactly on the
issue of divine retributive Justice. The writer strongly and frequently raises
his voice against the existence of a relationship between merit and fate. What,
then, is a proposition like the following doing in his book? *"God confers
wisdom, knowledge, and joy on the saintly man, while on the sinner He lays
the burden of accumulating and piling up only for the benefit of him whom
He judges perfect!"* (2:26a).

From this hopeless state of affairs in the text, the only way out in good
historical method is to suppose that the work has been altered—corrected
and provided with glosses. Treatment of this sort is not unlikely in a literature
like the Bible, which was originally anonymous and handwritten, and examples
of such revision are numerous and familiar (especially in Job). It is no surprise
at all in the Book of Ecclesiastes, since—notoriously—the book's admission
into the Jewish biblical canon (see note 21 on page 90), which of course made
it an official text and protected it from such operations, was delayed for
perhaps three hundred years.[2]

Hence, I believe that before we can read the text of Ecclesiastes soundly,
a critical "purge" is in order. Without any great illusions about the results of
this purification or any other (conjecture is the congenital vice of history, and
a certain modesty and skepticism with respect to our evidence—even while
we doggedly hold to it as long as it is not proved erroneous—is the prime
virtue of the historian), I would not swear that the text refined by whatever
critic is authentically the text written by the ancient master. It does seem to me,
nevertheless, that, when thus pruned, he has a chance to present his thought
more clearly to us—us, especially, who are at such a distance from him.

2. Ecclesiastes and the Song of Songs, no doubt the last books to be included in the Jewish
biblical canon, were not accepted into it until the end of the first century C.E.

This then is the method, at the end of a long and painstaking study, by which one tries to restore the text that the author of Qoheleth felt compelled to write; the later glosses and corrections have been set aside and are indicated in footnotes. Let me repeat that although each exclusion is based on sound and solid reasons that could be listed one by one in voluminous commentary, in the final analysis the whole still remains a matter of conjecture. This rendition (which we could justify in all its details only with wearisome footnotes) "sticks" as much as possible to the Hebrew text, but equally takes care to avoid being heavy and mechanical: a translator has to rethink the text in his own language if he does not want to be replaced by one of those electronic gadgets that now—not too successfully—try to do his work.

THE TEXT

Theme	1:1	*The words of the Qoheleth, son of David, king in Jerusalem.*
	2	*Vanity of vanities, said the Qoheleth, vanities of vanities, all is vanity.*
	3	*What is left to man after all the labor he takes on here below?*
The Movements of Nature are Without Purpose	4	*A generation passes, a generation comes forth: but the world does not change.*
	5	*The sun rises, the sun sets: after which, it rushes toward the horizon to rise again.*
	6	*The wind turns to the South, then returns toward the North, and goes on changing ceaselessly; and thereafter, it resumes its rounds.*
	7	*The rivers flow to the sea, and the sea is never filled; yet, the rivers continue all the same flowing there without cease.*
	8	*All discourse is endless: but one never succeeds in saying everything. The eye has never seen enough, the ear is never filled with hearing.*
	9	*Whatever has happened will happen again, what has been done will be done all over again: nothing is new under the sun!*

10   *When one says of something: "Now, there is some-thing new!" it had already come about, nevertheless, in all the ages that preceded us.*

11   *But one does not keep in one's memory former times. And moreover, the future itself will not be remembered by those who come afterward.*

"Philosophy"
Is Useless and
Saddening

12   *I, the Qoheleth, have been king of Israel, in Jerusalem,*

13   *And, by means of wisdom, I devoted myself to the study and research of all that goes on under the sky—a wretched activity that God leaves to people to busy themselves with.*

14   *I have reflected on all the acts that are performed under the sun: they are all vanity and pursuit of wind.*

15   *"What is twisted cannot be straightened.*
     No value can be set on what is lacking!"

16   *And inwardly, I concluded: "This is how I exceeded in wisdom all those who went before me, ruling over Jerusalem; thus my heart has come to know much wisdom and science,*

17   *and thus I pained my spirit in the study of wisdom and science, of folly and nonsense: and now I realize that that too is chasing wind!"*

18   *For the more wisdom one has, the more misery one has, and whoever increases his knowledge adds to his suffering.*

Knowing
How to Live
Is
No Better
Than
Senselessness

2:1   *Then I said to myself: "Come! I shall try happiness! Taste pleasure!" That too was vanity.*

2   *And I said of laughing: "Senseless!" and of happiness: "To what purpose?"*

3   *I resolved to accustom my flesh to wine—without my heart ceasing its practice of wisdom!—and to pursue folly until I saw what happiness there is for the children of men to seek all the days of their life, under the firmament.*

4   *I undertook magnificent works; I had houses built for myself and vineyards planted for myself;*

5   *I had gardens and parks made, and fruit trees of all kinds planted in them;*

6   *I had ponds made to water a grove planted with trees;*

7   *I purchased slaves and serving women, and I had servants born in my house; and I acquired a quantity of livestock, large and small animals, more than all my predecessors in Jerusalem.*

8   *I piled up silver and gold, and a royal treasure, and provinces; I provided myself with male and female singers, and—the delight of the children of men!—a princess, indeed, several . . .*

9   *In this way, I went far beyond all those who had reigned before me in Jerusalem, and my wisdom did not leave me.*

10   *I did not refuse my eyes whatever they demanded, I did not withhold any pleasure from my heart, and after all my turmoil, my soul found happiness: this was my reward for all my efforts.*

11   *But then, I began to consider all the works my hands had completed, all the trouble I had taken to make them, and I saw that all was vanity and pursuit of wind, and nothing lasts under the sun!*

12   *I sat down to reflect, indeed, on wisdom and on foolishness and senselessness, saying to myself: "What sort of man will succeed me [and rule after me(?)]?"*[3]

13   *And then I did understand that, indubitably, wisdom has some advantage over foolishness, just like light over darkness:*

14   *because   "The wise have eyes in their head,*
                  But the senseless walk in darkness!"
    Yet I know very well that the same fate lies in store for both of them.

---

3. The alleged Solomon here supposedly calls up the image of his successor, the sad and "mad" Roboam, under whose reign the schism between the North and the South broke out (see page 40 above).

15 And I said to myself: *"The same end the fool has awaits me too? But then, what good is it to have been a sage?"* And I decided inwardly that that also was vanity.

16 *There is no more memory of the wise man than of the fool: a few days pass, and already one as well as the other has been forgotten. Alas, the wise man dies exactly like the fool.*

17 *Then, I was disgusted with life, for I felt all that happens here below is ill done, because all is vanity and chasing wind.*

18 *I was disgusted with all the labor I had gone through under the sun, whose results I must leave to my successor.*

19 *For who knows whether he will be wise or senseless? Either way, he will be master over all the gain of the efforts I made and the wisdom I applied here below. That too was in vain!*

20 *And inwardly I became desperate over all the trouble with which I had toiled under the sun.*

21 *For, finally, consider a man who wears himself out with wisdom, skill, and effort: and must he leave all he has to one who has never labored? That too is vanity, and a great woe.*

22 *In fact, what is left to a man in the end after all the turmoil and all the motions his heart went through here below?*

23 *His days are but suffering, his work is filled with misery, even at night his heart does not take rest: and all for nothing!*

24 *In truth, there is no happiness for a man but to eat and drink and let his heart taste the pleasure at the end of his efforts. And all that, I am convinced, comes from God:*

25 *For would people be able to eat or rejoice, if it were not by His grace?*

26[4]

---

4. V. 2:26a. *Correction.* To the man whom he judges good, God gives wisdom, knowledge, and joy. But on the sinner He imposes the work of gathering and heaping for the [sole] benefit of him He judges good.

26b—That too is vanity and chasing after wind! [Probably a misplaced verse line.]

Life Consists	3:1	*There is a moment for everything, and a time for*
in Contrary		*every undertaking, here below:*
Actions,	2	*a time to give birth and a time to die;*
Whose		*a time to plant and a time to uproot what one has*
Results		*planted;*
Cancel One	3	*a time to kill and a time to nurse;*
Another		*a time to break down and a time to build;*
	4	*a time to weep and a time to laugh;*
		a time to mourn and a time to dance;
	5	*a time to cast stones and a time to pick up stones;*
		a time to embrace and a time to refuse kisses;
	6	*a time to seek and a time to lose;*
		a time to preserve and a time to waste;
	7	*a time to tear apart and a time to sew;*
		a time to be silent and a time to speak;
	8	*a time to love and a time to hate;*
		a time for battle and a time for peace.
	9	*What is left to him who acts, from that which he has*
		done?

None of This	10	*I have meditated on "that activity which God has left*
Touches on		*to people to busy themselves with":*
Divine	11	*all that He does is admirable and timely; but though*
Perfection,		*He has given over the entire universe to the human*
but Proves		*mind, man still does not understand the work God*
Merely That		*brings about.*
Man Is Small	12	*I have realized that there is no happiness for them*
		except to be glad and obtain joy in life.
	13	*And further, if one eats, drinks, and tastes the pleas-*
		ure at the end of his work, that is a gift of God.
	14	*I know that whatever God does is definitive: we have*
		nothing to add to it, we cannot take away from it.
		God acts in a way that puts us in awe of Him.
	15	*What happens has already happened, what must be*
		done has already come about: God goes and fetches
		what had disappeared.

16–17[5]

5. Vv. 3:16–17, probably transposed; to be placed after 4:1.

18   *I inwardly concluded, with respect to human beings:
      "It is that God wants to keep them far away and show
      that basically they are like animals!"*

19   *In fact, the fate of men and beasts is the same: beasts
      die, and men die likewise; they have the same Breath-
      of-life; and men have no superiority whatever over
      the animals, but all are vanity.*

20   *All go to the same place, all were made of dust, all
      return to dust.*

21   *Who could know whether the Breath-of-life of people
      ascends [at death], while that of the animals goes
      down toward the earth?*

22   *Thus I understood that there is no happiness for man,
      outside the joy he draws from his work: that is his
      portion. And no one will lead him to see what comes
      about afterward.*

The
Wickedness
of People

4:1   *Then I turned my attention to all the wrong that is
      done here below.
      Look upon the tears of the oppressed, with no one to
      comfort them. Their tormentors' hand is full of brute
      power, and no one forces them to return what they
      steal.*

3:16 *I have also seen, here below, the place of judgment
      held by iniquity, the seat of justice invaded by crime*

17[6]

4:2   *And I called the dead happy, for they are already
      dead, surely happier than the living who are still alive.*

3   *And happier than the one and the other is he who has
      never yet existed, for he has never seen all the evil that
      is done here below.*

4   *I have understood that all the trouble men take and
      all the effort spent in doing things arise only out of
      mutual envy. That too is vanity and chasing after
      wind.*

5–6[7]

6. V. 3:17. *Correction.* I said in my heart: "God will judge the just and the unjust, for there is
a time for every matter, and [a judgment] for every act."

7. V. 4:5. *Gloss.* The fool folds his arms, but eats his own flesh.

7   *I observed another vanity here below:*

8   *Here is someone who lives without companion, without sons or brother, who nonetheless never ceases to trouble himself and never beholds enough riches.*

-    *Then for whom do I wear myself out and deprive myself of joy?*
     This also is vanity and a wasted effort!

9–12[8]

13 *When a king is aged, but he is a fool and will not take counsel any more, it is better to have a youth of low birth, who has much wisdom,*

14 *though he be released from prison to rule, and though he was born poor while the other sat on the throne.*[9]

15 *Indeed, I have seen all the beings who walked under the sun appear before that youth, when he occupied the throne in the place of the other.*

16 *The crowd of those who first assembled was immense, but their descendants no longer delighted in him. . . . This also was vanity and pursuit of wind.*

4:17–5:8[10]

---

8. Vv. 4:9–12. *Gloss.*

9   It is better to live together than alone, for then there is more return for one's endeavors.

10 If both fall, one lifts up his companion; however, woe to the one who is alone and falls without anyone to pick him up.

11 If two lie together, they are warm, but the one who is alone does not feel warmth.

12 It is easy to overpower someone who is alone, but two resist an aggressor, for "a cord of three strands is not easy to break."

9. This probably refers to a real event that was known to the author and the first readers of the book but of which we have no documentation whatever.

10. Vv. 4:17–5:8. *Glosses.*

FIRST SERIES: 4:17–5:6

17 Watch over your behavior when you appear in the House of God: standing before Him in utter humility is worth more than the sacrifice of fools, who can only do wrong.

5:1 Let your mouth not be quick, nor your heart be in a hurry, to speak before God. God is in heaven, and you on the earth, so let your words be few.

2   For he who is always roused is dreaming while awake, and he who talks much is a fool.

3   When you make a vow to God, do not delay carrying it out. Fools do not deserve any favor; therefore, keep your promise.

4   It is better not to make a promise than not to keep one.

5   Do not let your mouth condemn you by saying before God: "It was but a blunder!" Do you wish to anger God and wipe out your merits?

6a [Doublet of 5:2.]

6b Therefore, fear God.

Wealth Is
Heavy to
Bear,
Uncertain,
Terrible to
Lose, and
Decidedly
Useless

5:9 *When we love money, we never have enough money.
Nevertheless, he who loves money does not benefit
from it at all. One more vanity!*

10 *The more goods there are, the more people there are
who swallow them up, and what benefit comes to the
owner, apart from the sight of them?*

11 *The laborer's sleep is sweet, whether his fare be scanty
or abundant; but the satiety of the rich man does not
buy him sleep.*

12 *There is a grievous misfortune I have encountered
here below: the riches that a man preserves serve only
to harm him.*

13 *Riches disappear in a poor transaction. One begat a
son, and now one does not own anything anymore.*

14 *As he came from his mother's womb, he shall go
back, as naked as he left, keeping nothing from all
his toil that he might carry in his hands.*

15 *This is indeed the great misfortune: that we must
leave just as we came. And what gain do we acquire,
when we have worn ourselves out for wind,*

16 *having passed our entire life in darkness and grief, in
excruciating misery, suffering, and bitterness?*

17 *In truth, I have understood that it is better to spend
our time eating, drinking, and tasting the pleasure in
every effort in which we exert ourselves here below,
every day of life that God grants us: for that is our
portion.*

18 *Yes, every man to whom God has given riches and
goods, and whom He permits to enjoy them and to
take his part from them, and to draw pleasure from
his work—receives a benefit from Him,*

19 *for in that way at least, he does not think too much
about life, but God entertains him through the joyfulness of his heart.*

SECOND SERIES: 5:7–8

7 If you observe in the land that there is oppression of the poor, and denial of right and justice,
   do not be surprised. For above the ruler has been placed someone else who has oversight,
   and above them, another who is still higher up.

8 What is needed in the land, instead of all this, is a king for a cultivated territory [?].

6:1 *There is yet another evil that I have observed here below, which often befalls men:*

2 *Someone is endowed by God with riches, treasures, and glory, so abundantly that he lacks nothing of whatever he could desire; and nevertheless, God does not permit him to enjoy it, but a stranger is to profit by it. This is a terrible vanity and evil!*

3 *After all, if a man have a hundred sons and live for long years, and the days of his life are innumerable, if his heart is not filled with happiness, and in the end he does not even get a burial, I say that a miscarried fetus is better off than he.*

4 *It came down here for nothing, and goes away into darkness, where its name remains buried:*

5 *but if it has not seen the sun at all or known anything, at least it did have more peace than that man!*

6 *If he live twice a thousand years without tasting happiness, do not both of them meet in the end?*

7–9[11]

Again the
Inexorable
and Perfect
Power of
God; Any
Attempt to
Counter It
Is Useless

10 *What happens has already been named, and One already knew what it would be, and man is not able to dispute with Him who is stronger than he is....*

11 *The more you contend, the greater you make the vanity: and what does one derive from it?*

12 *Can we know where a man will find happiness during his life, all the days of his life of vanity that he passes like a shadow? After all, who will tell man what will happen next here below?*

7:1–12[12]

---

11. V. 6:7. *Gloss?* All of man's toil serves his mouth, and even so his desire is not satisfied.

8–9 *Erratic verses.*

8 What does the wise man gain over the fool? And what does the poor man gain who knows how to conduct himself before the people?

9 The sight before a man's eyes is better than the wanderings of desire. This too is vanity and chasing the wind. [Is verse 9 perhaps a gloss on verse 7, which might be authentic?]

12. Vv. 7:1–12. *Glosses.*

FIRST SERIES: 1–6a

1 A good reputation is better than a good ointment, and the day of death better than the day of birth.

13   *Indeed, consider God's work: who can straighten what He has bent?*

14   *Therefore, on the day of happiness, stay happy, and on the day of adversity, consider that God has made one as well as the other, so that man cannot know what lies in store.*

15   *I have observed the following two situations during my days of vanity: a just one who perishes despite his justice, and an impious one who lives a long life in spite of his impiety.*

16   *Hence, do not exaggerate in justice, and do not over-do the practice of wisdom: why make yourself ridiculous?*

17   *Do not be too wicked either, and do not act foolishly: why die before your time?*

18–22[13]

23   *I have examined all these things using wisdom. I said: "I want to be wise!" However, all things remained out of reach.*

2 It is better to visit the home of mourning than the house of festivity, for in the former you can see the end of every human being, and the living take it to heart.

3 Sadness is better than laughing: under the sad exterior the heart rests happy.

4 The heart of the wise is at home in mourning, the heart of fools in the house of pleasure.

5 It is better to listen to the warning of the wise than to the song of fools,

6a for the voice of fools is like the crackling of thorns under a pot.

6b [*Doublet or erratic verse?*] That too is vanity.

SECOND SERIES: 7–12

7 Oppression maddens the wise, and a gift spoils the heart.

8 The end of a discourse is worth more than the opening, and patience is better than pride.

9 Do not hasten to give in to sadness: sorrow has its home in the bosom of fools.

10 And do not say: "Why is it that former times were better than the present?" It is certainly not wisdom that makes you utter a question like that.

11 Wisdom is as good as an inheritance: it is a great benefit to those who are under the sun.

12 For wisdom offers protection comparable to that of money, and the advantage of being wise is that wisdom gives life to those who have it.

13. Vv. 18–22. *Glosses.*

18 It is best to hold on to the one without letting go of the other: whoever fears God will avoid all those dangers.

19 Wisdom confers on the wise more power than ten wealthy men in the capital.

20 There is not a single just man in the land who does only good and lives his whole life impeccably.

21 Do not believe everything you are told: you cannot even listen when your servant curses you.

22 As a matter of fact, you know in your heart that you yourself have often cursed others.

24   *That which happens is remote and unfathomable:*
      who will be able to understand it?

25   *Nevertheless, since I began to pursue and search for*
      wisdom and understanding, my heart realized that
      wickedness is folly, and foolishness insane;

26a   *and I found that woman is more bitter than death,*
      that her heart is a snare and a net, her arms fetters.

26b[14]

27   *This is what I discovered, so says Qoheleth, while I*
      was pursuing intelligence step by step,

28   *while my heart ceaselessly searched without reaching*
      it: one man in a thousand, I did find, but I have not
      found one woman among the sum total of these
      creatures!

29   *And I reached this conclusion: God made human*
      beings straight, but they are the ones who looked for
      all kinds of perversion.

Personal   8:1–8[15]
Justice   9   *I observed still more things when I turned my attention*
Does Not   *to all that happens here below, in this time when*
Confer Any   *people wield their power over others only to harm*
Advantage   *them.*

14. V. 26b. *Gloss or correction.* He who is perfect in God's eyes can escape safe and sound, but the sinner is caught by her [= the woman, mentioned in the text].

15. Vv. 8:1–8. *Glosses.*

FIRST SERIES: 1–4

1 Who but the wise man can disentangle things? A man's wisdom lights up his countenance, while anger deforms a face.
2 Pay heed to what the king says, and, for the love of God,
3 do not make haste to leave his presence, and do not get involved in something wrong, for he can do whatever he wishes.
4 The word of a king is powerful indeed, and who can say to him: "What are you doing?"

SECOND SERIES: 5–8

5 Who keeps the commandments will not experience anything bad. A wise heart discerns time and judgment.
6 For there is a time and a judgment for every thing. Man's evil weighs heavy on him
7 because he knows nothing at all of what must come to pass; who, in fact, could make known to him what is to happen?
8 No mortal wields power over the Breath-of-life, nor can he hold on to his breath; no one will be worth a thing on the Great Day; and for that battle, no leave will be granted. Then, wickedness will not save its perpetrator.

10   *Thus I have seen evildoers being carried [with great show] to their grave, while those who had acted in accordance with the law left the Sacred Place to be committed to oblivion in the City. That also was for nothing!*

11–13[16]

14   *There is a vanity that occurs on earth: we meet just people to whom the lot is meted out that is fit for evildoers and their works, and wicked men to whom the lot befalls that is deserved by the just. I say that this too is vanity.*

15   *So I commended joyfulness, because for man here below there is nothing good, except eating, drinking, and exultation. And let that accompany his work all the days of his life that God grants him under the sun!*

16   *When I applied my heart to learning wisdom and the contemplation of matters that occur in this world, to the point of losing sleep over it, day and night,*

17   *my gaze encompassed all that God does, and I had to recognize that man cannot comprehend the plan that unfolds under the sun. No matter what effort he makes in his search, he does not succeed in finding out, and even when the wise man would pretend to know, he cannot understand.*

Absolute
Uncertainty
of Life,
Before
the Utter
Defeat of
Death

9:1   *So all this I took to heart, and this is all my spirit realized: the just and the wise with all their works are delivered up to God. Love or Hate? No one knows. In His view all is vanity.*

2   *The proof of this is that there is only one destiny for all: for the just as for the godless, for the honest man as for the wicked, for the pure and the impure, for the one who sacrifices as for him who neglects the*

16. Vv. 11–13. *Correction.*

11   Because the judgment on misdeeds is not passed quickly, the heart of man fills up with desire to do evil.

12   The sinner (they say) does evil and prolongs his life. But I know very well that happiness is reserved for those who fear God and have regard for His presence,

13   while there will be no happiness for the godless, and, like the shadow, the godless will not prolong his life, for he does not have regard for God's presence.

sacrifice—the decent man has nothing more than the sinner, the one who blasphemes is treated like the one who does not blaspheme.

3   *This is a salient evil among those that occur here below, that the same fate comes to all. Furthermore, it is the reason why the heart of the sons of men fills up with the desire to do evil, and why foolishness settles in it for the duration of their life. . . . And thereafter they join the dead!*

4   *For who will escape it? But, for the living, there is still some hope:*
      "A living dog is better than a dead lion."

5   *Indeed, the living know at least that they have to die. The dead, however, do not know anything any more, and no longer have anything to gain. Their very memory is gone,*

6   *and likewise, from now on, their love, hate, and desire do not exist any more, and they will never have a part any more in all that happens under the sun.*

7   *Well then, eat your bread cheerfully, and drink your wine with a glad heart, if God has blessed your work;*

8   *put on festive clothes always; do not be sparing with oil on your head;*

9   *enjoy life with the woman you love, all the days of vanity that you are given on earth; that is your share in existence and in all the trouble you go through under the sun!*

10 *Whatever is in your power—do it with all your might, for there is no action, no thought, no knowledge, no wisdom any more in Sheol, where you are going. . . .*

Total
Disproportion
Between
Merit and
Fate

11 *Again, I observed that here below the swiftest do not win the race, nor do the strongest win the battle; bread does not come to the ablest, nor riches to the thoughtful, nor favors to the learned, but time and misfortune strike all without distinction.*

12 *No one knows his hour, but like fish in the net or birds in the snare, they too are caught in an evil time that comes upon them suddenly. . . .*

13   *Again, there is something I have seen here below that distressed me greatly:*

14   *There was a small town with a handful of people in it. A mighty king laid siege to it and erected strong assault towers against it.*

15   *Now, in that town was a poor, thoughtful man who saved that town by his wisdom. But not a single person took heed of that man!*[17]

16   *So I said: "Wisdom is surely better than power, and yet, the wisdom of that poor man is despised, and people do not listen to his words!"*

9:17–
10:4[18]

10:5   *I have observed an evil existing here below that is caused, one might say, by the carelessness of the Sovereign:*

6   *a fool is raised to the highest station, while excellent people remain at the lowest rank.*

7   *I have seen slaves on horseback, and princes walking on foot, like servants. . . .*

8–14a[19]

---

17. This case is similar to one seen earlier. See note 9 above.
18. Vv. 9:17–10:4. *Glosses.*

FIRST SERIES: 9:17–18 and 10:4

17   In quietude, one hears the words of the wise more than the shouts of the king of fools.

18   Wisdom is worth more than the instruments of war, but one single sin annihilates much good.

10:4   —If the anger of the ruler rises against you, do not leave your place: calm averts great follies.

SECOND SERIES: 10:1–3

1   Dead flies give a foul ferment to the perfumer's fragrant oil. In the same way a little foolishness diminishes the value of much wisdom.

2   The wise man has his heart to the right, the fool to the left.

3   Even when a fool saunters in the street, he lacks sense, and all can see it: "He is crazy."

19. Vv. 8–14a. *Glosses.*

FIRST SERIES: 8–11

8   Whoever digs a pit risks falling in; whoever breaks down a wall may be bitten by a snake.

9   Whoever quarries stones may find misfortune; whoever cuts down trees may find danger.

10   If the iron is blunted and the cutting edge has not been sharpened, one needs to apply twice as much force [and to repair it is a use of wisdom(?)].

11   If the serpent bites for lack of the snake charmer's art, the charmer gets no reward.

SECOND SERIES: 12–14a

12   What the wise man pronounces wins favor for him, but the fool's lips lead to his perdition.

13   As soon as he begins to speak, it is foolishness, and the end of his talk is evil foolishness.

14a   But the fool speaks on and on. . . .

14b *So man does not know what will happen to him, and no one can disclose the future for him.*

15–11:4[20]

11:5 *Just as you will never know the way the "Breath-of-life" follows to enter the bones in the womb of the pregnant woman, no one can find out the plan of God who makes all there is.*

6 (See the end of note 20.)

The Last Vanities: Decrepitude and Death

7 *Still, the light is sweet, and the eyes delight in seeing the sun!*

8 *May he who lives for many years pass them cheerfully, but without forgetting that the days of darkness will also be many. All that happens is vanity.*

9a Rejoice, child, in your young age, and may your heart give you pleasure in the days of your adolescence. Follow the impulses of your soul and the desires of your eyes:

9b[21]

20. Vv. 10:15–11:4, 6. *Glosses.*
FIRST SERIES: 10:15–17 and 20
15 The fool's labor exhausts him, and he does not even know his way home any more.
16 Woe to you, O land whose king is but a child, and whose princes start carousing in the morning!
17 Fortunate are you, O land, whose king comes from a good family, and whose princes eat at the proper time, to regain their strength, and not to indulge in revelry.
20 Do not curse the king, not even in thought; do not curse the powerful, not even in the secrecy of your room; the birds of heaven could carry your voice, the winged creatures proclaim what you said.
SECOND SERIES: 10:18–19; 11:1–4, 6
18 Where laziness is lodged, the frame of the house caves in; where hands are idle, the leaks multiply.
19 One prepares bread for enjoyment; wine gladdens life; and money answers all needs.
11:1 Throw your bread upon the waters; after a long time, you will get it back.
2 Let seven other people, or even eight, have a share of what you have: you do not know what misfortune may come upon the earth.
3 When the clouds are filled, they pour rain over the earth; but whether a tree falls north or south, it stays where it fell.
4 Whoever gapes at the wind does not sow, and who keeps watching the clouds does not harvest.
6 Beginning at the dawn sow your seed, and until the evening do not let your hand rest: you do not know which will prosper, this or that, or whether both together will be fruitful.
21. V. 9b. *Correction.* But know that with respect to all this God will call you to judgment.

10   *remove misery from you, keep suffering far from you, for youth and the morn of life are vanity.*

12:1   *And remember your Creator in the days of your youth, before the evil days come near and the years of which you have to say: "I find no pleasure in them!"*

2   *Before the sun's effulgence, the light, the moon, and the stars are darkened, and the gloomy clouds return again after the rain,*

3   *before the day when the watchmen of the house tremble; when the athletes stoop, and the few women left to do the grinding cease from work, when the women who look through the windows are dimly seen,*

4   *when the doors on the street are closed, when the sound of the millstone softens, when birdsong ceases, when the singing girls fall silent,*

5   *when one is afraid to be in the hills, one is terrified to be on the roads, one rejects the almond, the locusts fatten themselves, capers lose their strength,[22] because man is about to gain his abode of eternity, and the mourners already make their rounds through the street.*

6   *Before the silver thread is cut, the golden cup broken, the pitcher broken at the spring and the pulley worn out at the well.*

7   *Before the dust returns to the earth, from which it had been drawn, and before the Breath-of-Life leaves to rejoin God who had given it.*

8   *Vanity of vanities, said the Qoheleth, all is vanity!*

Epilogue   9   *The Qoheleth was a very great sage, who always taught wisdom to the people and adapted many proverbs that were profound.*

---

22. Many of the images given here in the tableau of the decrepitude of old people still speak directly to us: the hands, which protect and defend the person, have begun to tremble; the body itself stoops and shrivels up; teeth cease from work and fall out; the eyes become dim and lose their sight; the old person dwells more and more within himself ("the doors on the street are closed"); he feels dizziness, he is afraid to walk alone for fear of falling. . . . Other images, though evidently in the same key ("almond," "cricket" or "locust," "capers"), quite escape us now.

10   *The Qoheleth searched for valuable words, and wanted to frame discourses of truth.*

11 [23]

12   *In the final analysis, my son, let me warn you: there is no end to the writing of books, yet too much study wears down the flesh.*

13   *Here then is the end of my discourse: When all is well understood, fear God and keep His commandments. Every man can do that!*

14 [24]

THE MEANING OF ECCLESIASTES

Despite the relative clarity critical study has provided, Ecclesiastes still is not easily accessible. We cannot forget that we are dealing with the work of a Semite, and, what is significant, a Semite of the past. People like him did not reason in the way we do. *Our* reasonings are done to show clear ideas, laid out around a central, visible line of thought; they aim primarily at the mind. *Their* reasonings, which are extraordinarily concise, without transitions, without middle terms[25]—whose absence always leads us astray—incline toward the point where mind and heart meet: they make us think of musical variations on a theme. If one agrees to *feel* rather than see what is said, they present a proof that is less clear, but more profound.

As for ourselves, incurably rational, we find it hard to give in to that imprecise yet searching course of reasoning without trying out some transposition into clear language. This is our stumbling block: and indeed it is problematical to transform a piece of music into syllogisms.

Here is why the opinions of exegetes who have tried to "clarify" Ecclesiastes can differ literally from one extreme to the other.

---

23. V. 11. *Gloss.* The words of the wise are like goads, and writers of collections, like fastened nails.

24. V. 14. *Correction.* For God will bring every deed, whether good or bad, into the judgment over all that is concealed.

25. [Translator's note: Formulated by Aristotle in his *Prior Analytics*, the middle term is the crucial element in the syllogism, which leads properly to the conclusion. An example of a simple (or categorical) syllogism: (1) All animals are mortal. (2) People are animals (= the middle term). (3) People are mortal.]

There are those who transform the book into a "breviary of optimism"—
a thesis that, in my opinion, is a glaring blunder and betrays a lack of literary
judgment that is commensurately a rare and interesting phenomenon . . . for
how could a writer who wished, above all, to inculcate optimism conclude
his book with such a vision of decrepitude and death?

Is the author, then, a pessimist first and foremost? Some have believed so,
and there is merit in their case. It is true that this book as a whole is dis-
consolate and that it hardly encourages action. But in spite of all that, one
can scarcely imagine an Israelite of the third (or even the first) century B.C.E.
trying to show us step-by-step that "life is not worth living." People then
were less complex than that, less "old" than ourselves. Above all, there are
the passages that strike a different chord: the ones in which Qoheleth invites
us to eat well and drink well and to rejoice when the occasion arises. For
there are good times, he thinks.

Might not this discord between optimism and pessimism hint that the real
discussion occurs at a higher level? I opened the present chapter with an
exposition of the problem of evil in Israel, for that, I believe, may help us find
the basis of the ancient sage's teachings.

If the question were only whether life as such is good or bad, why call on
God so frequently, why insist on His rule over things, why reiterate *"we
cannot understand the plan of God, who makes all"?*

> *I have examined all these things using wisdom. I said: "I want to be
> wise!" However, all things remained out of reach.*
> *That which happens is remote and unfathomable: who will be able
> to understand it?* (7:23–24)

"All these things," or, as he has it elsewhere, *"all that happens under the
sun"*: our idiom would call it the sum of what occurs in nature and in history;
the author of Ecclesiastes is the first philosopher of Israel, and from that point
of view, a Greek influence upon him is practically certain.[26] If he cannot

---

26. See especially I. Lévy, "Les croyances égyptiennes, grecques et juives sur la vie d'outre-
tombe," in *Revue de l'Université de Bruxelles* 4 (May–July 1929): 24ff., on Ecclesiastes' acceptance
of certain "beliefs of Hellenic spiritualism." One will also remark that the author is the first in
Israel to give to *hokma*, "wisdom," in addition to its traditional, "practical" sense (see page 172),
a "speculative" meaning, close to the Greek *philosophia* (see, for instance, 1:18 and especially
7:23ff.). The text of 3:21, *"Who could know whether the Breath-of-life of people ascends* [at
death], *while that of the animals goes down toward the earth?"* is reminiscent of the *pneûm' apheis
eis aithera*, the "breath ascending to heaven" (Euripides, frag. 971), and the Pythagorean and Stoic
ideas on the residence of "souls," upon death, in the air. (See, for example, Erwin Rohde, *Psyche:*

reconcile *"all these things"* with his comprehension, it is because, on the one hand, as a good Israelite he wholeheartedly believes in God who is perfect, just, and good (the fable of Qoheleth the skeptic was launched into the discussion by Ernest Renan[27] and is undeniably the product of an obsession) and, on the other hand, he has found that evil is everywhere, and useless, pure and simple, are the efforts of nature and man; useless, wisdom and knowledge, activity, politics, wealth, and intellectual, moral, and religious perfection; life itself is futile, concluding in the idiocy of old age and the endless torpor of death. Certainly, there are moments: it is pleasant to eat and drink, to love your wife, and to rejoice at heart; one is happy to live and "see the sun" (11:7). If that were the sum of it, all would be well, all would be clear and comprehensible. But evil exists, and to the sober and lucid observer, it obviously has the upper hand. There, for the religious spirit, is the terror! This is what the author of Qoheleth sought to understand—and he admits defeat.

But he adds an explanation of his failure, and thereby, I believe, he joins Job: *"I have meditated on 'that activity which God has left to people to busy themselves with'"* (3:10).

Thus he summons wisdom, "philosophy" (in 1:13 he even says: *"a wretched activity,"* half ironically, as scholars sometimes like to do in evoking their specialty):

> *all that He does is admirable*[28] *and timely; but though He has given over the entire universe to the human mind, man still does not understand the work God brings about. . . . I inwardly concluded, with respect to human beings:*
> *"It is that God wants to keep them far away and show that basically they are like animals!"*
>
> (3:11 and 18)

In a colder language that is almost brutal, language of a philosopher rather than a poet, here we have the fundamental idea of Job: the absolute transcendence of God, before which, no matter what happens, the only

---

The Cult of Souls and Belief in Immortality Among the Greeks, trans. W. B. Hillis, 2 vols. with consecutive page numbering [New York: Harper 1966], 446–50, nn. 44 and 62 of chap. XII.)

27. [Translator's note: Joseph Ernest Renan (1823–92), influential French philologist and historian.]

28. The Hebrew word is yafe, which, like Greek kalos, denotes all that is so well-shaped that it is a pleasure to look upon.

sensation and the only mental reaction one can have are admiration and affirmation.

What surpasses even Job is that this affirmation arises not after an examination of the singular suffering of the just—which, after all, is a secondary problem for the metaphysically concerned mind—but after the most complete and frightening catalogue of universal evil.

In the religious development of Israel, where absolute monotheism and the total perfection of God take precedence, there was not, and there could not be, a higher and more just response to the problem of evil than that of Qoheleth. And whatever personal feelings a historian of religions may have vis-à-vis the religion and the teachings of the ancient Jewish sage, he will have no trouble admitting that those teachings are among the summits in religious thought and the religious experience of mankind.

For Readers Who Wish to Engage in a More Diligent Study of the Bible

If we limit ourselves only to contemporary works and those in which sheer confessionalism or apologetics do not make themselves unbearably obvious, the literature that turns around the Bible is still copious to a degree that far surpasses the Bible's translations "into all languages of the world." Scholarship on questions concerning the Bible is international, and in a brief list one could not begin to name all works in French, German (especially German), and English that are relevant to the topics addressed in the present book. Moreover, from year to year, and, in fact, from one day to the next, the scholarly literature increases, enforcing a limit (to some extent arbitrary) on the array of titles in any selection.

In this English translation, it will suffice to name the following French titles:

L. Mouloubou and F. M. Du Burr, *Dictionnaire biblique universel* (Paris: Desclée et Cie, 1984).

Introductory work on the *internal critique* of the Biblical text is not as rife in the literature in France as it is in Germany and the English-speaking countries. Of note, however, are the third edition of a large, instructive, and solid work, L. Gautier, *Introduction à l'Ancien Testament* (Lausanne: Payot, 1939), and a differently conceived, smaller work, A. Lods, *Histoire de la littérature hébraïque et juive* (Paris: Payot, 1950).

For archeological data, see the translated work by Roland de Vaux listed below.

In consultation with Professor Bottéro, the translator adds the following choice of works in English.

Paul J. Achtemeier, general ed., *Harper's Bible Dictionary* (San Francisco: Harper & Row, 1985).

Harry Thomas Frank, ed., *Atlas of the Bible Lands*, rev. ed. (Maplewood, N.J.: Hammond, 1990).

Johannes Pedersen, *Israel: Its Life and Culture*, 4 pts. in 2 vols. (London: Oxford University Press; Copenhagen: Povl Branner, 1946–47). Pedersen is one of the great philologists of the twentieth century. This particular work sheds a great deal of light on the meanings of key terms in classical Hebrew.

Samuel Sandmel, *The Hebrew Scriptures: An Introduction to Their Literature and Religious Ideas* (New York: Oxford University Press, 1978).

Robert H. Pfeiffer, *Introduction to the Old Testament* (New York: Harper, 1941).

Roland de Vaux, *Ancient Israel*, 2 vols. (vol. 1: *Social Institutions*; vol. 2: *Religious Institutions*) (New York: McGraw-Hill, 1961). English trans.: Darton, Longman & Todd.

William Foxwell Albright, *The Archeology of Palestine* (Harmondsworth, Middlesex: Penguin Books, 1954).

Norman H. Snaith, *The Distinctive Ideas of the Old Testament* (London: Epworth Press, 1983).

John Bright, *A History of Israel*, 3d ed. (Philadelphia: Westminster Press, 1981).

Delbert R. Hillers, *Covenant: The History of a Biblical Idea* (Baltimore: Johns Hopkins University Press, 1973).

John van Seters, *In Search of History: Historiography in the Ancient World and the Origins of Biblical History*, (New Haven: Yale University Press, 1983).

Marvin H. Pope, *Job: A New Translation with Introduction and Commentary* (Garden City, N.Y.: Doubleday, 1979).

Sara Denning-Bolle, *Wisdom in Akkadian Literature: Expression, Instruction, Dialogue*, Mededelingen en Verhandelingen van het Vooraziatisch-Egyptisch Genootschap "Ex Oriente Lux," XXVIII (Leiden: Ex Oriente Lux, 1992). This work is of special interest for the wider context (including classical Greece) in which the author views the biblical as well as the Mesopotamian wisdom literature in dialogue form.